MOSAIC IN THE FOUNTAIN

By BERTITA HARDING

PHANTOM CROWN
ROYAL PURPLE
GOLDEN FLEECE
FAREWELL, 'TOINETTE
IMPERIAL TWILIGHT
HUNGARIAN RHAPSODY
AMAZON THRONE
LOST WALTZ
SOUTHERN EMPIRE: BRAZIL
AGE CANNOT WITHER
THE LAND COLUMBUS LOVED
MOSAIC IN THE FOUNTAIN

MOSAIC IN THE FOUNTAIN

BY
BERTITA HARDING

Everything has a cause and the cause of anything is everything. . . .

TIMOTHY TURNER

GEORGE G. HARRAP & CO. LTD
LONDON SYDNEY TORONTO BOMBAY

TO

MY BROTHERS AND THE CHILDREN

SINCE THIS IS THEIR CHILDHOOD TOO

First published 1951
by George G. Harrap & Co. Ltd
182 High Holborn, London, W.C.1

Dewey Decimal classification: 928.1

Composed in Garamond type and printed by Western Printing Services, Ltd, Bristol. Made in Great Britain

CONTENTS

I

GIPSY LURE

No one can choose his place of birth.

We cannot guess even remotely whether accident or design governed our conception, though this fleet instant in our individual eternities is of the greatest moment. We are not consulted. We arrive. We are here. Willy-nilly.

In view of this random contingency it appears mystifying that most of us attach an almost fanatical importance to the geography of our origin, and that from so patently fortuitous a circumstance should spring the formidable passions of national love and hate. With the exception of the emigrant who, of his own volition, turns his back upon the land that bore him to seek his fortune elsewhere, the average citizen takes a righteous pride in that which he could neither remedy nor pick. We, alone of earth's creatures, worship our cradle; it is given to the human race to nurse a jealous fire in its breast for even the most outlandish and intolerable spot, provided it be hallowed by a personally gratifying obstetrical event.

Our mother felt this way about her native Hungary. Not only did she regard its capital, Budapest, as an entrancing place, but she felt genuinely sorry for people who had not been born there. Transient visitors to the Magyar scene earned her particular pity. "They have to go away again," she would sigh, with a look of condolence. "This is not their home!"

Hungary had been *her* home, or rather that of her ancestors, the Counts of Károlyi-Nagykárolyi, for nearly a thousand years. Even her Christian name, Sarolta, abbreviated to the softly musical Sári, was of ancient Asiatic derivation; it had been brought into Europe by barbarian hordes that once galloped across the steppes of Tartary with Attila the Hun.

Except for school terms spent in town, much of Sári's childhood had for its setting an estate in the hills of Buda, overlooking the small village of Solymár. Here, with her brother Károly and a younger sister Irma, she learned to ride, hunt, fish, and to dance the wild *csárdás* of the region. She also grew proficient in the use of traditional *czigány* profanity, for the country was overrun by gipsies from the Balkans and the Levant. These tattered nomads swept across nineteenth-century Europe in appalling numbers, jogging their carts from Rumania through Hungary, across the Lombard plains to the far shores of Spain. They were a stange, exotically savage crew, imaginative and poetic in their pleasure, which was music—but fierce and cunning in their trade, which was horse-stealing and the kidnapping of small children. Such children, if fair of face, could be trained as artists or circus performers; but, if plain, they were maimed into monstrosities who brought in a tidy income as professional beggars.

In Solymár people feared and hated the gipsies. When the grey-covered wagons appeared on the horizon herdsmen ran home to spread the alarm. Instantly all village mothers stopped their work and ran forth to gather their little ones off the streets. Then, as the creaking caravan crossed the deserted market-place, householders peered through shuttered windows and crossed themselves, while muttering curses under their breath.

The gipsies paid back in equal coin. Enraged by the villagers' reception, they glared at empty courtyards and doorways, spitting out maledictions of such calibre that each year Solymár's not inconsiderable vocabulary was perceptibly enlarged.

"Clodhoppers and fools!" bellowed the Romanies, remembering always to add a genealogical predicate of most unsavoury character. "You think we'd bother to visit your stinking hovels? By your King's buttocks, we've better things to do! We're passing through, we are, and holding our noses while we're about it!"

With this, they rumbled on, but only just beyond the village limits, where, on a convenient hillock, they set up their tents and settled down for a week's encampment. Fiddles were dusted, the cymbalom was tuned up, and the fortune-teller's booth nailed together. Next a small sawdust ring was fashioned for the display of every category of mount, from blooded Arab to plebeian nag. Lastly kettles were set to boil over open fires, while the tribe lolled about in picturesque languor to await developments.

It was never a long wait. Incurably curious, the villagers were already on tenterhooks. True, they put up a stern front on account of the aspersions cast on the King's buttocks (Hungarians are overwhelmingly royalist and can brook no contumely against their dynasty, enthroned or otherwise), but before sundown of the second day a compromise was made with conscience. Romanies, reasoned Solymár's inhabitants, were rascals without knowledge or refinement, hence their jabber carried no weight. There was certainly no harm in looking them over, strictly for purposes of study, as one did the more fearsome and malodorous creatures in the Budapest zoo. It went without saying that such contemplation ended invariably in noisy carousals and much bibbing of heady Tokay wine. At the conclusion of Gipsy Week the villagers were usually left nursing numbed heads and yawning pocket-books, while their nomad visitors made off with a substantial intake of cash.

Although city-bred, Sári's family was equally susceptible to the malignant Romany charm. The head of the house, Atya (Hungarian for 'father'), could not resist the siren song of a *Prímás* violin quivering in the warm summer night air. Anya, the children's mother, found it still harder to keep out of sight and earshot of the encampment, for each season the grimy, olive-skinned tribal women were said to bring fabulous cashmeres, silks, and jewels from the lands beyond the Caspian Sea. That the cloth which draped these swarthy females turned out more often than not to be cheap Turkish calico, while brooches, ear-pendants, and bangles were of the most crudely hammered Smyrna brass, in no wise dampened Anya's enthusiasm. She went each time, only to be trapped into some purchase that later brought a blush of mortification to her cheek, for even Zoltán, the coachman, and Marishka, the cook, refused to wear the signet-ring or chain that overnight turned dim with verdigris.

Anya was fine and delicate, with the gentle air of a great lady. In her youth she had been a court attendant at the Királyi Vár, the Royal Palace, in Buda. She had witnessed the betrothal ball of the young King-Emperor Franz Josef and Princess Elisabeth of Bavaria. There were in her possession several keepsakes commemorating this occasion: a fan, a handkerchief bearing the crested initial of the Imperial bride, a Biedermeier shawl. But the most precious of Anya's trinkets was a *carnet de bal*, or dance programme, covered in royal blue velvet and adorned with tinted miniatures of the dynastic pair. Inside this *carnet*, printed in gilt letters, were the dances of the period: the polka, the mazurka, the polonaise, the Hungarian *csárdás*, and always the Vienna waltzes of Johann Strauss. Beside each dance there was a space for a ballroom partner to sign his name. When first she inspected her mother's treasured memento, Sári was overcome with dismay; Anya must have been something of a wallflower, for her dances were not nearly all taken. The children brooded over this. Golden-haired, emerald-eyed Anya, with the white hands and the fragile, seemingly boneless, wrists, a wallflower? It was impossible. At last they ventured a question. Or rather, the older two pressed small Irma into service, prompting her to ask their mother about those dances.

Anya replied with dignity, drawing herself up to her not very considerable height. "Those dances? Oh, I spent them on a terrace in the moonlight. . . ." From the luminous look on her face it was possible to gather that she had had a very lovely time indeed, a conclusion which the children hugged to their young bosoms and cherished for what it might be worth, since they would far rather think of their mother as a belle of the court than a wallflower.

For a long time it was Sári's despair that she did not possess her mother's golden beauty. Her own locks were almost black, matched only by the shadowy depths of her dark eyes. Irma likewise missed blondness, though she had inherited Anya's green iris, under lashes of breath-taking length. Károly alone was fair, excessively slender, sensitive, and marked for early tragedy. He attended the Lyceum in Budapest, preparing for a musical career. At twenty he married and a short time later, during a strenuous concert tour, was carried from the podium of the Musikhalle in Prague where he had collapsed over his violin. The young widow brought the body back to Solymár for burial.

Anya had gone from them earlier, a victim to that characteristic recklessness which caused her to revisit gipsy camps despite the certainty of being robbed, or to walk hatless in the rain. On a berry-picking expedition to the woods that bordered the estate, she had been overtaken by a cloudburst. Instead of running for shelter she had called to her daughters:

"Come on out! Kick off your shoes and wade in the grass—it's wonderful!"

With squeals of glee all three of them had splashed and pranced among the dripping acacias, while from the canopy of heaven a deluge descended on their heads. The result was a first-rate bout of pneumonia. The children recovered. But Anya, barely thirty-three, said farewell to life.

2

SÁRI AND HER LION

ATYA MARRIED again.

Oddly, he chose a lady from the southern province of Siebenbürgen, where there was an isolated settlement of Saxons and Swabians transplanted from their Germanic habitat during the religious wars of the sixteenth century. Though 'Magyarized' by law, these settlers and their descendants after them constituted a foreign element in the body of Hungary, for they stubbornly retained the dress, traditions, and speech peculiar to their land of origin. If they learned Hungarian at all it was with great effort and inconspicuous success; the jargon they spoke became inevitably an atrocious mixture of dialects which only fellow-Swabians or Saxons could understand.

Atya's new wife proved an exception to this rule. She had attended school in Budapest, where her slow but dogged mind grappled with city ways and city accents. Quite plain in appearance, she was not beset by admirers. Marriage to a widower, with a small orphaned brood that needed looking after, appeared to be her best prospect. She accepted it with alacrity.

He was not very much in love, poor Atya, and the Swabian lady knew it. But she had integrity and a sense of obligation. She became a good stepmother, albeit a strict and not very amusing one.

Her name was Sophie, and in later years she was to be known to her step-grandchildren as Grossmama. Long before that time, however, the family circle was augmented by the birth of Sophie's only offspring, a daughter named Cornelia. This child, the issue of parents well past their prime, soon became the spoiled darling of the household. Like a lioness concentrating on her lone cub, Sophie devoted her every waking thought to the dimpled baby girl.

Sári and Irma luckily spent their school years away from home. Being spared the doting tyranny that shackled Cornelia, the older sisters flowered into happy young-womanhood. At seventeen

Sári was in love. The young man of her fancy came from the French border town of Saarlouis, in the Rhenish Palatinate, where his émigré Huguenot ancestors had settled during the reign of Louis XIV. A student at the Mittweida Institute of Technology in Saxony, he had come to Budapest on his summer vacation. His name was Johann Émile Leonarz de Liége. His age: nineteen. His avocation: travel.

Railway journeys cost money, and students—in those days as now—did not have much in their pockets. But this was no handicap to anyone with imagination. The continent of Europe was small and wanderers betook themselves across it from one end to the other on 'cobbler's steeds'—their own shoe-leather. It was thus that Sári's enterprising young man had set out, marching straight through Bavaria and over the border into Austria.

He persuaded a Danube skipper to take him on a river-boat. Scenes drenched in ancient lore now drifted past his eager eyes as the craft sailed leisurely downstream, past Mautern (known as Mutaren in the saga of the *Nibelungen Ring*) and Castle Dürnstein, then Vienna itself and Pressburg of countless fables (the Czech city of Bratislava). Castle Dürnstein, erstwhile prison of Richard Lionheart, held a personal interest for him as his own Gallic name, Leonarz, together with its innumerable variants—the German Leonhard, the Norse Lennart, and the Italian Leonardo—were derivatives of the illustrious epithet. This did not mean that the Plantagenet Crusader was common ancestor to all who bear a 'leonine' patronymic. Long before the days of Britain's Richard, courage—and at times mere braggadocio—invited comparison with the lord of beasts.

The river journey ended at Budapest, where Sári stood on the dock beside her father. Atya was an official of the Danube Shipping Company and he frequently witnessed the movements of passenger-boats. On such occasions it was inevitable for travellers and officials to meet at the captain's hospitable board. It was thus that Sári found her young man.

To be sure, their meeting was of the briefest. That same night a free boat-ride to Belgrade offered itself, which could not be refused. Despite a distinctly amorous flutter in his heart, the youth departed. After all, he had his travelling to do. But he promised to write.

It was fully two weeks before the slow river-post brought news that Sári's young man had reached his farthest goal, Constantinople. In Constantinople the first thing he had done was to sample Turkish coffee. "It's so strong," he wrote, "that your spoon remains standing in the cup!" He also purchased an Ottoman fez which, worn at a rakish angle, made him feel like an Oriental pasha. Finally he did some exhaustive sightseeing until his eye fell upon a calendar, and he realized with a start that it was high time to return.

He would have preferred retracing his steps by way of Budapest, so as to see Sári again. But the journey up-stream was interminably slow, and he would never reach Mittweida on time. He must cut diagonally across the Balkans and make straight for the Austrian frontier. But his plan for so direct a course was thwarted by the difficulty and fascination of the journey.

This time the region was more primitive, and he did not have much luck with his hitch-hiking. Through Greece and Macedonia traffic consisted mainly of ox-carts, whereas the heights of Montenegro could be scaled only by pack-mule or on foot. But it was glorious adventuring. Olympus, the Acropolis by moonlight, Thrace, King Nikita's small capital of Cetinje, all would remain engraved on his memory. But the best was yet to come, as from mountain cliffs he descended to the table-lands of Serbia and reached Belgrade, known in the Slav tongue as Béograd, The White City, which he had seen only briefly on his earlier voyage down-stream.

Beholding this White City, which lies on a promontory overlooking the confluence of the Danube and Sava rivers, he became dazzled by the panorama. He paused to consider that various delays had already upset his schedule and, since he would be late anyway for the opening college term, he might as well miss that term altogether. On further reflection it came to him that as long as he was missing the first term he could dispense with the second also. Thus he would be his own master for one whole year.

An immediate handicap presented itself in the fact that he did not speak Serbian or know a soul in the whole town of Belgrade. But he would remedy that. A language could be learned and there was always work to provide for one's keep. He resolved to try both.

Fortune was with him. This was the last decade of the nineteenth century and the dawning of the machine age in the Balkans. Throughout Western Europe incandescent lighting had just been discovered: in England and France people turned little buttons and gasped at the miracle of incandescence, while in Germany experiments were being made with tramcars operated by this new power. Gradually the Balkans, too, felt the impact of science, and Sári's young man had little difficulty finding employment with a pioneer electrical firm. He thus helped bring modern lighting installations to Bosnia and Herzegovina, to Belgrade itself, and to the city of Sarajevo, where, not many years later, the spark of world conflagration would be struck.

Since his employers, Ganz and Company, had large offices in Budapest, there were frequent visits to Sári. These included week-ends at Solymár, where relatives and friends took stock of the young man's qualifications. Self-respecting Hungarians held with no international alliances. Particularly was their ban directed against Russians and Prussians, Slavic square-heads all, as could be seen by the similarity of their names. But Western Germans of the Palatinate or South Bavaria were practically Austrians; though inferior to Magyars, they could be tolerated. In addition there was the fact that Sári's young man was embarking on an impressive new career, engineering, which overawed Solymár's rural gentry. Hungarian lads of good family turned mostly to diplomacy, the Church, or the breeding of fine horses. A fellow who knew about electricity might be a very good catch indeed.

"Has he a title?" Sophie (who hadn't one) wished to know.

Atya took her down several pegs. "Among us, here in Hungary, titles come twenty to the dozen. But it's not every one who can explain a kilowatt!"

The betrothal was celebrated then and there, although wedding plans must await the bridegroom's completion of his studies at Mittweida. During the intervening two years Sári did not lack suitors, who wrote expansive stanzas upon the pages of her poetry album, several brush artists among them even going to work with water colours for the embellishment of their respective sonnets. But neither lyric verse nor daintily etched marigolds and myrtle caused her to waver in her choice.

The marriage took place in 1896, at Budapest, with a vast company of relatives attending. Among the latter were two brothers of the bridegroom, who made the journey from distant Saarlouis, arriving barely in time for the ceremony.

3

THE FAMILY BEGINS

THE HONEYMOONERS went on a trip through the Austrian Alps. It was Sári's first excursion beyond Hungarian borders and she was never to forget the wonder of it. Her homeland, except for the Tátra Mountains in the north, consisted predominantly of gentle hills and the vast fertile plain of the Puszta. The Alpine scenes she now witnessed were of an awesome and majestic splendour, reminiscent of pictures she had seen of the Swiss world of William Tell.

The first stop of the journey was Vienna, in those days one of Europe's most glittering capitals, though still overshadowed by the seven-year-old Mayerling tragedy. While the Volksgarten, the Ringstrasse, and the Wurstlprater teemed with gaiety, there were few lights in the Hofburg and the great castle of Schönbrunn. With Maximilian of Mexico and Archduke Rudolf the cycle of Habsburg disasters was only half run; violent death awaited Empress Elisabeth two years hence at Lake Geneva, and Franz Ferdinand sixteen years after was to be slain in a Bosnian street. The Emperor Franz Josef, though in residence, was rarely seen in public nowadays. The era of night-long revelry, when the handsome young sovereign had led every polka and quadrille or twirled a fast Lanner and Strauss waltz, was gone for ever.

The blissful Sári and her groom, of course, took little account of mournful history. On the surface it was Vienna still, where pavement cafés rang with laughter and the *heuriger* wine spilled from glasses that were swung in three-quarter rhythm.

Next on the itinerary was Salzburg, the Mozart city, with its quaint medieval streets and mighty fortress-castle. Here, beside the rushing Salzach river, the young couple spent an idyllic fortnight. Music and drama festivals were already the town's chief attractions, but there were also enchanting minor trips to be made to Bad Gastein, Sankt Wolfgang, Gmunden, and Zell.

During the young couple's absence Atya had located a cosy apartment near Gellért Hill, which would be just right for Sári's first experiments in housekeeping. But no sooner had furniture movers and decorators left the premises than the honeymooners found themselves faced with an abrupt change of plan. The firm of Ganz and Company had dealings with the important Siemens Works at Nuremberg, and it was imperative that some one fluent in the German tongue be placed as representative in the Bavarian city. Without even unpacking their trunks the travellers took once more to the road.

It was one of those apparently unimportant moves made in youth, without consciousness of deep, uprooting consequences that were to encircle half the globe. With this seemingly insignificant step the young pair had embarked on a road to high adventure.

During the next few years five children made their appearance in fairly close succession. The first of these was a girl, named Katrin Alexandra after her paternal grandmother. There followed two boys, Sylvester and Arnim, and another girl, Mady. The youngest in line was myself, Bertita Carla Micaela, to be nicknamed Minka.

We lived at this time in a cramped, gabled medieval house of the ancient Meistersinger town, within a stone's throw of the Pegnitz river and the crenellated walls of the Burg. Here stood the famous Five-cornered Tower with the adjoining museum that contained an imposing array of torture instruments from the Dark Ages, among them the "Spiked Cradle" and the terrible "Iron Maiden." To offset these cruel reminders of a gloomy past the modern portion of the city smiled upon the vistior in all its quaint and flawless charm. From here the world's best Christmas delicacies, pretzels, gingerbread-men, and marzipan went forth in prettily decorated tins, while tinsel, Christmas-tree ornaments, and toys of every description carried the name of Nuremberg to the ends of the earth.

Since our father was presently employed by the firm of Siemens and transferred to its large plant in Berlin, only the older children retained any lasting impression of the picturesque ctiy of our birth. A mere baby at the time of the Berlin move, I remembered nothing. Yet, through a fabulously big postcard album kept by our mother, I grew intimately familiar with this unknown place; here was a Nuremberg all my own, with artificial snow dripping from the tavern known as the Bratwurstglöcklein, a bit of metallic dust embellishing the fountain called Schöner Brunnen, cut-outs of red mica lighting up the windows of the Albrecht Dürer Haus.

Of Berlin, which did not lend itself nearly so well to picture-postcard exploitation, Mama's album showed few views. We moved to the fashionable Grunewald section, as tenants rather than owners of a moderate-sized villa. Daily I was wheeled in my pram under the great forest trees, while the older children raced round me with their rolling hoops.

In Berlin I took my first steps, clinging to the hand of Valli, my nursemaid. Valli was huge, round-cheeked, big-bosomed, and full of laughter. Fond of children, she also loved policemen, and it was this latter foible which very nearly caused her to inflict a lifelong injury upon my unwitting person. It happened one late afternoon when our parents remained in town for the theatre and a midnight supper. Feeling herself unsupervised, Valli extended our walk far beyond the usual hour so as to enjoy the conversation of Herr Knorcke, the constable on our beat. With falling dusk her conscience bestirred itself, and she made up for lost time by returning at the double. Why she did not pick me up, in the interests of haste, remains a mystery. Instead, the witless girl dragged me by the hand, while my short toddler legs endeavoured to keep pace with her. At a street crossing the idiotic thing happened. Lifting me by one arm, she pulled the shoulder-joint out of its socket.

Again this event is known to me only from hearsay. I remember neither anguish nor pain, though there must have been a good portion of both. As told many years later, Papa and Mama returned that night to find me tucked neatly under the covers, but with the wrenched arm hanging limply between the bars of my crib. Stern interrogation below stairs elicited from the blubbering nursemaid a confession of what had occurred.

Actually the damage was quickly repaired by an orthopædist who that same night snapped my shoulder back into place. But our parents were unable to calm down. They had already faced tragedy with two of their children—before our transfer from Nuremberg both my sisters had died in a diphtheria epidemic. The accident that had befallen me now could not be taken lightly. It led to our parting with Valli.

A governess named Fräulein Marta took her place. Ordinarily this type of domestic employee is neither fish nor fowl, being above the educational level of a servant, yet not on a social par with her masters (an oblique circumstance amply exploited in the novels of Arthur Schnitzler). Happily, in our home no such quandary existed. Fräulein sat with us at table, joined our mother and father in the parlour, and, when company came, was introduced as one of the family. Before long she and our parents shared a fraternal glass of wine in the ceremony called *Bruderschaft*, after which they addressed one another by their Christian names and employed the familiar *Du.* My brothers and I were enjoined to look upon the Fräulein as our aunt and to call her *Tante.*

The change required some reflection on the part of Sylvester, who from babyhood had been a gravely thoughtful fellow, adhering staunchly to whatever he learned. Thus he now compromised by saying, "*Fräulein Tante.*" Sylvester had another trait, peculiar to himself alone. From earliest childhood he displayed great formality, speaking of himself—like royalty—only in the third person. If he overheard some one inquiring, "Did Sylvester dirty his blouse?" he stepped up and answered with slow solemnity, "Oh, no—Sylvester does not do that!" They, the grown-ups, referred to him that way, so he did too.

In her new status the Fräulein was given full authority over us, including spanking privileges, which our parents preferred to dodge. To her credit it must be said, however, that she was a humane pedagogue. Only in extremity did she resort to physical chastisement, and then of a light-handed, feminine sort. When serious mischief was involved, especially on the part of my high-spirited brothers, Papa would have to be summoned to take over. As such duties were distasteful to him he often resorted to a fierce glare in place of active discipline. But there were times when the glare did not suffice and treatment must be applied to that part of the anatomy which is "more honoured in the breech than in the observance," at least in the case of the boys. As far as I was concerned, Papa failed ignominiously; my misdeeds were the Fräulein's responsibility, to deal with as best she might. For, if I did not wilt immediately under one of Papa's angry looks, he hastily withdrew.

4

WE MOVE TO MEXICO

WE HAD lived in Berlin a little over two years when an extraordinary offer was made to our father through his employer and personal friend, Werner von Siemens. From an overseas country called Mexico there had come a request for a dependable engineering expert to direct the construction of a power plant. The choice had fallen on our father.

The news did not find favour with Mama. Having set up three homes within the short years of her marriage, she felt unable to face another move. Also, she had never, throughout her sojourn in Germany, lost a poignant longing for her native Hungary. The thought of now putting an ocean between herself and her loved Danube country seemed too much to bear.

"Very well," said Papa, "we won't go!" The matter was dismissed. However, it did not end there. In letters to Budapest the project was discussed, and Atya passionately censured his daughter's shortsighted attitude. "You are standing in your husband's way!" he protested. "Besides, a trip like that will be only temporary; you'll be back home again before you know it. . . ." And now he added a clinching argument. For several months the Austrian Foreign Office had engaged in negotiations with the Mexican Government for the return of certain Imperial jewels, left behind after the downfall of Maximilian and Carlota. The House of Habsburg was even now looking for a trustworthy person to undertake this task. What did Sári think of performing such a service for Maximilian's brother, the Emperor Franz Josef?

It was a purely rhetorical question, as our grandfather well knew. Having reared a royalist family he could not expect his daughter to reject so splendid a challenge. By the next post Sári requested detailed instructions, and in a fortnight's time the die was cast. With crated furniture, boxes, trunks, governess, and children, our parents set out upon their double mission.

"Why not leave the little ones in Solymár till your return?" suggested Grandmother Sophie.

"Oh, no," Mama said quickly. "If we go, we all go together."

The sailing date was set for early spring. We went aboard the Hamburg-American liner *Albingia*, crossing the Atlantic in the wake of that long-forgotten and dismal Habsburg venture. Our goal was Veracruz, the sun-baked tropical harbour where, more than a generation ago, Maximilian and Carlota had landed. Almost four centuries earlier Cortés and his Conquistadores had set foot on the same desolate shore.

Only from hearsay do I know that the voyage proved stormy, that the ship's master was a Captain Rantzau, and that our party included a tutor who coached Papa, Mama, and the Fräulein in a strange new tongue: the Spanish of Latin America, spoken without the lisped consonants of Castile. The New World, so the teacher explained, had adopted the language of the Conquistadores, who were not Castilians but coastal people from the province of Andalucía. Evidently, Andalucians did not lisp.

On arrival in Veracruz our parents were confronted with the same dismaying sight that once had caused the Archducal pair to wince: lined up on flat housetops and cornices sat the gaunt black vultures known as *zopilotes*, waiting for carrion. In the absence of more modern hygienic provisions these hideous birds had, from time immemorial, served as the port's sanitary police. Though horrible to European eyes, in the tropics Nature had use for scavengers.

Losing little time, we set out for the capital, Mexico City, which lay a day's train-journey up the plateau. The route we traversed had been followed by Maximilian and his bride in a rumbling stagecoach, while the Spaniards before them had come as centaurs, astride beasts with iron hoofs the like of which no Aztec brave had ever seen. For us there were narrow-gauge English tracks, a mahogany-panelled railway carriage, and a snorting wide-funnelled locomotive.

The journey led steadily uphill, past sleepy Indian towns and fields of agave, known in Mexico as *maguey*. As the terrain mounted and grew steeper, snow-capped volcanoes appeared in the distance. The train chugged across aqueducts and over bridges, through tunnels and along a maze of serpentine curves that thrilled our father's engineering eye, but made our mother ill. Soon other passengers grew terrified by the widening precipice that yawned outside the carriage windows, so that a porter was kept busy pulling down shades and reassuring every one that derailings and other calamities "almost" never occurred. He likewise did a good business selling souvenirs, photos, tiny glass trains or lanterns filled with coloured confections, and tissue-paper streamers on a stick (to ward off flies). Most effective among these panic chasers was a special kind of sweetmeat made of a rich almond short-cake mixture and packaged in cornhusk tubes. With an almond cookie melting on one's tongue it was possible to forget even the spine-chilling ravines that might at any moment lure the little locomotive into their depths.

Orizaba, at the foot of snowy Citláltepel, was reached by noon, and, as the train had no dining-car, we stopped for lunch at the town's most presentable inn. Here, too, Maximilian and Carlota had paused on their journey to the capital; he to make a speech (in somewhat garbled Spanish) from the balcony of the town-hall, and she to nurse insect bites, sunburn, and bruises obtained during the bouncing stagecoach ride.

After the short noonday interruption our upward passage continued as we now approached the most hair-raising portion of the trip. Mexico City lies at an altitude of almost eight thousand feet; and the rise from flat sea-level to the lofty plateau grew ever more menacing. Female passengers who risked a peep behind fluttering shades fainted forthwith, nor could the toothsome almond cookies (even if the supply had held out) abate the general hysteria.

At last the summit of the cordillera was reached and the table-land of Anáhuac came into view. After a brief descent the train rolled safely over level tracks along a picturesque waterway known as the Canal de la Viga. Near by the giant volcanoes Popocatepetl (Smoking Mountain) and Ixtaccihuatl (The White Woman) rose to shuddering heights, their frozen caps piercing the clouds. But the ancient Aztec city nestled peacefully in the valley, its towers and cupolas aglow under the evening sun.

We recovered from the rigours of the trip at a comfortable hotel in the Avenida Isabel la Católica. Here a secretary from the Austro-Hungarian Legation and the Mexican representative of Siemens came to call. With their combined aid we were established in a small Spanish house, staffed with native servants, in the suburb of Santa María. The neighbourhood, though residential, looked grim and dreary, since all buildings were set flush with the pavements and only an occasional bougainvillea vine tumbling over a housetop revealed the presence of flowering gardens within.

Despite cramped quarters, Papa and Mama plunged into their new life with zest. The furniture was unpacked and placed in as nearly the pattern we had known in Europe as possible. Particularly the bedroom of our parents was the same, no matter where we lived. There were the two walnut beds with Gothic headboards pushed together as one, so that a vast, tasselled, maroon spread covered them both. On either side stood marble-topped night tables, each with a silver candlestick representing a halberdier with helmet and pike, the latter providing a grip for the taper. These candlesticks had been a wedding present from Papa's first employer, Herr Ganz. Over the headboards hung a wall-bracket lamp, shaded in red Japanese silk and calculated to encourage a lifelong family vice—reading in bed. Next, there were two mirrored wardrobes, each with a single wide door that locked with an enormous key. But by far the proudest item in this ponderous chamber was the great chest which, with marble surface and an added marble shelf under a towering mirror, served as a washstand. Plumbing in those days had already come indoors, but fastidious people still held on to their portable pitcher and basin sets. Mama was particularly proud of her equipment, which included a dainty covered soap-dish, toothbrush holder, and hairpin receptacle, all tinted in pale lavender and embellished with realistic iris blooms.

The rest of our household furnishings included a depressing dining-room with a carved sideboard that boasted an upper structure like a cathedral, with niches and miniature balconies to hold prized porcelains. Similarly in our parlour there stood a big red plush sofa with a shelf running above the headpiece, where vases and delicate figurines of Meissen shepherdesses rested in precarious array.

It was the fashion, too, in that day of frilled and cluttered living, to place ornamental tables of highly polished nickel or gleaming brass (topped with gewgaws known as *nippes*) in every available space. These tables were often mere stands or pedestals on convoluted Baroque legs, quite high, and sometimes tiered in two or three levels like a palm with spreading fan leaves. Since every respectable home in Mexico possessed this French version of the what-not—in unbelievable variety of design—it was the delight of my childhood to visit other people's parlours and to gape with fascinated eyes at their bric-à-brac.

In the end our possessions drove us from the little house. Shortly after getting settled, the Fräulein had received a sad letter from Berlin, telling of her brother's grave illness.

"His asthma," she sobbed. "It's such a tragedy—he is a fine pianist who might have had a great future."

The word "pianist" captivated our mother, whose Hungarian heart fed on music. Couldn't something be done to save the unhappy young man? People with pulmonary trouble went to Switzerland because of the altitude. Then why not Mexico City?

Papa was startled. But, unable to withstand tears—and the Fräulein wept copiously—he agreed to cable passage money to Berlin. Before another severe European winter set in, the ailing youth was to embark for Veracruz.

Not until their impulsive decision had been acted upon did our mother and father ponder its consequences. Where, in the miniature house, was another adult to be quartered? With a cook, chambermaid, and gardener (for a laughable patch of back yard), we were falling over one another. Any addition, even a canary in a cage, must cause the little structure to burst at the seams. In short, we had to move.

Luckily the district of Santa María touched another residential neighbourhood called San Rafael where, on the street of Manuel María Contreras, Papa located a large and rambling corner house with an immense walled-in garden. Here we were able to spread out, with cats and dogs added to the *ménage*, as well as the canary. Also, since Papa and Mama rode every morning, their horses could be stabled on our grounds. The gardener, answering to the astonishing name of Jesús, took on the additional duties of a groom.

It was not long before the Fräulein's brother arrived. He was a slender, fair, aristocratic youth, quite unlike his plump and rubicund sister. So as to make him feel at home, my brothers and I were instructed to address him as Uncle Bichteler. He was a shy man, yet with exquisite manners. We loved him at once.

With Uncle Bichteler music entered my life. When his long white hands touched the piano keys I was transported into a realm of sensory delight heretofore unknown. We had not been told, my brothers and I, that he was ill. And, indeed, after six months of Mexico City sunshine he ceased to be ill. Before long he even joined our parents in their morning ride, alternating with his sister, for whom Papa had acquired another horse.

Not far from our street of Manuel María Contreras lay an ancient causeway known as La Verónica, which connected this part of town with the forest of Chapultepec. In the centre of that forest looms the castle on the crag, on the very site where once stood the palace of the fabulous Montezuma, where later lived the Viceroys of Spain, still later Maximilian and Carlota, and where, since Juárez, the Presidents of Mexico have held sway.

From almost any angle of the inner city the lordly mansion was visible, its single turret and bastioned medieval walls forming a strange contrast to the Florentine balconies and terraces of later origin.

Surrounding the castle in a radius of three miles stood the thousand-year-old trees known in the Aztec tongue as *ahuehuetes*, which means The Old Men, since from their lofty branches long fronds of Spanish moss hung thickly like a mass of tangled grey beards. It was a story-book forest in which a child might walk with plausible prospects of meeting Little Red Riding Hood and her wolf, or a witch that hobbled about a delectable Gingerbread House. For us who in Solymár and in Berlin's Grunewald had already experienced the magic of a European wood, this sylvan retreat held a breathless enchantment. Running along humus-laden paths, we beheld the leafy canopy overhead, shutting out the sky so that a mystic darkness spread all about, pierced only here and there by oblique shafts of sunlight. At times the spell of that forest was so overpowering that I burst into tears of mingled ecstasy and fear. Only one who has walked very young under trees and listened to the soundlessness of his own footsteps, almost unreal and disembodied, can feel the shiver of delight evoked by such a memory.

It was along the wooded paths of Chapultepec that we children first heard the story of Maximilian and Carlota. The laundress Dolores, who on off days did duty as second maid, had charge of our airings in the park. She pointed out the fabled pool, deep and crystal clear, in which Montezuma and his court had bathed. But it was when she told about Mexico's brief Habsburg interlude that the old woman got into her stride. To be sure, she did not know the European machinations and political intrigue operating behind the scenes. Hers was a simple plot: in the palace above us had lived a tall, fair prince, the Emperor Maximiliano, and beside him his Empress, Doña Carlota. They had been happy, these two, happy and in love. Fiestas and merriment made up their days. And then, tragedy had come. The Emperor had been annihilated by his enemies, while the Empress fled across the seas and was never seen again.

Here in this small bare truth lay the secret of all legend and folklore. So must the ancient ballad-singers have fashioned their songs, and so must those greatest of narrative poems, Homer's *Iliad* and *Odyssey*—or even the Bible itself—have come into being: through the creative power of the spoken word. "Empty barrels make a hollow sound," said an old Hungarian proverb. In girth,

Dolores looked astonishingly like a barrel. But we knew that she was not an empty one.

In a more direct way our parents became linked with the Maximilian theme almost from the start. Mexican families with whom they made contact appeared steeped in their country's tradition; such names as Macías, Torres-Rivas, Teresa, Terraza, Escandón, Rubio, Limantour, Pimentel, Romero-Terreros, and Rincón-Gallardo had enjoyed their highest lustre during imperial days. The more patrician of these clans still boasted some doddering and picturesque figure who might have stepped straight out of another century, some great-uncle or aunt who had belonged to the courtly entourage of Chapultepec. At Mama's afternoon teas there appeared at times several grandes-dames, former ladies-in-waiting to Carlota. These wrinkled octogenarians sat in the parlour, their taffeta robes spread about them, while our mother made conversation (Mama was no linguist) in fluent Magyar, experimental Spanish, and bad French.

On these occasions it often happened that I was called into the parlour to make my curtsy and then to depart. Only, I never departed. I always stayed to hear what the old ladies had to say. And it was now that the characters of Maximilian and Carlota assumed for me a flesh and blood reality. Up to this point, even when I gazed at the heights of Chapultepec, the Emperor and Empress had been figures of legend and fantasy not unlike the fairy-tale creatures that peopled our nursery world. But now it becmse suddenly clear that Maximilian and Carlota had truly lived, for here were eyewitnesses who remembered them.

This was modern, industrialized, republican Mexico under President Porfirio Díaz! Who cared about that far-away, forgotten Maximilian Empire? Yet the old *damas de honor*, the ladies-in-waiting, had nothing else to talk about. They were still proud of their former connexion with royalty, boasting about it and preening themselves in its lost glow. This one felt that she had been Carlota's particular confidante, while another fancied herself as the once celebrated belle of the court. A third and fourth emphatically begged to differ. Thus in testy tones they quibbled and quarrelled over their teacups, stirring the dead past in its ashes and restoring it almost tangibly to life.

My brothers and I absorbed these scenes like avid little sponges. The graphic antics of the court ladies, when added to the stories told by the Indian maid Dolores, furnished a precious ballast to be stored away in that "glorified attic of the imagination" of which the poet Edgar Saltus spoke.

5

THE MAXIMILIAN STORY

The Maximilian drama was known to our parents only in broad outline. As Europeans, they saw it in a European light; that is, primarily, as a reckless and typically dynastic exploit which had unhappily miscarried. They were quite unfamiliar with New World conditions, particularly with respect to the United States Civil War, which had actually precipitated the entire Maximilian episode. Without this War of Secession during the 1860's the Habsburg interlude in Mexico would never have happened. It was the American conflict between North and South which made Maximilian possible, at least as temporary occupant of a hypothetical Aztec throne.

Following the outbreak of hostilities within the borders of the "Colossus of the North," an internationally unpopular principle called the Monroe Doctrine was forced into abeyance. The authorities in Washington were far too busy with domestic problems to engage in policing the entire Western Hemisphere. This meant that European Powers interested in gulping yet another slice of the New World might do so while the United States was not looking.

One country so inclined was France, ruled at that time by Napoleon III, a Bonaparte who lived under a handicap: it was not an easy thing to be the undistinguished nephew of a world conqueror. France had fed on glory under Napoleon the Great, and she wanted more of that dish. She looked to Napoleon the Little to give it to her. Alas, he was not cut after the heroic pattern; he was not even a good politician. But he knew what France wanted of him, and so he had agents scattered over the globe to ferret out an opportunity for the deed sensational.

America's Civil War gave him his chance. Alert advisers called his attention to the fact that south of the Rio Grande there was a rich unexploited country called Mexico, which would make an admirable colony for France. Napoleon immediately saw the point. An overseas expedition would enable him to pluck this juicy plum, thereby restoring Bonaparte prestige throughout the world. But he had no handy excuse for intervention in Mexico; one must, for future history-books, find a pretext.

It was Napoleon's stock-jobbing, bastard half-brother, the Duc de Morny, who thought out a solution. A scallawag Swiss financier named Jean-Baptiste Jecker had been complaining in the Paris Press that certain of his Mexican investments had gone awry. Now, if Jecker could be clothed with French citizenship, argued Morny, his cause became the cause of France. It was beautifully simple! Napoleon resolved to act at once.

Before he got very far, a fly—or rather, two flies—appeared in the ointment: England and Spain wanted a share in the rapacious undertaking. The Governments of both these countries also produced creditors with Mexican claims that were long overdue. In short, Napoleon's dream of personal conquest went by the boards as, under Lord Palmerston's cool strategy, the three Powers agreed on a joint expedition. It was to be a cosy little debt-collectors' war.

The joint invasion forces landed at Veracruz in 1861 and started for the highlands. It was now that, to their vast chagrin, Spaniards and Britons found themselves outnumbered by their French allies; the wily Napoleon had rushed advance detachments of the Foreign Legion into Mexico to ensure an advantageous foothold. Angrily England and Spain withdrew. They would remember this nine years later, when, at the *débâcle* of Sedan, the fallen French monarch had need of them. The war of 1870 against Prussia cost Napoleon his throne, with not a finger lifted in London or Madrid to save him.

For the moment, having a free hand in Mexico, the French undertaking prospered. With the aid of a second commander, Marshal Bazaine, the invaders reached Mexico City, drove the Indian President, Benito Juárez, out of office, and took possession of the land.

Things had been easy so far. But now that Mexico was in his power, Napoleon needed some one to rule the new colony for him. Unfortunately he did not have, like his famous uncle, a flock of brothers and cousins with whom to people the thrones of the world. He had only a five-year-old son, Prince Loulou, and an illegitimate brother, the Duc de Morny. Neither Morny nor Loulou would do.

But now a brainstorm struck him. There were always any number of pleasing and debonair Austrian archdukes about—young men who danced the Vienna waltz divinely, made friends easily, and (a handy qualification in this case) found themselves often in the ranks of the unemployed. One such candidate for Napoleon's overseas throne might be the Archduke Ferdinand Maximilian, brother of Austria's young Emperor, Franz Josef.

The proposition required crafty handling and a persuasive eloquence, talents in which the French sovereign excelled. With high-flown language he offered Maximilian the crown of a presumably imperial Mexico, assuring the startled prince that across the ocean a strife-torn and war-weary nation yearned for the blessings of monarchic rule.

Actually, nothing was further from the truth. But Napoleon's best ally shared Maximilian's bed: Charlotte, former Princess of Belgium. During their brief Florentine honeymoon Charlotte had changed her name to the Italian Carlotta; now, with Latin American prospects in view, she removed yet another consonant, for the correct Spanish spelling. As Empress Carlota of Mexico she would outrank even her father, Leopold I, who was only a king. Indeed, Maximilian shared the plight of all patient husbands whose wives want to get on in the world.

Finally, there was the most potent driving force of all: Napoleon's consort, the Spanish-born Eugénie, whose fiery heart could never forget that a large part of the Western Hemisphere had once belonged to the Crown of Castile. If Mexico was lost to Spain, Eugénie would bend every effort to win it for her adopted homeland, France. She pelted Carlota with goading letters, calculated to help Maximilian make up his mind.

Needless to say, the matter was arranged. After a token plebiscite under French auspices, Maximilian was presented with a five-page manifesto purporting to be the will of the Mexican people. He accepted this at face value since, obviously, there must be some truth in five sheets of flowery and grandiloquent prose.

In good faith the new Emperor and Empress set out for their overseas realm, where they expected to be received with open arms. Landing at Veracruz on May 28, 1864, they found themselves facing a hostile land that had made no provision for welcome. One look round the fever-ridden and desolate port told them that here they were not wanted: they should never have come. Of course, the logical thing would have been to return to Europe immediately. But they had their pride to consider. Desperately Carlota argued: perhaps, if they took their courage firmly in hand and pressed forward instead of back, they might yet win the friendship of this inscrutable Aztec race on whom they were imposing themselves.

Quelling his doubts, Maximilian agreed. And so they pressed forward, up to the plateau and Mexico City, where they did win native hearts by the simplicity and sincerity of their own ways. In the capital and its environs Maximilian and Carlota grew to be well loved. But out in the provinces, where people did not know them, they were soundly hated. In the provinces, too, waited the Indian president—Benito Juárez—for the hour of revenge.

Fate did not keep him waiting long. In the great country to the north the Civil War came to a close, and the Monroe Doctrine was taken from the shelf for preliminary dusting. Presently official Washington looked southward across the Rio Grande and raised angry eyebrows in the direction of Paris. What, American Secretary of State Seward wished to know, was the French flag doing in Mexico?

Napoleon was badly frightened. He wanted no trouble with the United States, and decided to wash his hands of the luckless Mexican venture. In this he was wise, for he could not afford to throw the French people into a war against the fully mobilized American forces. But so troubled was his conscience that he did not let Maximilian know which way the wind was blowing until it was too late. By the time the duped Habsburg grasped the full measure of his plight the Foreign Legion was already taking to its boats, while only a handful of Frenchmen remained in the country. It fell upon Maximilian to rake the chestnuts from the fire of Napoleon's kindling.

In a last, desperate gesture, Carlota tried to save the day. On the heels of the fleeing troops she sped to Paris, to plead her husband's cause. But at the Palace of St Cloud she found herself knocking on closed doors. Pushing her way past restraining guards, she faced Napoleon and Eugénie, only to discover that they were her friends no longer.

Would anyone else in Europe help? Even the portals of the Vatican were slammed in the wandering Empress's face; after this final blow she collapsed in gibbering despair, unable to pursue her mission further. While Belgian relatives locked the mad Empress away in the moated castle of Bouchout, outside Brussels, the world learned of Maximilian's lonely fate. He died on June 19, 1867, before a firing squad on the Hill of the Bells at Querétaro, as that which he had never wanted to be—a usurper.

The tragi-comedy had ended, and the curtain rang down, with only a brief epilogue to follow. There had been left behind in Mexico an assortment of Imperial possessions: Carlota's bracelets, her necklaces and diadems, as well as Maximilian's military orders and decorations, among them the exalted order of the Golden Fleece. These things the House of Habsburg wanted back.

At the time of the tragedy the political climate of Mexico was far too hostile for a return of the gems to be attempted. Almost four decades elapsed before another generation could look upon that chapter in the nation's history with tolerant and comprehending eyes. By the turn of the century Mexicans regarded Maximilian no longer as a culprit, but as rather a gallant and even heroic figure; historians began to stress that the doomed Habsburg could easily have saved his skin by making a timely escape, yet he had remained at his post because he had pledged his word to France.

Carlota also wrested from posterity a measure of compassion. Though her ambition to be Empress had plunged Maximilian into the foolhardy venture, she had stood staunchly by him in the face of ruin. Nor did she, after the shots at Querétaro, frivolously rebuild her life. A victim of melancholia, she spent the balance of her years making herself into a monument to the memory of a lost cause.

From so charitable a perspective towards the past, modern Mexico arrived at a generous decision with regard to the Habsburg gems. Every last piece would be allowed to return to Vienna, provided the Austrian Government followed a prescribed diplomatic procedure.

It was this "procedure" and its startling ramifications which, for a considerable time, dominated our life in Mexico. So it was that, while our father was absorbed with the construction of a hydro-electric plant at Necaxa which was to furnish power for Mexico City, Mama set out on her search for Imperial treasure.

6

SEARCH FOR JEWELS

WITH A zestful optimism, not unlike that which had characterized the reckless Carlota, our mother threw herself into her Mexican adventure. Confidently she had embarked from Europe on a peregrination at the end of which beckoned the Habsburg jewels, ready for her to pick up and return in triumph to the Hofburg. In actual practice the undertaking was not quite so simple. Upon calling at Castle Chapultepec to gather up the Imperial possessions, Mama discovered that there were none to be gathered. The obliging government of Don Porfirio, it now developed, had no objection to a return of Maximilian mementoes *if* such mementoes could be found. The bothersome search must be undertaken by the Habsburg emissaries themselves at no expense to Mexico. As for Imperial heirlooms, whatever had escaped destruction during the siege of Chapultepec would be widely scattered and difficult to trace; at the time of Maximilian's downfall the castle had been looted by Juaristas and much royal treasure had disappeared.

Rebuffed by official authorities, Mama bethought herself of the most logical source of information, the surviving old courtiers and ladies-in-waiting whose loyalty to the Empire remained unsullied. With tact and caution she broached the subject at her next afternoon tea. The response was gratifying on the part of the proud *damas*. Agog with excitement, they revealed the hiding-place of treasured keepsakes that had remained in their trust since the disbanding of the palace personnel. Did the Empress Carlota have need of these things? Quickly a pile of rings, bracelets, pearl collars, and diadems mounted on our parlour table.

"Take these," exclaimed the eldest lady, Doña Francisca Escandón y Landa, "and tell our beloved Señora that she could not have left them in better safekeeping!"

Naïvely the aged crones imagined that Carlota's reason had returned and that the royal trinkets were destined for Castle

Bouchout. It might even be, they speculated, that Her Majesty would have need of an entourage with which to set up a new court. The *damas* were not averse to travel, if there appeared the slightest chance of gravitating once more in an imperial orbit.

When told it was the Emperor of Austria who requested the gems they were a trifle crestfallen. "Ah, that Francisco José!" they commented acidly. "When Maximiliano needed help no army came from Vienna to his rescue. But the jewels, that is another matter!"

Gently our mother explained that Austria had never been a maritime Power whence armies could be dispatched on short notice overseas, and that in any case the Maximilian venture had been a Napoleonic rather than a Habsburg responsibility. The request for the jewels, she added, had been prompted purely by family sentiment.

This statement allayed suspicions and restored a measure of harmony. With renewed zeal the old ladies rummaged through their chests and cupboards, divesting themselves of their hoarded treasure. In addition they hinted that other pieces might be found at the Monte de Piedad (Federal pawnshop) in the cathedral square in the centre of the town.

For years the Monte de Piedad had been a cherished survival of Spanish civic administration. Instituted by the viceroys of Mexico during colonial days, more than three centuries ago, it served a civilized and humanitarian purpose. Here families of wealth and position, who might fall upon lean times, could, without loss of face, pawn their valuables for long-term loans. Periodically the Government held auction sales at which the original owners could redeem their belongings or dispose of them in a profitable exchange.

Losing no time, Mama marched to the famed pawnshop, where, to her delight, she was able to unearth a part of Maximilian's silver hollow-ware. This table service of heavy Christofle plate had been a gift from Napoleon and Eugénie to the vacillating Archduke at the time of the first Mexican negotiations. In response to Maximilian's demand for proof that he was wanted overseas the French sovereigns had heaped presents upon him, with the implication that these came from Mexico.

Most of the silverware had vanished through the years, but the *petit déjeuner*, or "breakfast," set of the Emperor had found its way somehow to the Monte de Piedad. It consisted of a small individual coffee-pot, a sugar-bowl, a salver, and a pitcher for milk (in those days the opulence of cream was unknown even to royalty). Each piece bore the Imperial initials *M.I.M.* (Maximilian I of Mexico) with the crown engraved above them. The salver, of later manufacture than the rest, was stamped with the name of a Mexican silversmith in place of the Parisian hallmark; also, unlike the French pieces, it was of solid silver.

The Empress Carlota too had owned her separate breakfast set, but this had returned to Belgium with her. The pieces left in Mexico gave silent testimony to the assurance with which the Empress had departed; far from anticipating disaster, she had expected to bring help from Europe and to save her husband's cause. Meanwhile, whatever vexations might plague Maximilian during her absence, he had to have his coffee. Carlota left instructions with Tüdös, the faithful Hungarian valet, to keep the polish bright on the Napoleonic plate. It was kept bright, even in the Emperor's prison cell on that last dawn at Querétaro.

Besides the silver hollow-ware other Imperial objects showed up at the Federal pawnshop, among these a pair of epergnes from the banquet hall of Chapultepec and two exquisite examples of crystal stemware. The latter, also of French origin, consisted of a claret glass and a champagne goblet, both with the etched cipher and crown, already noted on the silver. The champagne goblet was of so-called "court design," tall and narrow like a miniature vase, rather than the customary wide chalice.

The Monte de Piedad also did a flourishing business in oddities that had no Habsburg connexion. There were pre-Maximilian curios to tempt the shopper's fancy; antique carved furniture, ecclesiastic vestments, viceregal jewellery, and bric-à-brac of that late Spanish Baroque known as Churrigueresque. All this was housed in the same ancient structure erected during the post-Cortez era, which had withstood the ravages of many a political storm. To-day, as long ago, the Federal pawnshop in Mexico City remains the antique collector's happy hunting ground.

Another spot where our mother browsed for historic treasure was the Thieves' Market or Volador (literally: The Place Where Things Fly To) which was located on the same cathedral square —to-day's Zócalo—diagonally across from the Monte de Piedad. Unethical though it be to approve an establishment that thrives on robbery, the Thieves' Market enjoyed a venerable notoriety. Like the pawnshop, it had been founded more than three centuries earlier by the Spanish viceroys, and for a similarly persuasive reason: the salvage of cherished possessions. Unburdened by artistic considerations, thieves look for a quick turnover of their booty. In the case of stolen jewellery they care little for perfection of design or craftsmanship, thinking only of melting down the gold or silver content and selling it by weight, or breaking precious stones out of their settings and splitting them into more marketable fragments. In this way æsthetic values are destroyed, fine workmanship is lost, and a barbarism committed.

To prevent such desecration the far-sighted Spanish authorities established a trading-post for stolen goods. Here the rascals could bring their wares, and—under a limited immunity, governed by the speed with which they appeared—could sell them for a nominal fee. Thus anxious owners were able to recover their valuables intact, without forfeiting more than a customary finder's reward.

Thanks to this arrangement our mother fished up the most prized of the Maximilian pieces, the collar and pendant of the Golden Fleece. This diamond-studded decoration, once broken apart, could never have been replaced.

Twice, while Mama was at the Thieves' Market, she lost her own watch and our father had to buy it back for her. But this did not dampen her fervour. Daily she canvassed the robbers' den until every last bit of Maximilianiana had been winnowed out.

It was rumoured that during the collapse of the Empire much Chapultepec loot disappeared into the provinces. This could not be traced at all. Through decades to come there would be bits of Habsburg crockery—a soup tureen, a cup and saucer from the simple every-day table setting—cropping up as far north as Monterrey, and across the border in Texas, Arizona, and New Mexico. Particularly was the famous "Lapis Lazuli Collection" widely scattered. Of this there remained in Mexico City only the Emperor's watch, a bracelet belonging to Carlota, and some ear-rings all marked by the same diamond encrustment of crown and initials upon a background of blue stone. Maximilian's tie-pin and signet-ring, as well as Carlota's smaller signet, have more recently been discovered in the United States. But present-day impoverished Habsburgs have no funds to spend on family mementoes; the once-coveted objects have lost in marketability, much to their current owners' chagrin.

One phenomenon that greatly baffled our mother was the recurring appearance of so-called Maximilian watches. Apart from the above-mentioned authentic one, these others ranged from copper and silver cases to thinly washed gold. Since they all showed a remarkable similarity in design it presently became clear that disreputable jewellers were making them up from old Empire coins, particularly the well-known Maximilian peso, with the Emperor's profile on one side and his coat-of-arms on the other. These counterfeit monstrosities were being turned out by the dozen and snatched up by gullible tourists whose finances surpassed their historical acumen.

Lastly, the search for Habsburg memorabilia wound up on a somewhat delicate note. In the front parlour of the Teresa home adjoining the suburb of Tacubaya our mother came upon a fern-stand surmounted by an ample silver bowl, embossed with the familiar crest. Her gasp of surprise was received appreciatively by the hostess, who, with true Latin candour and aplomb, explained that this was indeed a most intimate utensil from the boudoir of Chapultepec: an Imperial chamber-pot. "There are four of them," she continued amiably. "The other three belong to some cousins of mine. Would you like to see them?"

With an effort at insouciance Mama declined, but the señora insisted. "They are absolutely authentic, except for the second handle, which was attached by our silversmith in order to permit —er—other uses."

It was the second handle which furnished our mother the chance for a tactful withdrawal. His Majesty the Emperor of Austria, she confided, wished to purchase only such dynastic paraphernalia as had not been (begging your pardon!) tampered with.

The fernery, in short, remained on its stand.

7

EXCURSION TO NECAXA

ANYONE LIVING in Mexico is at one time or another touched by the Maximilian theme. Throughout our neighbourhood children heard the same stories from their nursemaids that my brothers and I were being told by Dolores and her sister Cruz, who was our cook. Yet the particular aspect that concerned our own family —namely, the search for the imperial heirlooms—remained unknown to Sylvester, Arnim, and myself. It was also kept from the servants, since our parents wished to avoid any gossip concerning the accumulation of valuables under their roof. At the slightest rumour our house could have become a target for burglars, and the routine of canvassing the Thieves' Market might have had to start all over again. In short, our parents watched their conversation. During the noon meal, which was the only one we shared with them, talk turned about matters of livelier interest, such as Papa's construction plans for the Necaxa dam.

Papa had become consulting engineer for the Mexican Light and Power Company, and his field work took him on frequent journeys to the semi-tropic regions of the state of Puebla. This provided exciting holidays for the whole family, for we often went along to camp in one of the Company's guest-houses. The trip from Mexico City took some eight hours by rail to a small terminus named El Carmen, within sight of the Laguna watershed. Here we were transferred to a miniature track which led up to La Mesa, the Necaxa tableland, where the administration cottages stood in two neat rows. Round about, as far as the eye could see, there was a world of lush emerald green, dotted with an incredible profusion of flowers. All of the blooms were moisture-loving: hydrangeas, orchids, callas, and a unique pale-green rose. It rained nine months of the year in Necaxa, yet there was no hint of gloom. Daily a bright sun broke through between cloudbursts to highlight a glittering, dew-sprinkled paradise. At such times windows were quickly opened and all bedding was hung out in a constant battle against mildew. The novelty of this problem held a certain delight for us children; we enjoyed the gasps and shudders that accompanied bedtime on days when the sun had lagged in its task. City-bred, we sensed here for the first time an intimate dependence upon nature. Day and night we were in a great presence.

Necaxa held certain dangers, particularly for children. There was the hazardous terrain, consisting of immense elevations and breath-taking precipices, with only narrow strips of habitable areas at the top. The Mesa, where the guest-houses stood, was a narrow promontory surrounded on three sides by a sheer drop of more than twelve hundred feet. Heavy wire fencing closed in the safety zone, but this did not thwart our urge to climb and pick flowers on the other side. As a result our playtime had to be rigorously supervised either by the Fräulein or the local service personnel.

A second menace was the insect and reptile life of the low regions that yawned in steaming jungle heat about our breeze-freshened elevation. On daily hikes or horseback expeditions along lushly overgrown mountain paths we came into contact with these denizens of the wilderness. Uncle Bichteler started a collection (in alcohol) of the more lurid specimens. This created a minor sensation, since Uncle Bichteler had always been regarded as a thin-skinned æsthete. His startling competence in trapping iguanas, copperheads, scorpions, and a huge hairy tarantula earned him even greater respect than that accorded his musicianship. Slender, with candid eyes and a sensitive mouth, he resembled pictures of the poet Shelley or the latter's Germanic counterpart, Schiller, rather than a stout-hearted naturalist with a faculty for seizing loathsome fauna by the neck. Hereafter we looked with awe at Uncle Bichteler's tapering pianist hands.

More than any of us, Papa understood and enjoyed Necaxa. To him the mountain gorges and great waterfalls were a technologist's delight, since their vast hydro-electric potential opened a vista of attainable progress. Where the layman might see a panorama of imposing grandeur, our father visualized humming turbines and dynamos at successive levels of the tumbling precipice that circled La Mesa. Daily he visited Salto Chico and Salto Grande, two magnificent waterfalls that roared over the cliffs. Once we were allowed to join him on a perilous descent, by cable platform, alongside the racing sluiceway which ended in a spitting maelstrom before being harnessed to the power plant below. On another occasion he took us with him to inspect the tunnelled shafts through which workers were sped to their jobs in a matter of minutes, though the drop in elevation was a quarter of a mile. With the change of altitude we experienced an immediate contrast in climate; in fact, the sun might be shining brightly at the tunnel entrance while a torrential downpour greeted us at its exit. Native workers, most of them Indians from two near-by villages—Tenango and Huauchinango—were prepared for both contingencies, since they carried at all times a rain-cape made of palm rushes and a broad-brimmed peaked hat. The native rain-cape with its crisp fronds standing off in all directions made its wearer look like an upright porcupine, while the peaked hat with turned-down brim confused the picture by suggesting an overgrown beetle. This functional Necaxa hat differed radically from the typical Mexican sombrero of travel-poster fame; where the former shed moisture by its conical design the latter's up-curving brim collected water like a fruit tray. My brothers and I, of course, owned Necaxa hats, butter-yellow and woven out of pliable palm-fibre.

It was in Necaxa that I first heard English in daily use. An American construction engineer named Cooper lived on the Mesa with his wife and daughter. They were well-bred people, reserved yet friendly, with whom our parents enjoyed a happy association. The little girl was of an age with Sylvester; hence she played with the boys rather than with me. But I admired her immensely because of her long blonde curls and the bangs across her forehead. All through childhood I remembered those bangs, yearning to wear my own hair in so charming a fashion. But Mama was adamant. "That is the style for poodles," she declared, "not people."

Another thing my brothers and I liked about the Cooper child was that she owned a donkey. This angelic beast took all of us on its sun-warmed fuzzy back, ambling along the flower-bordered footpaths at a cautious, gingerly pace. The delicate tattoo of its hooves won my four-year-old heart, while I was still in awe of the snorting and stamping creatures in Papa's stable. If I could only have had bangs and a little grey donkey my happiness would have been complete.

In yet another respect Necaxa proved important to us, for it was here that we lost our Fräulein. She fell in love with one of Mr Cooper's assistants, a Mr Paul, who promptly asked our parents for her hand. This was an unforeseen development which created considerable commotion. Mama insisted on a wedding in Mexico City, complete with traditional flim-flam, since the young couple would thereafter lead an isolated life away from metropolitan glitter. Fräulein, meanwhile, wrote frantic letters abroad in an effort to engage a new governess for us.

We left Necaxa and returned to the house on Manuel María Contreras, where wedding preparations were started. The ceremony was to take place during early summer, in our garden, with an evening reception at the Crystal Pavilion of Chapultepec. Among the guests would be a neighbouring couple with two boys, the younger of whom was called Nené. Since Nené was my own age and we had been playmates for some time, it was decided that he should serve as a page while I was a flower-girl. We were to be costumed as a miniature bride and groom.

Not very clear in our understanding of these events, Nené and I believed that we too were being married. This was entirely acceptable to us, for we were very fond of each other. We sat one whole afternoon in the garden swing, talking about it.

Nevertheless, before the great day was over our idyll exploded on a discordant note. For some obscure reason, which could have been their secret yearning for a daughter, Nené's parents coddled him in egregious fashion, showering him with toys suitable to his sex and a girl's playthings as well. Thus, apart from marbles, air-pistols, or an archery set, he had pots and pans, a parasol, a perambulator, and a fully equipped doll's-house. Like two little girls, he and I played house, cooked, spanked our dolls, or gave them medicines to cure their colic.

On the afternoon of our Fräulein's marriage, however, I experienced a sudden awakening. Every child at the reception was to receive a special favour. In the case of Nené and me this turned out to be a pair of dolls, each with a small valise of interchangeable clothes. Now, Nené's possessions had heretofore never startled me, since they had already been his when we first met. But the *new* dolls were identical. Did this mean that Nené and I were identical? Having shared a nursery with my brothers, I knew that this was patently absurd. It was all right for Nené to have a doll, but she ought not to be wearing *exactly* the same frock or wig as mine. Something within me boiled at the idea.

Before the evening ended I took action. It had been agreed with Nené's parents that my brothers and I would spend the night at their house, since our servants were at Chapultepec to watch the dancing. This arrangement gave me the opportunity for my misdeed. Nené's family had a reputation for extreme piety, which was borne out by the fact that a private chapel with altar and prayer-stools adjoined the children's nursery. As I was being put to bed Nené and his brother disappeared into this chapel for their evening orisons. A moment later the maid turned out the light and left the room. I was alone with Nené's wealth of toys. Cocking one ear towards the devotions in the adjacent chamber, I reached for his new doll and divested her of every stitch of clothing. Next, without remorse or shame, I stuffed the loot into the small valise that belonged to my own doll, whereupon I dropped into a sound and untroubled sleep.

The next day there was hell to pay, when Nené proclaimed his loss in ear-splitting yelps. My dereliction was of course discovered, and our Fräulein, before starting on her honeymoon, was called upon to administer a final disciplinary spanking, after which —weeping herself—she kissed me good-bye. In addition, I was obliged to return each stolen object, with fitting words of contrition and apology. It was extremely humiliating.

Oddly, that same night something happened for which there could be no redress. The servant girl who had got me ready for bed removed a gold locket and chain from my throat, despite my protest that this was never done at home. The following day she dressed me without returning locket or chain. But, in the tumult already raised by my own disgraceful conduct, Papa and Mama were in no position to inquire after the "lost" trinket. The locket, heart-shaped and ornamented with a small ruby, had been a present from my godmother, Camille Fehér de Vernet. Its loss made an acute and lasting impression.

But, to cap the above train of vexations, Nené made a devastating announcement. He refused to marry me.

8

SCHOOL-DAYS

SYLVESTER AND Arnim had reached school age. Up to now they had been tutored by the Fräulein, so that they could read and scribble their alphabet. But after the marriage festivities were over and the governess had departed, our parents were faced with the problem of the boys' education. Possibly influenced by our contact with the Cooper family in Necaxa, Papa decided on a private school run by an Englishwoman known simply as Miss Neems.

I have no idea where this school was located, but I clearly recall that my brothers presently returned from classes, chattering in an extraordinary new tongue. It was quite different from the language spoken by the Yankee-born Coopers, particularly in one respect: every sentence seemed to open with the crisp announcement "I say!" It was "I say, is it raining?" or "I say, have you my umbrella?" Our parents, who knew no English, were greatly impressed. Still, it appeared rather silly to say that you were saying something when it was obvious no one else was.

As for myself, I learned parrot-fashion from my brothers. Listening to their conversations, it was not long before I grasped sufficient meaning to join in. Needless to add, I also could not open my mouth without announcing "I say!"

At times my brothers' growing vocabulary was beyond me. Thus on one occasion they maintained that an insect which in Spanish has the lovely name of *mariposa* is in English a butterfly. A fly in the butter? I did not like it at all. And, what was more, I did not believe it. The language of Miss Neems was new to Sylvester and Arnim, and they had perhaps heard wrong. The word might possibly be "flutterby"? At any rate, flutterby I made it, and flutterby it remained for me until many years later when, in a Philadelphia boarding-school, I learned that butterfly was, after all, right. This was a disappointment to me, since I still feel that flutterby is so much nicer.

Miss Neems's school was to leave a permanent imprint upon

our lives in quite another way. After only a few months of attendance Sylvester, the elder of my brothers, skipped a class. In addition, at the end of the school year he topped his fellow classmates and received an engraved fourteen-carat gold medal for "exceptional scholarship." It was an absurd award for one so young, but that was the way Miss Neems did things. Hers was an academy for little gentlemen, whom she treated as pint-sized adults.

At home Sylvester's medal made a great hit. The shiny badge, shaped like a Maltese cross, was boxed in a dark velvet case like some order of high rank. Mama in particular took pride in it. For a considerable time thereafter, when visitors came to our house Sylvester's medal was passed from hand to hand and volubly admired. At such times I learned to recognize an awed and bewildered look in Arnim's large grey eyes. Arnim had no medal.

Barring the normal bruises and physical pains of childhood, this was my first experience of spiritual suffering. It hurt me, with a sharp stinging hurt, to see a distinction made between my brothers. This distinction was certainly not Sylvester's fault. Indeed, in years to come his brilliance was to extend far beyond the scope of Miss Neems's prophetic recognition. But it descended on my small heart with a heaviness that I cannot explain. This is all the more puzzling as it would not have occurred to me to be jealous of my gifted elder brother. I was the baby of the family, and the only girl. Mine was an enviable and unchallenged state.

It was not so with Arnim. He stood between. And it seems to me now that, long before he himself grasped his situation, I had already sensed it. Years later a stanza by Elizabeth Coatsworth came to my attention, ending with the lines:

> The only honest democrat
> Is a young child—or else a cat!

My horror of injustice threw me instinctively to the side of Arnim, so as to create some sort of balance. He had no medal, I reasoned, so perhaps he ought to have *me*. At the same time this was a source of torture, since it set Sylvester apart in a loneliness all his own—a loneliness not mitigated in my eyes by adult accolades. Though I could not yet read, write, or even think in more than elementary terms, I could feel. And what I felt was the danger of a cleavage among us, the children, who were one flesh. It did not come to me that way—our being one flesh. The feeling was obscure, ambiguous, and I had no knowledge of the source of its strength.

As it happened, these early agonies were soon interfused with a problem all my own. At breakfast one morning I was told that on this day I would enter kindergarten. Since Miss Neems's school had no provision for children my age, Papa transferred the boys to the American School of Mexico City, which simplified our daily transportation. Trotting beside Mama, with Sylvester and Arnim on either side of us, I eagerly entered the strange, noisy building known as the Colegio Americano. It was great fun up to this point. But I was not prepared for what followed. For no sooner had a tall bespectacled lady separated my hand from Mama's warm grip than I found myself suddenly abandoned. Sylvester and Arnim had dashed off along a vast corridor to their separate classrooms, while my mother's figure—somehow, in these surroundings, not looking a bit like Mama—passed through a far doorway and vanished from view.

I was terrified. Looking round me, I saw a room full of chattering youngsters whose language I could not understand; the smattering of British English I had picked up from my brothers forsook me in this first mass encounter with American speech. It was not that I caught a tonal distinction between two language forms, but that I faced a dual crisis: the normal shock of childhood's first parting, sharpened by unfamiliar sounds that cut me off from all contact with my world.

The teacher was amiable and kind. She leaned over and addressed words to me which, in their rising scale, sounded like questions. I answered in snatches of Hungarian and of the Viennese dialect spoken by Mama, thereby clogging the linguistic wheels still further. The harassed teacher shook her head. By this time neither she nor I had the sense to establish an easy rapport in Spanish. While I bawled with mounting consternation the poor woman cast a worried glance at her other charges, who, unstrung by my behaviour, might at any moment break out in mass hysteria. In the end she did the only thing possible: she took me to the principal's office. Here, once my identity had been established, it was ascertained that I had two brothers enrolled in upper classes. One of them, Arnim, was fetched.

At sight of him my world, which I had thought annihilated, came miraculously back to life. In the midst of a sob an indescribable sense of rescue lifted me out of my primordial despair. Gulping with hiccoughs, I was now overcome by shame. What a blessing that they had not called Sylvester! Already a certain superiority attached itself to my elder brother, so that I dreaded his censure or discountenance. Arnim said nothing, but with his handkerchief he dried my tears. Then he took my hand and we walked home. Abashed but happy, I trotted beside him.

The episode did not sit well with Papa and Mama. I was given a day to think things over and then, on the third morning, I found myself again entering the Colegio Americano. This time Arnim sat with me through the whole morning, setting up blocks, cutting out pictures, and weaving gay little mats from strips of coloured paper. I was fascinated, and my fears had vanished.

Thereafter my days were filled with activity. I particularly enjoyed the air of suspense imparted by the teacher to each morning's schemes, from the tracing of bold landscapes in bright crayons to the looping of wool thread through punctured cardboard. The latter was an embryonic form of embroidery which brought great satisfaction as each child could take home a bit of finished handiwork. But my endless delight was the famous set of Froebel blocks, a square wooden box containing four smooth cubes. Every morning before these cubes became building-stones for the erection of a pyramid or column the teacher issued an invitation:

"Now let's all start the day by playing the piano!"

At this we pulled the lid out in its groove to about half an inch, turned the box upside down, and drummed with our fingers on the tiny protruding 'keyboard.' I don't know why this bit of spoof gave me such pleasure! Sometimes we chanted in piping voices to our own busy 'accompaniment.' But the mood of enchantment was deepened when our fingers worked in silence while we were exhorted to "think" a tune. This summons to the imagination, in all seriousness to regale itself with a private concert, was the rubbing of Aladdin's lamp. It opened a passage to the intangible but quite real world of the mind.

My term in the Colegio Americano must have extended into the month of February, for I clearly recall a festival called George Washington's Birthday. On this occasion every one in the school, whether American or not, received a lollipop in the shape of a hatchet, a sticky ball of marvellous pink popcorn, a paper hat, and a little star-spangled banner. In addition, we had been taught a tune, the first line of which ran: "Sing a song of Washington!" It was a paraphrase, I discovered many years later, of *Marching through Georgia*.

Altogether I was having a beautiful time among my daily associates when suddenly, in early spring, the pattern of life changed. Mama had completed her search for the Maximilian jewels. We were going back to Europe.

9

RETURN TO EUROPE

TRAVEL PREPARATIONS had been going on for some time. In Mama's little red salon, off the parlour, daily consultations were held with the seamstress Celestina, while steamer trunks and valises stood about in every room. A special velvet-lined chest with thickly padded trays was handled with some secrecy; in it, though we children did not know it at the time, the Imperial collection was carefully stowed into fitted compartments which would preclude damage in transit. After the chest had been locked it was sealed with a cachet from the Mexican Government, waiving customs inspection by the port authorities at Veracruz.

Whether by choice or coincidence, we had reservations on the *Albingia*, the same ship that had brought us to Mexico originally. But the first voyage was not duplicated in every respect, for at the last moment Papa found it impossible to go along, except to escort us as far as the harbour.

On the morning of our departure from Mexico City we rose in darkness, at four o'clock. It was tremendously exciting. I remember standing on my bed while being dressed by a very tearful Dolores who at intervals plied me with a crisp buttered roll and a glass of hot milk. After this haphazard breakfast she buttoned me into my brown velours coat, which had a wide collar of cream-coloured lace. Dolores was by this time sobbing out loud. Not comprehending her grief, since my young wits hardly grasped the immensity of the journey ahead, I patted her cheek. Then, either from boredom at the servant's emotional performance or because my breakfast had been gulped down with unaccustomed haste, I was overtaken by a reverberating and quite unintentional belch. This brought the good woman out of her damp despair.

"*Niña!*" she cried in horror. "*Qué barbaridad!*"

I knew, of course, that belching was indeed a barbarity. Well-bred people, I had been taught, prevented a lapse of this nature by the application of something called self-control. Well, self-control must have failed me. Or rather, the treacherous mishap occurred before I could anticipate it and put up an adequate defence. In my embarrassment I grinned.

Up to now Dolores had been shocked but not angry. The grin unhorsed her, however. Forthwith she turned me over and administered a sound smack on the peplum of my beautiful coat. I did not feel the chastisement, but my dignity was outraged. The incident greatly eased the sting of parting.

Elsewhere in the house the rest of the family had been up since three o'clock (I had been wakened last), so that we were ready to set out by half-past four. A black brougham drawn by two horses took us to the San Lázaro station.

It was still dark. Except for a few hucksters on their way to market the town was asleep. Beggars lay huddled in doorways, shivering under the chill night air, for it was March and a cold wind blew from the mountains. Under every corner lamp-post snored a blue-coated policeman, his képi cocked over one ear, while a round oboe-like whistle dangled from a cord round his throat.

These clay whistles, used by *los gendarmes* of Mexico City during the Díaz régime, were the delight of every child. Their eerie sound, half-way between a gurgle and a hoot, cut through the night with notes of spine-tingling melancholy. They were blown every hour, not for purposes of alarm, but as a checking-up device among the guardians of the public weal. In every precinct the patrolman on the beat set off a blast, proclaiming to his colleague in the next block "I am awake, *amigo*! Are you?"

Each succeeding fellow took it up with a flourish, passing on the splendid news through the whole neighbourhood, whereupon they all buckled beside their lamp-posts and went back to sleep.

From the carriage window my brothers and I now watched these dear friends the policemen, whom we alternately loved and feared, for they were imbued with awesome powers. When we were well behaved the servants used to report this to Don Hermenegildo, the watchman on our corner, who thereupon rewarded us with a penny stick of *charanuzca* (a pale caramel-coloured toffee), while naughtiness brought threats of arrest and punishment, with the fiercely moustached Hermenegildo glowering at the front door and shaking an ominous stick.

In the first glimmering of dawn, however, the dozing gentlemen of the gendarmery had lost all vestige of either benign majesty or menace. Like so many flour-bags they drooped against the posts in a blissful trance from which only the clangour of the first church bells would rouse them. Though we were too young to grasp its irony, we had long been familiar with a Spanish term of peculiar fitness; from Madrid to Buenos Aires the Hispanic world referred to its police force as *Los Serenos*, the "Serene Ones."

At the San Lázaro station a secretary from the Austro-Hungarian Legation awaited us. He had been assigned to our party as an escort, to assure diplomatic immunity against prying inspectors in the ports of Spain, France, and Germany, which the *Albingia* touched on her journey overseas.

At the gangplank in Veracruz we saw our parents wipe their eyes as they embraced. The realization that Papa was not coming along threatened to set off a woeful outburst on the part of my brothers and myself. But the ship's governess, trained to meet emergencies of this sort, spirited us aboard to the children's playroom. Here other youngsters were already at work on hobby-horses, stationary bicycles, and other gymnastic paraphernalia.

While we were thus occupied our mother settled herself in her state-room. She put a lace cover on the dressing-table before spreading out her silver brushes and toilet articles. Next she tossed her own little head pillows on the bed and sprayed a bit of *Divinia* cologne into the air, so that in no time the cabin had become identified with her.

Our heavy luggage was, of course, stored in the ship's hold, but the treasure trunk stood behind a curtain near Mama's bed. We were mystified by this, but no explanation was offered. The secrecy that prevailed regarding the contents of the trunk had no political import, since both Mexican and Austrian authorities were in accord regarding the transfer of the imperial gems. But there would be danger of theft, particularly as the ship neared European waters. Had we children known the heirloom story we would most certainly have chattered and put international jewellery robbers on Mama's track.

Thus it was not until our adolescent years that we heard the story of the heirloom search, and even then it was couched in the simplest terms.

"There were some things belonging to the House of Habsburg," explained Papa, "which your mother was asked to include in her baggage."

"And did she?" we asked excitedly. "What sort of things? What did they look like?"

At this Mama would relent and divulge a few descriptions of diamond brooches, pearl collars, and emblazoned insignia, bedded in layers of velvet. "They were a pretty sight," she would muse with a far-away look.

More than this we were not told, since not much more really happened. But there was, to wind up the tale, the audience with Emperor Franz Josef at Schönbrunn Castle outside Vienna, where the presentation of the recovered heirlooms finally took place.

While we children played in the palace gardens our mother was received in the white and gold salon of Maria Theresa, where His Majesty stood waiting.

"*Ein lieber alter Herr*," Mama described the Emperor in reminiscing. "A dear old gentleman—he looked so handsome and straight in spite of his great age!"

The meeting had been grave and formal. The octogenarian monarch, visibly moved at sight of his brother's belongings, had scanned the collection in silence. When he spoke at last, Franz Josef pointed out that he wanted only those things which had been originally Habsburg possessions. He wanted nothing that belonged to the Empress Carlota's Belgian family or that had come into Maximilian's hands as a gift from the Mexican people. Such pieces, he felt, should be singled out and restored to Brussels or Mexico City respectively.

In addition, Franz Josef desired nothing that had come from France. And there was, of course, among the collection the *petit déjeuner* set, given to Maximilian by Napoleon and Eugénie as an inducement to plunge into the Mexican venture. Carefully Mama had unwrapped the silver pieces and placed them upon a tray. But Franz Josef would not touch them, for he looked upon the French sovereigns as the betrayers of Maximilian and he wanted no reminder of their duplicity. For this reason, and since no further instructions were given as to its disposal, the *petit déjeuner* set returned to Mexico and was later recovered by an uncle, Don Enrique Bornhoeft, for our family.

Before closing the interview, his Majesty turned to an equerry who held a small, gold-lettered case. It contained the Signum Laudis, a decoration awarded for service to the Crown, which the Emperor placed in Mama's hands.

With this, our adventure of the Habsburg jewels had ended.

10

HUNGARY AGAIN

HER MISSION completed, Mama headed for Budapest. We picked up our bags at the old Bristol Hotel and drove in a fiacre to the docks of the D.D.S.G. (Danube Shipping Company) where the night boat waited. En route through the town my brothers played a well-known game, which consisted of repeating the shipping firm's name as a single multisyllabic word: "*Donaudampfschifffahrtsgesellschaft.*" This Germanic practice of compounding terms *ad absurdum* was ridiculed in a popular dance-tune entitled "I am the Captain-of-the-Danube-Shipping-Company" or "*Ich bin der Donaudampfschifffahrtsgesellschaftskapitän!*" Amid such polyphonic entertainment our mother found the carriage-ride something of a strain.

For me that brief trip to the river docks is associated with another slight incident. As we mounted the fiacre my brothers had lost no time in pre-empting for themselves the two available windows, while Mama sat in the middle with me at her knee. It was now that Sylvester felt himself seized by a gallant urge. Surrendering his place to me, he said, with an air of worldly surfeit, "You take the window. I know Vienna!"

He was nine years old, and he had passed through the Austrian capital exactly twice, in a closed carriage from docks to railway station at the age of six. This early experience entitled him to the solemn assertion "*Ich kenne Wien!*"

The river journey in the long European dusk led through scenes of legendary beauty. Immediately beyond Vienna's city limits lay the forest and game preserves of Lobau. Next, in quick succession, the ancient towns and the ruins of feudal castles—Petronel, Altenburg, Hainburg, Röthelstein, Theben (Porta Hungarica)—passed before our eyes, while in the distance the first low slopes of the Carpathian mountain range came into view. Beyond Bratislava the Danube bed widened into the Hungarian plains. After the confluence with the river Raab the mighty stream passed Komárom and curved majestically about the ecclesiastical town of

Esztergom, seat of the Bishop-Primate of Hungary. Here were two names my brothers and I loved to roll on our tongues, "Komárom and Esztergom, Komárom and Esztergom," but by the time our ship touched these picturesque towns darkness had fallen, and we were fast asleep in our narrow bunks.

In Budapest the boat docked at the Petöfiter landing berths on the left bank, or Pest side, of the Danube. Here Grandfather Atya, Grossmama, and a cordon of relatives awaited us. There were new faces: Aunt Irma had married an architect named Mauder, who stood beside her with their small son, Ferenc. Aunt Cornelia boasted a new beau, a lieutenant of dragoons.

Amid shouts and exclamations we were marshalled into a droshky and, followed by the others, sped to the railway station. Here we took the local train which crossed over to Buda and the near-by hills of Solymár.

"At last," said Mama, "the holiday part of our trip has begun!"

In Solymár, where our mother had spent her girlhood years, nothing had changed. Atya's old country house stood ruggedly fenced against the low hills, with vineyards and fields of ripe wheat shimmering about it like a golden sea. Across the road just beyond the front gate we saw again the lovely acacia forest where Zoltán, the coachman, spent his off-hours whittling. Here, too, the goatherd Imre grazed his flock and at times took on Grossmama's geese as well. We loved the acacia forest. Over its soft grassy ground the village children ran barefoot, breathing the woodland air that had a way of lingering in the senses. Again the magic of a wood held me spellbound. Years later I would be able to close my eyes, perhaps only for a fleeting second, and smell again the sweet acacias.

For my brothers and me Solymár was a warm, earthy heaven. We rummaged through the house, inspecting every corner, from Atya's cool wine-cellar to Grossmama's gabled attic. The kitchen, with its display of copper cauldrons and Baroque tiled oven that reached to the ceiling, absorbed our attention no less than Aunt Cornelia's bedroom, where an almost life-size Sistine Madonna (the three-quarter detail, without saints and cherubs) hung in a wide gold frame.

In the garden a host of surprises beckoned. There were cherry-trees, heavy with promise, while near-by plums, gooseberries, peaches, and apricots vied for attention. At harvest time Zoltán rounded up villagers to help with the picking, while Marishka, the cook, stored the garden's treasure in great baskets and bins for winter canning.

To one side of the orchard there was a sheltered terrace, where the daily *Jause*, or afternoon coffee, was served. Here Grossmama's flower-beds attracted butterflies and bees, which were reflected in the mirrored depths of a big red sphere. Near by was a tiny grotto before which a bronze statuette of d'Artagnan, with troubadour lute and plumed hat, stood guard.

But best of all we children loved the fields, where peasants in bright boots and kerchiefs laboured under the hot Hungarian sun. Their implements were ancient—hand scythes, pitch-forks, and threshing flails—which they wielded with authority and grace. Towards evening, as the big hay-wagons creaked downhill amid shouting and laughter, we yearned to join in the gusty proceedings. Our greatest desire was to exchange city clothes for the colourful garb of country folk. To our vast delight this wish was one day granted.

It happened on a Sunday in July when Zoltán took us down into the village on a visit to the Widow Pilmann, a peasant matriarch with seven stalwart sons. It was easy to assemble a properly fitting *csikos* (herdsman) outfit for each of my brothers, since the Pilmann cupboards held an inexhaustible supply of fringed trousers, streamered hats, and white sheepskin greatcoats. For me a special search became necessary among village families with daughters my size. At last four starched petticoats were fitted round my middle, topped by a ruffled skirt, tight bodice, and a marvellously garnished headdress. The latter, known as a *párta*, was the large and particularly ornate kind from Mezökövesd reminiscent of the high Russian *kokoshnik* except for the mass of many-coloured flowers in place of Muscovite jewels.

A distinction existed between "regional" and so-called "national" dress. The former was not worn by city people; it belonged to peasants of different localities, each with its own traditional and undeviating design. The latter, donned by gentry and aristocracy in a spirit of patriotic masquerade, permitted fashion vagarics as to quality of material, colour, and ornament. Regional dress, identified with daily living, was coarse of weave, sturdy, true. National dress too often underwent modification to comply with a demand for spurious operetta prettiness.

The same contrast prevailed in the styling of feminine coiffures. Peasant women and girls skinned back their tresses into the tightest of braids, while their city sisters wore loose, fluffy locks. My own transformation into a Solymár villager thus began with a painful brushing which swept every last blonde wisp off my forehead and left me with a feeling of having been scalped. So quaintly grotesque was my appearance that Mama whisked me to the nearest photographer for a souvenir pose.

Alas, despite the costuming, my brothers and I did not really become a part of Solymár. This was owing to the peculiar curse hanging over children reared in foreign lands: they speak always the language of the spot most recently impressed upon their memory. For Sylvester, Arnim, and myself that spot was Mexico. Among ourselves we spoke only Spanish. We smirked and grew embarrassed if we tried anything else.

To be sure, all children exposed to travel at an early age become natural linguists, since the acquisition of new tongues requires neither genius nor even better-than-average intelligence. It is purely a matter of opportunity. Languages are picked up in transit, as it were; if one is thrust into an environment where people seem to be making strange noises, the best thing to do in self-defence is to make those noises back at them.

In our own case philology was dropped into our cradles, for we became bilingual from the start, since in our grandfather's house conversation alternated between Magyar and Viennese. The first of these, Hungarian, is a difficult Asiatic tongue; the second, Austrian, is German with a southern accent. My brothers and I at first employed both towards our parents, who exacted this from us and would not listen otherwise. In Mexico, however, Hungarian soon gave way to Spanish and was further blotted out by our brief contact with English. This defection set us apart from Solymár villagers, who gaped at us as though we had dropped from some distant star. We created a sensation in the sense in which freaks create a sensation.

It did not take us long to profit by this. Indeed, we strained and concentrated on new ways to further startle and beguile our beholders. One day we taught the Widow Pilmann and her pop-eyed offspring the manufacture of Mexican corn pancakes, or *tortillas*. This bread of the Indians had been prepared daily by our swarthy cook, Cruz, on the charcoal braziers of the house in Manuel María Contreras. The correct baking of *tortillas* is, of course, an intricate procedure. Dry maize is put to soak in water with just such and such a portion of lime. Next the grains are carried to a miller who will grind them into a mass called *nixtamal*, after which the Indian cook dusts off her *metate* (square, flat mortar and pestle made of lava stone) and lovingly refines the mixture to its final perfection. Now follows a phase that appeals to all children, namely, the shaping of small lumps of corn dough into thin pancakes. This is done by vigorous clapping of hands, a delicious sound heard all over Mexico at mealtimes, thrice a day. My brothers and I had often begged to take part in the clapping, and we were quite expert at it. But even our best *tortillas* seldom reached the table, for they had a way of turning grey in exact ratio to the increasing whiteness of our palms. Needless to say, in Hungary we had no better luck. The Widow Pilmann owned a sack of golden-kernelled maize and some lime powder used for making soap. But no one knew the proportions, and besides, there was no mill. Hopefully we substituted plain flour and water, only to find that the resultant paste defied patting. The *tortilla* lesson ended in failure.

We made up for it with a bullfight. During our short life in Mexico we had never seen an actual bullfight, since our parents disapproved of the sport and, in any case, we were too young for admission to the Mexico City arena. But all over our neighbourhood the children had played bullfight games, aided by servants' descriptions of what went on in the real ring. Papa's stable-boy, the raw-boned Indian rascal named Jesús, had been an ardent fan; he attended the Sunday performances and returned as often as not with some gory trophy. We had seen gaudily beribboned *banderillas* with steel points that had pierced a fighting animal's flank. Tassels from a *picador's* jacket or silken shreds off a *matador's* cape were also customary souvenirs. Finally Jesús fetched home innumerable articles that had no bearing whatsoever on bullfighting, but were thrown into the ring by angry or enthusiastic spectators. It was well known that the excitement of the fray caused men to part with note-cases, beer-bottles, pocket-knives, or their best Sunday hats, while women hurled bouquets, fans, lace mantillas, and an occasionally well-aimed slipper at the current villain or idol of the show. Once our groom returned with a dainty if mudspattered girdle which, he swore, had been tossed by a frenzied lady at the feet of the illustrious Gaona. He was Mexico's *matador* of the moment, acclaimed even in the bull-rings of Spain. As for the girdle, it became a sacred relic. Jesús hung it in his room beside the dried and slightly odorous ear of El Negro, the savage *toro* that had once gored Juan Belmonte, greatest of Spanish fighters. So we had a fairish idea of bullfights.

Putting their heads together, Sylvester and Arnim planned an exhibition to be staged in the Widow Pilmann's back-yard. A set of medium-sized antlers from Grandfather's hunting collection would be manipulated by me in a set of sternly rehearsed taurine manœuvres. Arnim was to serve alternately as *banderillero* and *picador*, changing to the latter rôle by mounting a broomstick horse. Sylvester, as *matador*, reserved for himself the elegant cape-work and the kill.

The Pilmann family and their neighbours gathered for the show. Zoltán, who supported all our enterprises, blew an opening flourish on a toy cornet. I charged into the arena.

"*Joi, Istenem!*" cried the Widow Pilmann at the snorting and bloodthirsty antics. "Oh, my God!"

As I stamped my feet to raise a convincing cloud of dust, Arnim reached for the festooned poker and tongs that had been borrowed from Grossmama's fireplace. He made gingerly passes at me while I galloped about the yard. Sylvester was preparing a crimson table-cloth for the swashbuckling *faenas* (feats) of the cape. From the improvised stands our audience cheered.

Owing to insufficient rehearsal or my improper timing, the opening round of our *corrida* proved only a moderate success. I was too ornery a bull. I went through my paces with such gusto and ferocity that Sylvester and Arnim had no time to display their talents with lance or cape. It had not been impressed upon me that in real fights the bull respects certain rules: he charges only when sufficiently annoyed by snarls of "*Arre, toro*" or at the sight of red cloth. But occasionally a high-spirited beast upsets tradition by going berserk and cleaning up the ring without regard for pageantry or finesse. Obviously, at a real show, with every *torero* lodged behind the safety barrier and the bull in complete command, the performance would be a total loss. I was this kind of bull. I ignored the code. It became evident that we must make a change if our good Solymár friends were to have any kind of a show.

There was a pause for reorganization. Then, in accordance with the new strategy, Arnim took over the antlers while I was entrusted with firetongs and poker. Zoltán stood by as assistant *picador*, lest I again got out of hand.

This time the performance went beautifully. Arnim was a gentle child, trusting and reasonable. He looked like our lovely Aunt Irma, having the same luminous green eyes framed by dark brows and lashes. As a fighting bull he was ostensibly ferocious, but always aware of the rules of the game. He made a noble *toro*. Twice my *banderilla* thrusts, which should have barely grazed him, ripped wide holes in his short breeches, but he pranced on with sportsmanlike disdain. So considerately did he attune himself to their needs that Zoltán and Sylvester covered themselves with glory in the execution of their specialities. At the climax Arnim 'died' in lone defeat, while his killers accepted the plaudits of the crowd.

"*Éljen! Éljen!*" shouted the customers. "Hurrah! Hurrah!" The bullfight had been an unqualified success. Our reputation was made.

Unhappily we could not leave well alone. Drunk with applause, we allowed success to go to our heads. There must be other ways to shine. Again my brothers deliberated while I complaisantly awaited the hatching of their next idea. It was a good one. We were going to fly. In America, Sylvester told the Solymár children, people were building aeroplanes. Had they not heard about the Wright brothers, Orville and Wilbur?

The Hungarians laughed. Such funny names! As for human beings purporting to fly, it was preposterous. And blasphemy, too.

Sylvester and Arnim went quietly ahead. They bargained with one of Atya's farm-hands for a wooden crate from the vineyards. With several lengths of wire and some gunny-sacking they fashioned wings that spread boldly from opposite sides. Two boards served as a propeller, and the top of a great haystack was selected for the take-off. To add realism, a passenger would be required. The boys looked at me.

"Minka will do," they decided. Arnim fetched a pillow from his bed and stuffed it into the box.

We climbed the steep end of the haystack by means of a ladder. The opposite side, sloping at a more moderate angle towards the field, would serve for the take-off, which was to be illustrative and theoretical rather than actual. All our games called for a large dose of imagination. In short, if the Wright brothers really *did* fly, this was the way it would look.

Everything was ready. At the foot of the haystack a cluster of red-cheeked village urchins gaped upward. Serenely confident, I let myself be lifted into the 'cockpit,' while my brothers emitted a strident whoop:

"Here she comes!"

They gave the 'aeroplane' a magnificent push and sent it hurtling through space.

How I missed breaking my innocent neck has remained a mystery for ever after. As it was, I was badly shaken up and broke two teeth.

As a demonstration in aeronautics, the performance was less than satisfactory. Solymár youngsters were toboggan experts during winter, when heavy snow cloaked their steep hills. "Wait till we get out our sleds," they cried. "We'll show you who can fly!"

II

OTTO AND RELIGION

I HAD A DOLL NAMED OTTO.

Otto was a sailor with a sturdy sawdust body and a variable succession of porcelain, celluloid, or bisque heads. Sometimes he was a fair Nordic, while at others his complexion changed to swarthier hues, depending on what luck we had with replacements. For he was not a shop doll, except from the neck up. Our mother had sewed him together out of bits of cloth several months before I was born. Since she could not know whether I would be boy or girl, she had compromised on the sailor-suit and a head with a coat of paint for hair; it would have been untenable to present a new-born son with a petticoat puppet in long curls.

Because his soft and flexible body was so huggable, I preferred Otto above all my other dolls. Unlike the factory-made product of hard, cold torsos and limbs, Otto responded to warmth. His cotton skin was always at room temperature. I loved him dearly.

He was really Otto the Second. There had been a previous Otto the First, belonging to my brothers, who had thoroughly worn him out. So versatile had this doll ancestor proved in his day that Sylvester and Arnim extended his usefulness far beyond intelligible limits. During toddler years they had fathered him with clumsy tenderness, but later he was employed as a dray-horse and a drum. There seemed to be no end of uses to which Otto the First could be put. His ultimate fate was disembowelment while pulling a load of goods-wagons.

The new Otto had an easier time of it. Although he was older than I (sometimes his changing physiognomy showed it, too, as the time he returned from the doll hospital with a black moustache), my maternal devotion was exemplary. I liked him especially during his blond and blue-eyed stages, of which he had several owing to Mama's windfall in acquiring at one purchase a number of identical heads. But once Otto also possessed an exquisite face with tender brown eyes, which opened and shut. I was just getting used to this duskier type when my little Mexican friend Nené poked his thumb at the orbs and pushed them clear through the back of the painted hair. This mishap occurred at a time when toymakers were beginning to give up the manufacture of separate heads. Dolls came in one piece. The rag variety entered the field of caricature, furthermore, with features embroidered in wool. Thus there was nothing for it but to mend Otto's last treasured face by stuffing the head with cotton wads so as to hold the loosened eyeballs into place. He could no longer sleep or even blink, but with a few brushmarks to cover up the scars on his cemented skull he emerged in astonishingly good fettle. Perhaps because his survival had been threatened I prized him the more.

Otto had navigated the Danube. He had crossed Europe and twice sailed the Atlantic. He was by way of being a doll of the world. Still, this did not lead me into pitfalls of indulgent parenthood. I reared him sternly and according to precept. On the whole, he behaved well, though at times he talked back to me in four languages, and there was always trouble about his bedtime. Also, he said no prayers, which came to shock me greatly. The matter of Otto's prayers derived from an experience which my brothers and I had with our Aunt Cornelia.

For several years now our Aunt Cornelia had been the belle of Solymár and, as the daughter of the village squire, she was considered a matrimonial catch. Rural swains of the district vied for her attention. But she had no use for these. They were peasant lads, utterly beneath her notice. Cornelia had been reared as a fine lady.

It was because of this that she did not approve of our village friendships, particularly with the Pilmann brood. Twice Mama heard from her about such associations:

"Sári, how can you let your children play with those peasant brats?"

Our mother passed over the matter lightly. "In Mexico they are saddled with fewer prejudices."

"You mean," gasped Cornelia, "they meet on equal terms with Indian halfbreeds—dark-skinned savages?"

Mama laughed. "Savages, no! Dark-skinned? Only Mexicans of purest Indian stock fit this description; most of them have such a large percentage of Spanish blood that their complexions are fairer than yours."

Aunt Cornelia was an olive-toned Magyar. The information that descendants of Montezuma and Attila had this much in common came as a surprise. Mama's next words were an added revelation.

"As for Mexican children," she said, "they are the most polite and well-reared in the world." She looked at us wistfully, as though we bore little resemblance to them.

A few days after this we gave Aunt Cornelia a shock. It happened on an afternoon stroll over the Solymár hills, and the reverberations were to cast a shadow on the balance of our visit in Atya's house.

Rural Hungary is dotted with small roadside shrines, as well as lonely crucifixes that rise in gaunt, carved artistry before the passer-by. Their presence is so ubiquitous that a landscape without some pious symbol would appear incomplete to Catholic Magyar eyes. On the edge of our grandfather's land, only a short distance uphill, stood one of these shrines. Before it a great tree spread its branches, while beside it there was the usual tall crucifix. The little chapel had been dedicated to Saint Anne, and Grossmama referred to it as the "Anna Kapelle."

My brothers and I must have seen this spot when we were quite young, even before our migration to Mexico. It is possible that Sylvester and Arnim remembered. But I didn't. Suddenly, as we walked uphill that summer afternoon with Aunt Cornelia, I looked up and saw a bluish-white figure, crowned with thorns and dripping blood from hands and feet, nailed to the black cross.

"Who is that man?" I cried in terror. "And why does he hang there?"

Our aunt was thunderstruck. She turned to my brothers.

"Have you ever heard about God?"

Of course they had! He was everybody's father up in heaven. He punished bad children and gave presents to the good, like the *gendarmes* in Mexico City. A benevolent, overgrown Don Hermenegildo, in fact.

"Then you boys, at least, know who Jesus is?" continued our aunt, more hopefully. She did not pronounce the name as we did in Spanish, with the accent on the last syllable. She said, "*Yeh-'zhush*," in Hungarian.

Now my brothers were stumped. There was Jesús, the manservant in our house on Manuel María Contreras. We knew him very well; but did our Aunt Cornelia?

"Answer me!" she insisted. Her voice grew shrill.

Sylvester and Arnim blinked. "Oh, yes," they stammered, realizing that they must make some sort of showing, or else our mother and father would be compromised in some strange way.

"Well——?"

"Jesús is our *mozo*," the boys beamed ingratiatingly.

This was good enough as far as it went, since our Aunt Cornelia did not know the meaning of *mozo*. It might have been Spanish for Saviour. The speculative frown across her nose granted such a hypothesis. My brothers had the wisdom to leave it at that. But something in my immature brain-pan began clicking. I wanted to help.

"Like Zoltán," I crowed importantly, "Atya's coachman!"

This finished our poor aunt. If a storm had come up at that moment she would not have been surprised to see a bolt of lightning strike us down.

Always when we walked she had held my hand in hers. Now she let go of it with a shudder. For a moment she did not seem to know what to do, and her uncertainty communicated itself to us. My brothers reached for me and took my hands between them. But we did not move.

The interval passed, and our Aunt Cornelia took a deep breath. She had regained her composure. Her lips tightened as they shaped a brief order:

"Home! And be quick about it!"

My brothers still held me between them. I felt their fingers close more firmly over mine as we marched downhill.

12

CATECHISM IN SOLYMÁR

MONTEZUMA AND Attila, indeed!" snapped Aunt Cornelia at our mother across the dinner-table that night. "Your children are heathens!"

Grave faces met this outburst as she proceeded to relate the afternoon's events. Grossmama, a lady of great piety, emitted a gasp while Atya took a gulp of wine and lapsed into appalled silence. Mama looked very alone.

Our grandmother found her voice. "Well, Sári," she asked in a tone of disbelief, "what have you to say to this?"

Mama ventured a little smile. "You won't understand, even after I tell you," she said. "Cornelia is right. The children have had no religious training."

"You mean, they've never been to church?"

"Never."

Even gentle Atya's eyebrows arched at this. "But, Sári," he warned, "haven't you shirked a serious responsibility? You were brought up yourself in a Christian home."

"It's a good thing we saw those children baptized," put in Aunt Cornelia. "Otherwise, if they catch a plague and die this week, they won't even make Purgatory. Straight to the fires of Hell they'd go!"

Our mother's face grew sober. "You really believe that? I shouldn't think you could picture a god less noble than his meanest creatures; no human being would punish an innocent child for the faults of its elders." She paused, and this time it seemed her turn to shudder. "For all eternity, too," she added almost under her breath.

"Blasphemy!" cried Aunt Cornelia.

At breakfast the following day every one said "*Jó regelt*" ("Good morning") with exquisite politeness, as heads bobbed in gracious nods. Disregarding our heretic condition, Grossmama held out a slender hand to be kissed. From the kitchen came steaming *Palatschinken* (pancakes) drowned in honey, our favourite dish. Everything was perfect, or nearly so.

Underneath, however, a hot flame smouldered. Not for a single moment since my childish ignorance had stirred up the fierce fires of religious controversy did Grossmama's and Aunt Cornelia's consciences find rest. The fact that we walked on the brink of perdition, unschooled in orthodox ritual and certainly remiss in Christian practices, disconcerted them greatly. They spoke to their confessor about us and thereby only aggravated their own panic. Father Miklos confirmed Aunt Cornelia's warning that we were headed for damnation if sudden death were to overtake us while in a state of gracelessness.

Grossmama in particular suffered at this thought, for she loved us sincerely. I was her special pet. At meal-times she liked to hold me on her lap and personally stuff my mouth with the best titbits off her plate. If we went to the village for an outing she tied a ribbon in my hair and slipped a handy korona (silver crown piece) into my tiny purse. She never tired of exclaiming, "My! My!" and "How wonderful!" when my brothers and I put on a bull-fight or an iguana hunt for her. And she was capable of sacrifice, as evidenced by her sympathetic attitude following my 'aeroplane' flight, during which I had nicked two milk teeth; bread-crusts bothered me for a time after this episode, so Grossmama, whose aged dental equipment could not have been of the best, valiantly swallowed the crisp morsels I pushed towards her and left me the tenderest bites.

It was her love for us that now caused the old lady to take steps towards our spiritual regeneration. Summer had gone, and with the arrival of autumn the Solymár village school opened its doors.

"Sári, wouldn't it be nice," Grossmama said innocently one morning, "if the children were not tutored this autumn, but spent a little time in one of our Hungarian institutions?"

"The Solymár school," Aunt Cornelia joined in quickly. "It's so convenient, and much less expensive."

Our mother looked startled. "Why, Cornelia," she smiled, "how democratic! The village school is attended only by peasants——"

Grossmama was ready with a reply. "The standards here are as high as in Budapest. No matter where the children continue their education, there won't be the slightest difficulty about catching up."

It seemed a sensible idea. My brothers and I were a restless trio, constantly in need of occupation. The novelty of our first appearance in Solymár had worn off. Our repertoire of Mexican diversions was threadbare with repetition, and our resourcefulness in thinking up fresh excitements had reached an impasse. Also, we were beginning to drop Spanish in favour of Hungarian; English had left us long ago. In short, to our Solymár playmates we were no longer interesting foreigners.

Grossmama's proposition pleased us immensely. On a bright Saturday afternoon she took us to the small stationer's shop in the square, where we were outfitted with long-sleeved smocks of the sort worn by French schoolboys. Copybooks, textbooks, slates, pencils, and pens were crammed into small leather satchels which were adjusted to our shoulders, so that we carried our classroom equipment soldier-fashion on our backs. Theoretically this was to encourage upright shoulders instead of the curved posture caused by lugging books under one arm. My school satchel was ornate, with a red plush lid that could be seen at a great distance. Although I was to be entered only in the first grade my supplies looked as important as those carried by my brothers.

We were excited. All day Sunday was spent in sharpening pencils, sponging the slates, and thumbing through the books in search of pictures. Endlessly we packed and repacked our satchels, trying them on and testing their capacity. We were enormously proud.

Grossmama seemed happy too. Unknown to anyone but Father Miklos and our Aunt Cornelia, she had purchased three elementary catechisms authorized by the Solymár diocese. Together with a black-bound prayer-book, these would be slipped into our packs when we set out on Monday morning for the village school.

Father Miklos taught catechism five days a week.

Under his guidance we met up with the Trinity in short order, learning that God was not One but Three. The whiskered individual of our fancy, with the authoritative air of a deified Kaiser Franz Josef, now gave way to the collective concept of Father-Son-and-Holy-Ghost. Here was a conundrum our mother had deliberately dodged.

Quite as she had feared, we were literal-minded and unaware of meanings behind meanings. We liked the Holy Ghost best, perhaps because He or It was the most incomprehensible. From snatches of folklore and servant tales we knew that ghosts were departed spirits that hovered in attics and vacant houses, striving to make contact with the living. They were mostly evil, since people were frightened by them. It was reassuring therefore to discover a "holy" ghost in God's immediate company, functioning for Good.

Our catechism had a picture in lithograph of the three celestial figures seated on thrones that were banked against a cloud. God the Father was depicted in the centre, with Christ and the Holy Ghost on either side. In studying this picture we could never dispel a sense of utter confusion, for Father Miklos insisted that the sacred Trinity—here visibly separated—still remained One. Each was the other and all were the Godhead. It was enigmatic, yet seemingly acceptable to the sober adult mind.

Father Miklos hurdled such problems by the simplest possible expedient: Faith. So wide was the scope of his belief that we were presently enveloped by it. Subtly a kind of comprehension dawned upon us that religion sprang from the heart and not the brain, that logic had no bearing on belief, and that cold reason was superfluous where man's simple urge for goodness was concerned. We sensed the impropriety of asking questions that challenged the credos of the soul.

Outside the theological field our curriculum embraced elementary arithmetic, writing, drawing, and—in my case—lessons in reading from a large-lettered book entitled *János és Juliska* (*John and Juliette*). These readings delighted me, for they concerned a small boy and girl who, among other things, went uphill for a pail of water, with dire accidents befalling them along the way. Children love calamity. I could hardly wait to find out each day what trouble *János* and *Juliska* would get into next.

My brothers soon moved on to loftier studies, including a simplified outline of history. This was of course presented in strictly Magyar setting and as seen through Hungarian eyes. The result almost at once coloured their playtime after school. No longer in their games did they impersonate bullfighters, Orville and Wilbur Wright, or the Aztec Prince Cuauhtémoc. They were heroes of the eastern steppes and their idol became Attila, Asiatic chieftain and leader of the barbarian horde. Together with the Pilmann boys and a boisterous army of village children they fought the battles of Mohács, Kossovo, and Buda, telescoping dates and military events with easy abandon. Prince Eugene of Savoy, Hunyadi, the Serb Tzar Lazar, and Suleyman the Magnificent all clashed in glorious combat, the outcome being always a highly satisfactory massacre of Turks. For five centuries Hungary had saved Europe from the Infidel. Her children knew no better game.

On the whole our period in the Solymár school proved a happy experience. We sat on narrow benches beside apple-cheeked youngsters in peasant dress, against whom our urban exterior formed a curious contrast. I particularly envied the little girls around me in their stiffly glazed blue aprons with square pleats carefully pressed into the material, where it had been folded, to proclaim the garment's freshness. (In just such an apron I had been photographed on the day when the Widow Pilmann dressed me in native costume.) The girls also had *babushka* kerchiefs tied in triangular fashion under the chin, exactly like the bandannas worn by working women in the sunny fields. I envied them their long braids, as my yellow hair was combed in the style of a Velasquez Infanta, shoulder length, parted on one side, and tied with a small ribbon. It did not suit Solymár at all.

"I want braids," was my constant plea, "like the blacksmith's Ilona!"

But Grossmama, who lovingly brushed my hair each morning—it was miserably soft, and tangled easily—made a chiding reply. "Your father isn't a blacksmith, and so you can't have Ilona's braids."

This seemed to make little sense. I wanted to argue. But the daily catechism class was beginning to take effect. Father Miklos strongly disapproved of taking issue with authority; in the interest of good upbringing, youth must not doubt age. Thus my brothers and I came to be indoctrinated with the cheerful delusion that adults were wise simply because they had reached adulthood. It was disconcerting in later years to discover that birthdays did not in themselves sharpen intelligence; the witless have a faculty of growing very old.

The fact remains that we were awed by our elders. To have contradicted Grossmama would have been heresy indeed. Thus, while I lamented that my father did not shoe horses so that I might tie my hair in two well-twisted plaits, down in the blacksmith's shack a tearful and sullen Ilona was perhaps at that very instant railing against her betters who would not permit the discarding of her kerchief and the running about with tresses streaming immodestly in the wind. To people steeped in ancient tradition the unbinding of hair belonged in alcove or bedchamber; it had an erotic tinge, associated among peasants—and poets!—with wedding-night intimacy. Quite likely Ilona's innocent petition, if she risked putting it forth at all, earned her a smart box on the ears.

For the rest, Father Miklos became a strong influence over our lives. He was a sociable and very human priest who went bowling with our grandfather twice a week and was not averse to an occasional drop of Tokay wine. Indirectly his authority invaded my playroom, where the doll Otto was made to feel the pious pedagogue's precepts. Grown aware myself, I now discovered a shocking godlessness among my sawdust children, with Otto, the eldest, the chief culprit. Otto said no prayers at night. In fact, for as long as I could remember, he had said no prayers in the daytime either. This would be remedied. With fervour I rehearsed my puppet family until their worldly souls were washed clean. Hereafter Elsa, Anna, Kathi, the red-bonneted Piroshka, and Otto himself were not tucked into bed without first completing extensive devotions.

I was not alone in this new passion for the spiritual life. My brothers, too, felt the impact of Father Miklos and they vied with each other to achieve a worthy blessedness. The little prayer-books Grossmama had bought lay on our night tables. Each evening before turning out the lights, Aunt Cornelia read aloud from a page entitled "Vesper Service," after which we recited in unison an *Ave Maria*, the *Salve Regina*, and the Lord's Prayer. With a beaming nod she then departed, warmed by the thought of our salvation.

Formerly, during our pagan past, the turning out of nursery lights had been the signal for a jabbering magpie feast. In the dark my brothers and I regaled one another with fanciful tales hatched extempore by our unfettered imaginations. No bounds were set to these recitals except that they must be entirely original, without recourse to conventional literature of the Hauff, Grimm, or Andersen school. If one of us struck a mental vacuum and strove to extricate himself by plagiarizing some familiar and hackneyed theme, there were boos and catcalls from the other beds. The listening two-thirds were uncompromising in their demand for fresh and unedited material.

Cut short by sleep, our story-telling bees were often resumed in the morning. Our breakfast usually included a bowl of thick porridge, which was admirably suited for designing diagrams and action pictures to illustrate our plots; we ate canals and trenches through our oats, built Alps or igloos in the custard, and then flooded everything with a beaker of Solymár goat's milk.

Our spiritual regeneration put a stop to this pastime. We found it necessary to drop the nightly narratives. Or rather, it was Sylvester who caused us to drop them. A serious child, he took things earnestly to heart. Having been made to realize that our evening prayers were directed to a supreme being, who was Lord of Heaven and Earth, he withdrew into sudden silence. For several nights Arnim and I addressed him in the dark, proposing some flamboyant tale. When he failed to reply we concluded that he must have fallen asleep, whereupon we continued the game in whispers. Apparently this was more than he could endure. After a few such evenings, when we again prodded him for co-operation, Sylvester broke his silence.

"I have just spoken with God!" he said with dignity.

The implication was unmistakable and compelling. Not only did he deem it unbecoming to descend from celestial spheres into profane camaraderie with an earthly brother and sister, but Arnim and I were not rising to a proper devotional level.

We were impressed. Without another word we dropped back on our pillows and pondered this new phase in our life with Sylvester. For his primogeniture had always set him a little apart; he wore the distinction that was his as an eldest son. Without impudence, but unequivocally, he allowed us to sense this distinction. It became manifest in the steadiness of his eyes, the gravity of his mouth, his unspoken leadership and responsibility. It showed also in our mother's rather special treatment of him, for there was a bond of understanding between these two that no one ever questioned. No privileges were extended to Sylvester in which Arnim and I did not have a share, yet there were subtle signs of rapport, even collusion. Our mother leaned on him in matters of trust, such as vigilance over our safety and the handling of money when we were sent uncompanioned on some errand. She had been heard to declare that our welfare never worried her so long as Sylvester was with us.

Sylvester's devotion to our mother was intense. He had an exaggerated faith in her powers. As a small child he witnessed the creation of the first Otto out of bits of cloth plus sawdust stuffing, and the wonder of it never left him. Thenceforth for many years he believed that with thimble and thread her fingers could fashion all his heart's desires.

It was this loyalty, in fact, which had at first threatened Grossmam's proselytizing programme. Vaguely aware that some veiled conspiracy against our mother was afoot, Sylvester had rejected any contact with Father Miklos. Only when Mama agreed to our 'conversion,' which she did quite readily on Atya's advice, would Sylvester have any part of it. Actually, Mama's freedom from bigotry did not bespeak an irreligious attitude; she was merely unwilling to push us into any sectarian groove before we were old enough to choose for ourselves. It was when Father Miklos pointed out that some fatal accident might overtake us before such a time, laying our eternal damnation on her conscience, that she had relented. She thought it an insult to God for pious believers to impute such injustice and cruelty to Him, but she did not want our mental outlook to be warped by daily dispute.

"Take them in hand," she had said gaily to Father Miklos, "and see what you can do!"

This had put an end to Sylvester's vacillation. He had grasped a lack of orthodoxy in our mother, but the respect and courtesy she showed the village priest proved conclusive. Sylvester could do no less. And, since there was an appalling lack of originality in Arnim and me, we followed suit.

It is possible that Mama's quiescence had been dictated less by virtuous impulse than by the knowledge that our stay in Hungary would not be for long. A letter had come from our father overseas, urging that we return before the European winter set in.

13

MAMA COLLECTS SOME RECIPES

It was difficult for Atya and Grossmama to accept the idea of parting. Our first sojourn in Mexico, although it stretched far beyond the expected time, had never been regarded as a permanent move. Our parents intended returning eventually to Europe, there to take up their lives where they had left off. This was understood from the beginning. The possibility that Mexico could one day become our home, in preference to the Old World, seemed unthinkable.

Yet this had come to pass. In the country of her birth Mama was homesick for a place more than three thousand miles away, on a sunlit Aztec plateau. She knew no explanation for her strange nostalgia, other than the fact that our father waited for us there. But the pull went deeper than mere human relationships, for it was something that happens to a great many people once they have been to Mexico. There is a magic about that land that never quite fades from memory. Perhaps it derives from Mexico's sapphire-blue sky, such as is seldom seen by Continental Europeans, which even in the rainy season holds drama as black storm-clouds paint portraits against its wide canvas. It may also be the sheer colour that is Mexico, primary, vivid, elemental, a landscape upon which Indian figures group themselves in natural murals everywhere. For us the charm may have lain in the music of the Spanish tongue, or in the beauty of a house with an inner courtyard—a patio—which opened to the sky, letting sun and stars look in upon our daily living. I don't know what it was, but our mother and father had fallen captive to the spell. There is a saying that anyone whose feet have touched the dust of Mexico will yearn for ever to return there. For us this proved entirely true.

While Mama began packing our trunks the family stood about in consternation. Uncle Mauder, Aunt Irma's husband, voiced a generally held opinion:

"You're pulling up roots—you've become emigrants! Do you realize the disgrace of it?"

This prevalent viewpoint had a logical foundation. Just as England's convict population took ship to Australia, much of the Continent's riff-raff had made off to the Americas, to seek, not honest freedom, but escape from the consequences of some misdeed. In respectable European circles a significant silence often greeted the announcement that the merchant Stephan X. or Lieutenant Y. or Baroness Z. had obtained passage for the New World. Automatically it was assumed that Stephan's accounts bore investigating, that the Lieutenant had been cashiered for gambling debts, and the Baroness was eloping with her husband's chauffeur. As for the nameless thousands who poured regularly from Europe's shores by steerage, cramming their crude belongings into hampers and old sheets, it was axiomatic that these must be misfits and incompetents. No loss to the homeland, they. Let them be skimmed off like the scum that tops a boiling stew, leaving behind what was useful and good. The time had not yet dawned when Europeans would admit the stupendous error of such shallow thinking. True, the vast westward flow of population contained a percentage of questionable fugitives, but the main stream was sound enough to build the sinews of a New World civilization in which the peasant, the aristocrat, and the intellectual had equal parts.

Uncle Mauder did not see the matter in this light. "What are we going to tell people?" he asked reproachfully.

Mama's laugh was taunting. "Tell them we have gipsy blood—that's nothing new in Hungarian families!"

With this she went to the kitchen for a conference with Marishka, the cook, who had promised to surrender some of her prize recipes. While Marishka dictated, Mama took down in pencil the ingredients for Hungarian stuffed peppers, known as *Töltöt Paprika*: the stuffing of boiled rice and equal parts of chopped pork and veal, topped by a thick tomato sauce that contained, of all things, sugar. The combination of hot green peppers (no paprika powder was used) and the sweet sauce produced a delectable dish. Another favourite was stuffed cabbage, which called for the same rice and meat filling, flavoured with nutmeg, rolled into a barely parboiled leaf, pinned with a toothpick, and fried until a golden brown (Turks and Armenians employ grape-leaves in a similar concoction). Marishka also prepared Viennese *Krautmehlspeis'*, a mixture of boiled noodles tossed in grated fresh cabbage that has been browned in butter; this dish could be eaten with salt and pepper as a main course, or topped with sugar as a heavenly dessert. There were other noodle masterpieces: fried noodles thickly sprinkled with sauté poppy-seeds, or potato noodles (half flour and half mashed potatoes) rolled by hand into thin sausages of an inch-and-a-half length, then boiled, drained, and tossed thoroughly about in browned bread-crumbs. All these noodle dishes were at their best with some ragout to provide an abundance of gravy. Most Hungarians depended on *Gúlyás* (known the world over as goulash) but Marishka considered this plebeian. Her speciality was the more delicately blended *Pörkölt*, a refined goulash without potatoes to coarsen the texture. Apart from its use in potato noodles, and pancakes (made of grated raw potatoes, flour, and egg), Marishka scorned the lowly spud.

Other data which Mama wrote down concerned chicory, endive, and cucumber salad, with a dressing of malt vinegar, oil, sour cream, and fresh dill. She also investigated the mysteries of pickle-making, which included the boiling of peeled cucumbers with mustard seed and spices, as well as a simple process of dropping unpeeled gherkins in brine and letting them stand in the sun until they pickled themselves.

Lastly, there opened up the almost unlimited field of Hungarian desserts, beginning with meringue puffs in vanilla sauce, through Christmas delicacies and *Strudel* in five varieties: apple, cheese, cherry, cabbage, and a sweet paste of poppy-seeds. Marishka also knew of a poor man's fritter called *Arme Ritter* ("insolvent knights"), consisting of stale bread dipped in egg batter, browned crisply, and served with sugar and cinnamon. But the triumph of Grossmama's table was a pastry that did not belong to Hungary at all: London cakes. This bit of perfection was achieved by lining a baking-tin with rich shortcake dough, spreading thinly with currant jelly, and topping this with thick meringue into which had been stirred grated almonds and nuts. After slow baking the cake was scored and cut into three-inch-by-one-inch strips. These were put in tins and, if properly hidden, could be kept for weeks.

Another dessert of foreign origin found its way to Hungary: Italian *zabaglione*. This was made of egg yolks beaten up with sugar and cooked in a double boiler, then served in individual portions flavoured with Chianti wine. Marishka preferred her own version, uncooked, with the fluffy egg-whites included, and a dash of heady *Barack* (Hungarian peach brandy) to lend zip.

In retrospect it appears that all these goodies were enormously high in starch and carbohydrate content, a thing frowned on by modern apostles of the slimming diet. Yet, oddly, not one of our

Hungarian relatives was fat. To be sure, all Solymár indulged in violent activities, particularly *csárdás* dancing, a pastime well calculated to melt poundage. At village festivals, when wine flowed in abundance and revelry lasted till dawn, Atya was usually too exhilarated to enter his carriage; instead, he climbed on to the coachman's perch and, with one arm around Zoltán, clicked his tongue and personally guided the horses home. Similarly Aunt Cornelia, after dancing through the night, found her legs willing to trot churchward for matins before dropping happily to bed. The appetites that went with so much movement were correspondingly hearty.

While our mother was busy with these gustatory notations Grossmama set out on a mission of her own. As a farewell gift she had placed an order with the Widow Pilmann for five feather-beds. The huge bags of bright red ticking, bulging with finest Solymár goose-down, arrived on top of a hay-wagon.

"*Istenem!*" cried our mother in dismay. "What's this?"

Grossmama beamed. "You're not to miss the comforts of home," she explained, "even though you want to maroon yourselves at the end of creation."

"But they don't use feather-beds in America."

"Rubbish," sputtered Grossmama in disbelief. "There's nothing like a soft goose comforter on chilly nights."

Our mother had no exact statistics at her command. Still, she insisted: "Mexico City is neither as chilly nor as hot as Hungary; it's two thousand metres above sea-level."

"So is Switzerland," said Grossmama. "Yet the Swiss use feather-beds. *They're* sensible people!"

In the end the billowy sacks were compressed into a special chest and sent off with our heavy baggage. A smaller case held the beautiful white linen slip-covers, scalloped and initialled, which Aunt Cornelia had contributed.

The villagers also sent gifts. From Béla, the baker, came a seven-layer and caramel-topped *Dobosch Torte*, besides a Greek honey confection called *Baklavá*. At sight of these goodies my brothers and I indulged in a greedy speculation. Could we not have threatened to leave earlier, then postponed the parting several times, so as to provoke repeated windfalls of this sort?

The actual farewells were painful. Even Atya's dogs, a St Bernard from the French Pyrenees, named Joyeux, and a Puszta sheep-dog called Bodry, drooped under the general air of melancholy. We had other pets: the talking crow of Father Miklos,

Zoltán's goats, the Widow Pilmann's wonderful black sow, Nuchi, and Grossmama's geese.

There was a special story about Grossmama's geese. These birds, a gander and two females, had been hatched shortly after I was born. Mere balls of fluff at the time of my baptism, they missed being roasted for the celebration. On the eve of our first departure for Mexico the birds did not appear to be quite fat enough for feasting, hence they were spared again. "We'll eat them when you return," said Grossmama in tones of solemn promise. Yet we came back to Europe and the old lady was still stalling. For, by now, the thought of executing her pets had become unbearable. *Die Gänseln*, as she called her darlings, were household fixtures. They wandered among the flower-beds, pampered and secure. The gander in particular was a big proud fellow of savage disposition; he hissed and honked at strangers, keeping them off the premises as surely as the most ferocious watchdog. Needless to say, he and his feathered wives had by now grown so tough that no one would have wished to eat them. To this day, however, the honking of geese transports me in spirit to the edge of an acacia forest and the sweet-smelling fields of Hungary.

Lastly, our farewells included a creature of our acquaintance whom my brothers and I never mentioned in the family circle, yet who crossed our path frequently as we came and went from the Solymár school. This was Brigitta, the village idiot.

Nobody seemed to know where Brigitta came from or who she might be. She did not live in Solymár, though she appeared there periodically, only to be charged with vagrancy and locked up in the local gaol. When her sentence was up she obtained her release and emerged again, usually pregnant. Since her feeble wits could give no clue, the identity of her assailant—or lover—remained always in doubt. Guards were placed before her cell in regular rotation. In fact, sturdy villagers volunteered eagerly for this chivalrous duty. Yet the result was always the same. Brigitta was with child.

"It's very strange," mused Solymár peasant bucks of every age and description. They seemed at a loss to explain the phenomenon.

The village women had less difficulty. "Very strange indeed!" they jeered. "We'll see that the wench gets put where she belongs."

They wrote a letter to Budapest, signed by Father Miklos and the postmaster's wife. After two weeks the letter returned, marked insufficient postage. By some oversight the postmaster had sent it out unfranked.

"Oversight, eh?" said the postmistress, purchasing a stamp herself and carrying the letter to the afternoon train.

This time it brought results. A welfare commission arrived from the capital, prepared to take the blonde, buxom, and quite barmy Brigitta to a charitable institution. But an astonishing controversy ensued. In a body the village elders took up the imbecile girl's defence against such high-handed interference by officials from another district. They pointed to a statute which declared that forcible removal of any person, male or female, by agents without jurisdiction in the territory constituted kidnapping.

The welfare commission, bent on an errand of mercy, wanted no entanglements with rustic law. If Solymár elders declined Budapest help in an obvious case of destitution, there was nothing the visiting officials could do. As a mere formality they asked Brigitta herself whether she wished to enter the Samaritan Home in the city, where she would have food, clothes, and medical care. But she shook her head and, glassy-eyed, turned a placid smile on her would-be benefactors.

"Oh, no," she told them, "I like it here!" Then, lowering her voice, she added confidentially, "Soon, I'm to take my walk. . . ."

By this she meant that she would disappear into the hills, as usual between gaol sentences, perhaps to exasperate the good parishioners of some other hamlet.

It was on these "walks" that my brothers and I had seen Brigitta innumerable times, lolling in the acacia wood or panting up the steep slope to the vineyards. She always grinned at us and waved a friendly paw. She seemed even a shade more amiable when Zoltán happened along. Zoltán was old, gnarled, and desiccated, but he had been among the public-spirited burghers who 'saved' Brigitta from confinement in the cruel asylum. He always waved back at her, whistling through his teeth. Nevertheless, when we asked if they were friends Zoltán said, "Nonsense—pick up your feet and get moving, you're late for school!"

Once, under the crucifix on the hill behind our grandfather's house, we found the feeble-minded girl with her most recent babe in her arms. She was swinging it back and forth, chanting a dissonant tune. But the next time we passed her the infant was gone. The rumour went that the village doctor had placed it for adoption. Under the crucifix Brigitta continued sitting for days, rocking her empty arms and crooning her lullaby.

When we bade her farewell she nodded. "Yes," her voice trailed off, "soon I'm going to take my walk——"

But not all our Solymár good-byes were tinged with gloom. My brother Arnim looked forward to the last day of school. Arnim did not like indoor life. He was gay, sunny, and of a pronounced artistic bent. As a boy soprano of exceptional pitch he took solo parts in the choir conducted by Father Miklos. He also had drawing ability and considerable ease at clay modelling, two talents foreign to Sylvester and me. On the other hand, mathematics and history gave Arnim ennui, since he preferred thinking of a dragonfly that he must create on paper in all the shimmer of its multicoloured wings, or of a fluted cornice on the Solymár church which might be reproduced with the plastic materials in his putty-box. As a result he had little use for school and loudly deplored the hours we wasted there. Still, his disposition made him a confirmed optimist. Hardly a day dawned when Arnim did not bound out of bed with the hopeful question: "I wonder if the school burned down?" The Spanish phrase he used implied almost a gambler's dare: "*A poco se quemó la escuela!*"

None of our schools were ever burned down. But Arnim never tired of asking.

On the last day in his Solymár classroom Arnim was exuberant. Invited by the teacher to expatiate on his personal plans, he rose importantly. "I'm going to be a *ranchero* in Mexico," he announced. "I'll sing to my herds, and then I'll paint the picture of a mountain. . . ."

The teacher, wishing to drive home an appropriate lesson in geography, broke in at this point. "What famous mountain is situated in Mexico?" When no one spoke, she prompted helpfully, "You've all seen it on the map, a volcano, Popo——"

At this the class broke into a disrespectful roar, for the opening syllables of the difficult Aztec word had an unfortunate connotation in German and Austro-Hungarian nurseries. It was a dialectic euphemism referring to the spanking area.

However, Arnim would not allow his lofty vision to be profaned. He came to the teacher's aid. "The name is Popocatépetl," he declared unperturbed. "It means The Mountain that Smokes."

14

FAREWELL TO THE DANUBE

IN HUNGARY, as in Tartary, China, and Manchuria, family names are placed before given names. Thus the eldest Pilmann boy who drove us to the station was called Pilmann József. We rode in an ancient springless vehicle that creaked in all its joints, but was big enough to accommodate us, grandparents and luggage included.

At the last minute Atya and Grossmama had decided to escort us part of the way to Vienna. First they would take us for a last round of Budapest sights: the Királyi Vár, the Gothic Houses of Parliament, the Turkish Bastion, and the famed baths of Szent Gellért, where Danube water was whipped by machine into foaming breakers. We crossed all the broad river bridges on foot, visited the Margit Island in midstream, the Angol Park, and the Szépmüvészeti Museum, where Grossmama's arches gave out. Leaving her in a near-by garden café with a cup of hot chocolate and *Schlagobers* (whipped cream) we went on to the Szent István Bazilika, to see the Sacred Hand.

The Sacred Hand was a relic of Hungary's patriarch king, Saint Stephen. Severed and embalmed at his death, it had remained dry and unwithered for ten centuries. Once a year great processions were held in Budapest, and the holy relic, resting in a glass coffer, was carried through the streets. At sight of it people crossed themselves and fell to their knees, renewing their vows of faith, since the hand's preservation was deemed—by papal edict—a miracle. As a special precaution the glass repository was carried on padded shoulders by four perfectly matched bearers who walked in slow measured steps so as to reduce vibration. The relic itself lay cushioned on thick silk, and the transparent walls around it were hermetically sealed.

"If the glass broke and air were admitted," Atya explained, "the hand would disintegrate into a mound of ashes!"

We stared in awe at the lean, greyish thing that had once been flesh. It sent the same shiver down my spine that I had experienced under the crucifix beside the Anna Kapelle.

In Budapest we took final leave of the family and headed for Lake Balaton, en route to Vienna. The Balaton halt was by no means on our direct line of travel, but Mama wished to go there for sentimental reasons. The famed resort was intimately associated with her own youth.

As everywhere in rural Hungary, the shores of Balaton were dotted with votive shrines and druidic spots hallowed by tradition. The lake itself is Europe's largest inland body of water, strangely quiet and opalescent, yet capable of sudden violence. As a child our mother had spent many happy summers wading in the mirror-smooth shallows or sailing with Atya through breakers churned to a white foam. She loved the Balaton as much as Solymár and Budapest.

From Balaton Lake we hastened on to Vienna for a brief call at the Hoftheater where my godmother, the Hungarian actress Camille Fehér de Vernet, was playing a long engagement. Aunt Camillushka, as we called her, loved us dearly and did everything in her power to spoil us, for she had no children of her own. Our youthful response to her affection was not untinged by opportunism, since she showered us with sweets and toys.

On our present visit she took us to her suite at the Hotel Erzherzog Karl, where we were regaled with bonbons and strawberry tarts. As we gobbled happily she clapped her hands in delight, praising our gentility, our cleverness, our looks.

Beyond doubt my brothers and I behaved our hypocritical best when in the presence of Aunt Camillushka. Such parlour manners you never saw! But, while Mama's embarrassment grew, the great Camille went into transports of delight.

"I know what I want to do," she exclaimed suddenly. "I will adopt one of them. My godchild—that's it, I will adopt my own godchild!" She lifted me from the floor and gave me an athletic hug, for, though she was petite, Aunt Camillushka had uncommon vigour.

Mama smiled politely.

"You don't believe me?" Aunt Camillushka challenged. "I am serious. I'll take out adoption papers right away. Please, Sári, you must give your consent!"

"How could my daughter share your famous name?" protested Mama. "She has done nothing to earn it——"

Camille bristled. "Oh, not my theatrical name," she said in a deprecating tone, "but the other, the legal one."

We knew what she meant, for Aunt Camillushka was in private life the Baroness von Marosffy-Fehéregyházy. I thought I would enjoy so splendid an array of syllables, and actually Camille went through with the arrangement. When I came of age the papers were put in my hands. But there was little snob value to be extracted from them, since no one outside Hungary was ever able to pronounce this fancy extension of my name.

From Vienna we went to Berlin, where Mama stopped to outfit us for the journey overseas. At a large department store near the Adlon Hotel my brothers and I tried on blue-and-white striped sailor's shirts, as well as jaunty rain-capes of a weatherproof material called Loden. We wore these capes right out of the store, as the autumn drizzles had settled on Berlin.

Bad weather did not stop Mama from showing us the sights. We visited the Tiergarten, which included one of the world's great zoological parks. Hailing an open landau, we rode along broad avenues with names familiar to every traveller: Unter den Linden, Wilhelmstrasse, Siegesallee. Twice a four-note motor-horn resounded and traffic stopped to let the German Emperor pass. We stared at Wilhelm II, so dark, sharp-featured, and somewhat forbidding as compared to the Father Christmas figure of Austria's Franz Josef. Yet the Hohenzollern monarch's smile was disarming as he acknowledged the cheers that greeted him on every street.

Our Berlin visit reached its climax in a dinner at the home of a Siemens official named Duffing, who lived in the wooded Grunewald area. Herr Duffing was an unctuous gentleman with a thin, nervous wife and three energetic children, a boy and two girls. The names of these children I have forgotten, but the afternoon we spent with them impressed itself indelibly upon my mind. We were off to a bad start from the moment Frau Duffing introduced us to her brood:

"Here are some little friends from Budapest, who have come to play with you." With an encouraging nod she abandoned us at the nursery door.

The Duffing offspring looked us over, then choked with suppressed mirth.

"That's Hungary," said the boy, nudging his sisters, whereupon their gaiety increased and they burst into open laughter.

"What is so funny?" Sylvester asked slowly.

They were holding their sides by now. "Why, *Hungarians* are funny! They're Mongols and Kalmucks, who smear themselves with rancid butter——"

We were outraged. "Rancid butter?"

"You come from a city called Butterpest, don't you? In Butterpest they've got nothing but rancid fat——"

"Shut up!" Sylvester lunged for the boy, who was a head taller.

"Two against one, eh?" sneered our tormentor as he sized up the husky Arnim who had stepped up to Sylvester's side.

We were shamed by these words, which made my brothers look like bullies. The young Duffings sensed our predicament. They grew cocky again and shouted:

"Yah, yah, Butterpest!"

At this moment the door opened and Frau Duffing's smiling head bobbed up and down as she propelled another visitor, a lad of about ten, across the threshold.

"Here you are," she told him with brittle cheerfulness. "Just join the others and have fun!" She cast a cursory glance in our direction. "Supper will be up directly," she twittered before rustling from the room.

We did not know the new guest, but it was evident that he lived in the neighbourhood and was on excellent terms with our young hosts. Instantly the latter encircled him and whispered in his ear, whereupon the chorus was resumed, this time with increased volume:

"Yah, yah, Butterpest!"

Now the proportion of fighters favoured the enemy and we no longer needed to pull punches. "*Arre, toro!*" bellowed my brothers. "*Corrida!*" And we dashed round the chamber in a mad bullfight stampede.

The young Duffings and their friend looked nonplussed, for we raced about at such speed that they were flattened out against walls and furniture, in an indiscriminate exchange of blows. Half-way through the fracas Sylvester recalled that the honour of Hungary, not Mexico, was at stake. Abruptly he broke out in a volley of Magyar war whoops. Now we were Attila and the Tartar Horde, galloping over the steppes of Asia and leaving destruction in our path. Toys, chairs, and sofa cushions littered the floor when, at the climax of these antics, the door opened again and Frau Duffing peeped in.

"*Ach*," she beamed, dodging a flying missile, "what a time you *are* having!"

The young Duffings pointed accusing fingers. "Mama, Mama——" they began, but before their accusations took form the lady had disappeared. In her place a stolid maid entered, pushing a tea-wagon with sandwiches, cocoa, and cakes.

Instantly the battle subsided. In quick accord we gathered about the cart and watched the maid fill up the cups with steaming liquid. A sandwich platter was passed round.

The food was delicious.

"Germany is the greatest nation in the world!" the Duffing boy now announced, appealing to the maid for confirmation. "Isn't it so, Gerda?"

The maid gave him a puzzled stare. "*Selbstverständlich*," she said. "Certainly." Her tone indicated that in so incontestable a matter interrogation was superfluous.

It was our turn to be flabbergasted. Here was something we had never heard before. Germany the world's greatest nation? Preposterous! Our elementary history-books in Solymár had taught us quite differently. Hungary, the thousand-year-old kingdom on the Danube, was indisputably supreme. And we said so.

But the Duffing boy had not done with his subject. Gerda's support led him to expatiate now at greater length. He had a keen mind for one so young, and he was well schooled in Germanic lore. His recital of his country's ancient and modern heroes made a formidable showing. We were confounded by such names as Ottokar, Hermann, Roland, Barbarossa, Carolus Magnus, Der Alte Fritz (Frederick the Great), and the current Emperor, Wilhelm II.

"And that isn't all," the other boy chimed in. "We have the best musicians, the best doctors, the best builders of Zeppelins... This Hungary of yours, what has it got?"

We floundered, for our education had been slipshod as compared to theirs. The few national figures that peopled our war games would hardly pass muster in such company as this. We might have mentioned the saintly King Stephen, the poet Petöfi, the painter Munkácsi, even Franz Liszt, but our combined memories were too paralysed at the moment to conjure up these names. Every second it became clearer that our hosts considered us very small fry indeed, and there was nothing we could do about it.

It was now that Arnim was struck by an enlightening thought. "Look here," he said with the air of a discoverer, "our father is part French and part German—all those big heroes you mentioned belong to us too!"

After a moment of hesitation I brought Mexico into the picture. As yet I had contributed nothing to the fray save a few minor bruises. This was humiliating. I thought I would redeem myself by blurting out, "We have Popocatépetl."

It was the wrong idea. Not only could our clever opponents distinguish a mountain from a swashbuckling idol, but German children shared with Hungarians the curious reaction evoked by the Aztec word. Assuredly, our side had suffered a death blow.

However slight this Berlin episode appeared at the time, in retrospect it throws a light on our development. For here, in the course of our infantile chauvinistic squabble, the first germ of a budding cosmopolitanism manifested itself in our behaviour. We had come to the Prussian capital flushed with Magyar pride, nurtured—by supposedly civilized adults—on the principle that our people, our background, our mode of life must necessarily be the noblest and the best. Why? Because they were *ours*, of course.

Then and there a trace of doubt assailed us.

15

SECOND WESTWARD CROSSING

IN BERLIN our mother interviewed a new governess, Fräulein Trude, who forthwith joined us on the express train to Hamburg. We reached the beautiful Hanseatic port in a heavy fog which shrouded the picturesque waterways of this Venice of the North. Pedagogically alert, the new governess gave forth with Baedeker information. She pointed out that we were here faced with 'Atlantic' or 'Ocean' climate, common to the British Isles, France, Belgium, Holland, and the North Sea coast.

"Too much condensation," said Baedeker.

We recalled the downpour in Berlin, but learned that this was exceptional and confined to a brief rainy season. Central Germany, Austria, Hungary, the Balkans, etc., had 'Continental' or 'Russian' climate, dry cold, dry heat, with extremes in temperature not uncommon. Berlin, Vienna, and Budapest were as hot—though fortunately not as cold—as Siberia. Europe's winters were happily tempered by the Mexican Gulf Stream.

We took pride in this, deriving from it a kind of proprietary attitude. To think that Mexican waters served as a heating plant for another continent! We counted the Gulf Stream thenceforth as our personal possession.

My brothers and I also had come to regard ourselves as experienced mariners, on intimate terms with life at sea. Two previous ocean crossings gave us assurance as we now mounted another gangplank and stepped aboard the Hapag liner *Kronprinzessin Caecilie*.

The ship's passenger list was cosmopolitan. Children with English and German nursemaids or with Spanish-speaking *nanas* walked the deck sedately, while a brass band played. The sirens joined in and the ship eased away from the pier. Moving down the wide Elbe river, we headed for the open sea.

A stop was scheduled at Plymouth, on the English Channel. The ship did not dock here but received passengers sent out from shore by tender. Among the newcomers were two little Swedish girls with their parents, and a smartly clad Belgian boy called Alain, who lived in Cuba. The latter walked aboard beside a dark, elegant lady whose furs and veil scented the air with perfume. Once in her cabin, however, the marvellous lady did not emerge again. Alain soon explained this.

"*Maman est malade*," he told anyone who cared to know. "*C'est le mal de mer.*" His accompanying gestures left no doubt regarding the nature of her indisposition.

Alain became the sensation of the boat, at least with its junior element. He was a handsome child, lively and full of enterprise, yet of gentle disposition. Only six years old, he possessed exquisite manners. But the real reason for his popularity sprang from the fact that he owned an inexhaustible supply of fabulous toys, which lay scattered in piles about the deck-chair his sick *Maman* did not use. There was a sturdy elephant of stuffed velvet, big enough to be sat on, with a howdah on its back. In addition, Alain had a model railway with scenic properties, signal-boxes, tunnels, bridges, and a network of nickel-plated lines. There was also a miniature Noah's Ark, besides a set of building-blocks, a tricycle, a bicycle, roller-skates, ice-skates, and an assortment of badminton bats, shuttlecocks, darts, arrows, and balls.

At first all this equipment had been stored in the luggage hold, with only a few articles left out for Alain's use during the trip. But after his mother took to her bed the boy grew lonely, and he made repeated descents into the bowels of the ship to excavate some of his spare supplies. As he emerged each day with fresh surprises all the other children clustered about in unabashed admiration. None of us had ever seen such opulence! Alain must be a princelet or a millionaire's son!

Grown-ups, too, speculated about the matter, and it was not long before the ship's grape-vine disclosed that the little boy's father was a rich sugar-planter from the Cuban province of Auza Oriente. Alain and his mother made annual vacation trips to London, Paris, and the Riviera, returning always with twice the baggage their tickets entitled them to.

"This time it's worse than ever," a stewardess revealed. "You haven't seen anything yet!"

We stared in amazement. "What do you mean?"

"He's got a rocking-horse below that's as big as a live pony."

This revelation was received with mixed feelings. A rocking-horse might be all right for a child of kindergarten age, but a boy of six? Well, perhaps this was something special, a toy broncho equipped with an inside mechanism that enabled it to run and kick and snort. We stormed Alain's play corner and begged to see his prize possession.

He was taken aback. "Who—who told you?" he asked sheepishly, a deep flush colouring his cheeks.

"Annele, the stewardess."

"I don't play with rocking-horses——"

We pressed him hard. "The purser watched it come aboard," we persisted. "Please, Alain, let us see it!"

He struggled manfully, but we finally wore him down. "Oh, all right," he admitted, "*Maman* bought it for me because she keeps forgetting that I'm not a *bébé* any more. But you mustn't think I play with it!"

After breakfast the next day we were on hand, uncertain whether our little Belgian friend would keep his word. Two hours went by without a trace of him. But before the eleven o'clock bouillon was served Alain appeared, followed by a considerable clatter.

"Here's Plomplom," he announced in a resigned tone, while two deckhands hoisted a carved equine wonder through the lounge exit.

We gaped in wide-eyed awe, for Plomplom was truly magnificent. He towered above our shoulders, curving a proud neck from which a wavy mane drooped gracefully over one side. The sculptured wooden body was dappled with bright paint, accented further by a red saddle, brass-studded halter, gilt bridle, and a pair of jingling stirrups.

"He came off the merry-go-round at Passy," explained Alain, lest we be horrified by Plomplom's size and girth.

But there was no danger of this. We were enchanted. Three at a time, we climbed on Plomplom's back and rocked to our heart's content. Shrieks and huzzahs rang across the sun-deck as Plompom, Pegasus-fashion, carried us on to high adventure. Not in its proudest days on the merry-go-round of Passy could a wooden horse have brought greater delight.

Alain, however, was moody. "I begin school this year," he said with quiet defiance. "I don't need a rocking-horse."

And one day the weight of his six years became too much for him. He could not bear the sight of Plomplom any more.

"Let's push him overboard," he proposed.

We could not believe our ears. The idea of lifting Plomplom from his wheeled base and pitching him into the sea was as preposterous as though we planned to do the same with the ship's grand piano or a card-table from the salon.

Alain was serious.

"Yes," he decided, "Plomplom goes overboard."

There was admittedly something irresistible about sending Plomplom splashing into the sea. The more we thought about the idea the better we liked it. And there were no grown-ups in sight.

"Come on, Alain," we cheered. "Let's do it!"

Without further pause the carved Pegasus was pushed up to the ship's railing, its forefeet pawing the air. The burnished mane fluttered in the breeze and the long flowing tail brushed our faces as we stooped to raise the rump over our heads. Now for a combined effort, a well-timed shove—and the glorious creature was catapulted over the top. A flash of gaudy colour gleamed momentarily in the sun. Then there was a dull plop followed by a disappointing bit of spray, as Plomplom settled between two tumbling waves.

Alain beamed happily. "Let's throw something else," he said, turning back to survey his play corner.

We watched in fascination as his eye fixed on the plush elephant. Seconds later the padded beast bounced giddily over the side, to join Plomplom in his watery grave. A woolly bear followed, and then a toy apothecary shop whizzed through space. After each heaving effort Alain brushed off his hands in a carefree gesture. We stared, dumbfounded.

It was when Alain crouched to rip up several lengths of railway line that our frozen stupor gave way to action. Caught in the spirit of things, we leaped to his side. Now everybody tore into the complicated works, snatching up papier-mâché scenic props, tunnels, repair sheds, signal-boxes, engines, goods-wagons, and carriages. In a kind of relay race we galloped to the railing, dumped our load, and returned, bouncing off one another as we tore along on our mad errand of destruction. Less than ten minutes must have elapsed before Alain's corner was bared of every object, including the steamer rug. A few stray building-blocks, balls, boxes, and broken crayons littered the deck gutter, but these were quickly disposed of in a final mopping-up action.

When it was all over, Alain settled himself comfortably in his mother's vacant deck-chair. He crossed both feet and let his eyes wander towards the horizon. Then, meditatively, he glanced over the surface of the ocean. The expanse of bluish-green water seemed to have wiped out all trace of his sunken treasure. No, in the distance two small spots of colour bobbed up and down: Plomplom and the elephant, still tossing in the ship's wake.

All at once a startled look came over Alain's face, as he sat up and undertook a frantic search of his pockets. He pushed aside the deck-chair and got down on his knees to inspect the clean deck-planks. But the thing that he was after seemed to elude him, for his expression now changed to acute anguish. He confronted us disconsolately and let out a piercing wail:

"I've lost my bean-shooter!"

He had thrown away a fortune in expensive toys, but it was the loss of his bean-shooter that made Alain feel poor.

Alain and his *maman* left us in Cuba. They were met at the pier by a tall man in a broad-brimmed planter's hat, who stepped from a Protos phæton driven by a liveried Negro chauffeur.

"Look!" cried several of the ship's children who had never visited the New World. "A blackamoor!"

My brothers and I were equally startled, for the only Negro we had ever seen wore a chef's cap on a package of breakfast cereal.

16

MEXICAN MOVING-DAY

At Veracruz our father and Uncle Bichteler met us with a fine surprise. In our absence they had, bachelor-fashion, explored Mexico City and come upon a far more suitable house in a new residential district called Colonia Roma. It was a four-storied structure (three floors and a gabled attic) just a block from the circular gardens of Miravalle. The street was called Colima and it lay nine squares from the avenue known as Calzada de la Piedad. According to Mexican custom this placed the house in Novena Colima or Ninth Colima Street.

Most foreigners are perplexed by the nomenclature of Mexico City thoroughfares. Not only is each block called a "street," but names change capriciously at quite irrelevant intervals, so that a single avenue is a composite of labels adding up to the same thing. For example, without the slightest alteration in width, direction, or quality of paving, the important Avenida Independencia runs along for a stretch, then emerges patriotically as the Street of the Sixteenth of September, commemorating the country's liberation from Spain. Similarly the old passage of Plateros (silversmiths) long ago blended into San Francisco (today Madero); a little farther it became Avenida Juárez, only to end up as Paseo de la Reforma. Yet they were the same street.

The reason for so much confusion derives from a certain expansiveness in the Latin character. An eloquent people, Mexicans can think up sonorous names faster than they can build boulevards; hence there is a surplus of the former. To take up the slack, available streets are subdivided into sections, each bearing another label. This makes for variety, but considerable strain on the memories of cab-drivers and postmen.

Added to the already teeming plurality of names there is the periodic urge on the part of city fathers to discard the familiar in favour of the new. In this manner whole neighbourhoods suddenly change identity, as in the case of suburban San Angel emerging in recent years as Villa Obregón.

Mexico City's main artery was, of course, the Paseo de la Reforma, known originally as El Camino de Carlota (Carlota's Road), since it was laid out by Maximilian for the Empress's daily drive from Castle Chapultepec to the cathedral. From the Paseo a wide avenue called Insurgentes led diagonally through the diplomatic quarter of Colonia Juárez to Colonia Roma, where our new home stood. Between these two residential sections lay the scenic suburban tram-line to Chapultepec, San Miguel-Chapultepec, Tacubaya, San Pedro, Mixcoac, and San Angel. Operated by a Canadian firm with headquarters at Toronto, this line gave service of a most pleasurable sort. Its cars were butter-yellow rather than the offensive orange shade customary then in most lands, and there were special open models for balmy weather. Three times a day express trams known as *Rápidos* came into service, geared to high speed as they carried rush traffic from the cathedral square to the wooded outskirts of the town. Everything stopped for the *Rápidos*, which crawled through the centre of the city, then gradually gathered speed until, beyond the Bucareli Clock and La Garita, there was no holding them. All the while, the normal jingle of tram bells was silenced so that the important tooting of the express could be appreciated.

A sense of importance seemed to attach itself also to passengers travelling with the *Rápidos*, whether they sat in the main power car or the breezy trailer. They looked upon the carriage trade and the occasional automobiles of that era with a distinct arrogance that was somehow in keeping with the toot.

In a way the *Rápidos* had a marked effect upon community life. There was a frustrated desperation at missing one, particularly at noon, when everybody in Mexico went home for the main meal. The very phrase "*Yá se fué el Rápido!*" ("The Express is gone!") conveyed a sense of forlornness, difficult to describe.

With passing years horses and carriages disappeared from the world's metropolitan areas. Cars and buses cluttered urban streets, making even tram-lines all but obsolete. Nevertheless, the *Rápidos* of Mexico City held their own in stubborn defiance of advancing time; for years they continued to snort fiercely along under the tall poplars that lined the well-fenced right of way. To-day their final extinction seems still somehow unreal.

In Colonia Roma we did not use the express trams. The distance to town being short, Mama preferred a victoria drawn by two bays. On Sundays it was customary to join the *corso*, or carriage procession, in Chapultepec Park. In fair weather our mother ordered the top put down so that she and Fräulein Trude could open their parasols and smile benignly at the populace, like royalty on parade. Everybody else on wheels did the same, which made rather an excess of royalty.

Sylvester and Arnim did not enjoy these drives unless they could climb on the coachman's box. Most of the time they preferred taking a tram to the amusement area of Luna Park, where they could fish in a magnet pool or attend a children's matinée at the Salón Rojo where French films were shown. An actor named Bébé, surely forty years old though wearing Dutch bangs and a Little Lord Fauntleroy suit, starred in an interminable series of juvenile comedies that were the rage during the same period when the silk-hatted Max Linder titillated adult fans.

I yearned to join my brothers on their outings, but when Mama tied a pink taffeta sash about my white dress of embroidered Swiss lawn, my chances were gone.

"I can't imagine," Mama erroneously imagined, "that you would prefer going with the boys, when Tante Trude and I have planned such a lovely drive."

It was almost impossible to counter so persuasive an assumption. I felt inordinately flattered that Mama, whom we regarded as a being apart from common mortals, should seek my companionship. Also, there was something compelling about the sash; its crisp perfection lured me invariably into a ladylike pose. The upshot was that I rode everlastingly through Chapultepec Park while my brothers split their sides at Bébé's latest prank or gasped at the exploits of a detective named Nick Carter.

Often there were band concerts in the park. At such times Mama and Fräulein Trude strolled down the Avenida de los Poetas or the Avenida de los Filósofos while I scampered ahead, rolling a genteel hoop. The forest grew familiar to me. My eyes were so accustomed to the giant trees with their blurred, moss-hung tops that I could not encounter them anywhere on earth without being transported instantly back to that ancient Aztec wood. It was the same with the flower odours of Mexico: rich heliotrope, the clove spice of carnation pinks, tropical jasmine, and the scent of roses over a rain-drenched coping. I was absorbing them with every breath.

But things were not right with the house picked by Papa and Uncle Bichteler in the street of Colima. To begin with, there were too many floors. Including the basement (an undesirable feature, since Mexico City is built on a swamp), no fewer than five stairways taxed the heart, an organ already sorely strained in that high altitude. We children enjoyed tearing from floor to floor in an endless game of hide-and-seek. Our particular delight was the mansard garret where we could hatch and enact Bluebeard plots of bloodcurdling detail, for the house was constructed in the incongruous style of an Alpine tower with infinite possibilities for Gothic villainy. But Mama was unappreciative. "Had you two been a pair of lighthouse-keepers," she told Papa and Uncle Bichteler, "you couldn't have picked a more unsuitable house."

Real estate was not expensive in the Mexico of that day, and, while looking for more appropriate lodgings, our father was taken with the idea of buying ground and building a permanent home. He found some fields for sale beyond Chapultepec in the sparsely settled community of San Miguel. The property was part of the immense ranches of La Hormiga, which had been bestowed during viceregal times by the Spanish Crown upon the families of Rincón-Gallardo and Romero de Terreros, respectively marquises of Guadalupe and of San Francisco. In Maximilian's day a new owner, Martínez del Río, took over, only to be expropriated by the anti-imperialist Juárez. Under the presidency of Porfirio Díaz an Englishman named Horncastle purchased some of the neglected acres, and it was from him, through the real-estate firm of Watson-Phillips and their agent Rudolf Groth, that our father obtained possession. Meanwhile, until building plans could be completed, we were to occupy a small country house near by, with walled-in garden, stables, servant quarters, and a somewhat dilapidated carriage entrance. Our temporary address was to be the third street of Gelati, No. 1007.

Moving-day in Mexico is an exhausting experience. To begin with, a surprising number of persons are tangled up in the process, some of them bent on honest toil, but the majority attending merely in a spectator capacity. On the morning of our transfer to San Miguel a van arrived with half a dozen porters tumbling out, all of them whistling in a great show of vigour. They rushed into the rookery on Colima Street and made straight for the kitchen, where they mopped their brows and asked for water. The cook, well trained in local customs, awaited them with a bucket of *tepache*, a refreshing pineapple drink. Liquids flow better when there is music; hence a guitar made its sudden appearance, and presently the kitchen rang with agreeable melodies while the men drank and worked themselves up into the proper *mudanza* or moving-day spirit.

Next there was a small religious ceremony to be performed. To leave a house—even so crazy a dwelling as our Swiss turret—is a sad thing. Lest a curse fall on the empty walls, prayers must be said before departing and a cross placed on the lintel until the last piece of furniture is gone. Similarly the new abode, which may have harboured evil spirits, is rendered safe by ritualistic incantations, while the same cross placed above the lintel blesses all who enter.

The moving-men were amiable and jovial fellows. My brothers and I were lifted on top of the van and taken to and fro, sitting on mattresses and burlap sacks, or else jammed in the driver's cab. Since the day was long and over-exertion was frowned upon, the loadings were light and several trips had to be made. This added immeasurably to our pleasure as we circulated merrily through the confusion, with a sense of adventure in our hearts.

The day did not end without mishap. On one of the loadings a careless workman detached the bathroom fixtures from the old house (built-in tubs were not yet the fashion) and transferred them to the waiting van. As he and two helpers carried our prized enamel bath across the pavement some one tripped and the heavy load was sent coasting down the street. Everybody scrambled to the rescue, gathering up spigots and pipe-ends, as well as the elaborate lion's paws that served as the tub's feet. It was during this mêlée that a bit of flying granite struck my hand, inflicting a small gash that managed to bleed profusely and create rather a stir. All six porters dropped their work to sympathize. The medicine cabinet, already stored away in the van, was extricated and set on the pavement, where Fräulein Trude functioned efficiently with antiseptic and gauze. The guitar player played like mad, and presently everybody was thirsty again, so the cook brought another bucket of *tepache*.

Altogether it was a memorable day and one that would retain an odd significance throughout my later life. Whenever in the course of foreign travels I have applied for a passport my request has met with the routine question: "Have you any identifying marks?" Alas, Nature provided me with no outward distinction. But, thanks to the tumbling tub-bearers, I have on the small finger of my right hand a cicatrix in the form of a neat crescent. While infinitesimal, it is enough to satisfy customs and immigration officials, eliminating the need for more intimate research.

As for our new location on Gelati Street, it held a particular joy for my brothers and me. The area of San Miguel bordered on the suburb of Tacubaya, so that we became season-ticket holders on one of the *Rápidos* that whizzed diurnally through our placid existence. A little inter-urban station known as La Condesa marked the end of our street. From a distance through the double row of shady trees we could see the butter-yellow express trains whisk by.

With passing time, however, the thrill of the *Rápidos* was superseded by the advent of our first automobile. This proved to be a French Protos, not unlike the car that had waited at the dock in Havana when our young friend Alain and his beautiful mother went ashore. We did not know it at the time, but Mama and Fräulein Trude had been greatly impressed by that handsome vehicle which put horse-drawn victorias definitely in the shade. Once our move from the Colima house had been accomplished, Papa agreed that the family must become motorized.

Various firms demonstrated their models, and he vacillated for a time between an Italian Fiat and a French Protos. But our memory of a Cuban sugar-planter rolling along the wharves in a shining contraption of red paint and polished brass carried the day. We would have a Protos, leather-upholstered and equipped with every device, from coach-lanterns and rubber horn to an elaborate tool-chest on the running-board. A swarthy but neatly uniformed chauffeur came with the car, since no amateur would have known how to manipulate the petrol-eating monster.

Owing to their novelty, automobiles in those days were favourite photographic subjects. Almost every one purchasing a horseless carriage posed for a camera even before taking the first ride. Papa was no exception. When the Protos arrived at our door a photographer had already set up his tripod while the assembled family waited in caps and linen dusters. As the vehicle puffed to a halt, Papa climbed into the driver's seat, arranging himself in a commanding posture behind the wheel. Next we scurried about him on to the high leather cushions, while the chauffeur was left standing superfluously in the street. Only as an afterthought was he summoned to drape himself across the tool-box, where he perched in evident discomfort until the camera clicked.

17

SAN MIGUEL CHAPULTEPEC

Our 'new' neighbourhood, known as San Miguel, was actually old, rustic, and picturesque in character. Here, on the outskirts of Chapultepec, lived Mexican families whose names had figured in their country's history for the past three centuries. On our own side of the street the Escandón clan dwelled behind a high garden grille while opposite, stretched out over untold acres, the tribes of Teresa and Terraza reigned in faded pomp. All these families had been closely associated with the Maximilian epoch, having furnished soldiers and statesmen for the Crown. With the downfall of the ill-fated Habsburg their star had waned, and in the reconstruction period that followed his rule they had obstinately withdrawn behind their ancient walls.

"The Terraza estate is the Empire in miniature," it was said throughout Mexico. In vain did curious passers-by try to peer through shuttered windows, hoping to catch a glimpse of the hidden life inside. There was nothing to be seen. From four separate streets huge green portals gave access to the walled grounds, yet we never heard the hinges screech nor saw a person come or go.

Occasionally the servants brought fantastic reports. A world in microcosm seemed to exist under the dark trees that rose above the walls. There was a family church, with sacristan, priest, and acolytes living on the premises. Towards the Tacubaya side a compact farm was operated, with stock, poultry, a dairy, and a winery. A small electric railway supposedly connected every part of the estate with the Casa Grande or main house.

"There's even a private burial ground," our old Dolores said, pointing out that no hearse ever came to fetch a dead Terraza to one of the public cemeteries.

In the opposite direction from our house, on what is now the street of Montiel, more cheerful conditions prevailed. Here lived a Swiss lady named Madame Gaby with her young nephew Carlos. Madame Gaby was well-read and a gracious hostess, in whose salon prominent personalities were often assembled. Among these was General Bernardo Reyes, a high-ranking figure of the Díaz era, who was godfather to Carlos. This relationship accounted for the many lavish presents received by the boy Certain it was that Carlos owned the best bicycle and the first fountain-pen among the children in the neighbourhood, which inspired a unanimous effort to win his favour. In addition, Madame Gaby kept a jar filled with almond pasties as sweet and good as her own disposition. While my brothers rhapsodized over the mechanical perfections of a nickel-plated wheel my admiration confined itself to the patisserie.

Only two doors away from Madame Gaby's house lived an English family named Boulder, with two blonde children, Eustace and Evelyn, aged nine and seven, who lived under a difficult disciplinary régime necessitated by their father's illness. Mr Boulder had cancer of the trachea and he breathed through a silver tube. Since the children were lively, they had to be sent outside their home to play. This brought them into contact with us.

Every one loved the Boulders. The little girl in particular captivated us with her ladylike air. She had an intense liking for flowers, and our neighbourhood was a riot of blooms. As a result Evelyn devised an original game which she played daily with the utmost gravity: Carnival Float. For this she enlisted the help of the Boulder gardener, who gathered up a mass of blossoms with which to decorate her pony-trap. With wires, ribbons, and tissue-paper every inch of the wicker vehicle was covered, holding marguerite, dahlia, magnolia, and gladiolus stalks securely in place. When all was done, even to the hub and wheel-spokes, Evelyn climbed aboard and slowly rode down the street, with the servant walking alongside and guiding the pony's steps.

"I am Queen of the Flowers," said the blonde child, serenely enthroned on her perch.

But a moment later she would jump to the ground and ask some other youngster who stood with mouth agape, "Would you like to be Queen of the Flowers?" Thus each little girl for streets around had a chance to ride in state, while the ribbon-decked pony jogged along at a patient trot.

Eustace, Carlos, and my brothers were unable to put up with such whimsy. They banded together and heckled us in Spanish, the language that was once more paramount in our daily life:

"Allí van las reinas del carro de la basura!" ("There go the queens of the rubbish-cart!")

This unnerved me and I retired from the floral procession. But not Evelyn. Poised and unassailable, she continued her favourite pastime, supervising the trimming of her little wagon and riding down the street in frozen majesty. It was a display of composure and self-confidence that utterly bewitched me.

There were in the San Miguel section other foreign families whose lives impinged indirectly upon our own. Three blocks away, touching the wooded fringe of Chapultepec, stood the spacious home of Baron von Hiller, whose wife was an American. This lady was said to come from a city called Philadelphia. The flowing syllables of that name captivated us, so that we incorporated it in our nightly supper narratives; many a canal was carved through our rice or mashed potatoes and gravy to a citadel dubbed Philadelphia.

Next to Baron von Hiller lived a gaunt Mexican widower with four small children, the eldest a girl of no more than six. They were dark-eyed and fine-featured, but extremely shy. For weeks they watched us from afar, never venturing outside the grilled door of their gloomy house. We knew nothing about them, except that the younger children called their big sister Rosalía. A cook or housemaid seemed to look after their wants, since we saw no aunt, grandmother, or governess around the premises.

One afternoon, while Mama was out and my brothers played elsewhere with their friends, I was sitting alone among my dolls when the garden gate was softly opened. A moment later the four orphans filed in meekly and stopped in front of the steps where I was busily rocking Otto and my flaxen-haired Sibylle to sleep.

"*Buenas tardes*," said Rosalía politely, nudging her sister and baby brothers to do likewise. The latter broke into a piping chorus, then fell silent, scuffing their feet in embarrassment.

I noticed that they were dressed up in an incongruous assortment of finery, as though everything they owned had been donned for the occasion. In addition, each child carried a large and unwieldy pack.

Replying to their greeting, my eyes focused on the bundles. "What have you there?" I asked.

At this they beamed. "Presents!" said Rosalía. Again she nudged the others, and they set down their load. "Presents for you——"

This was wonderful. Dropping my dolls, I rushed forward to inspect the boxes and baskets. The children stepped quietly back to let me rummage through the pile. Their eyes shone with pleasure.

An instant later an awkward situation arose, as my fingers extricated the most startling and unlikely objects assembled by the motherless youngsters as a neighbourly gift-offering. From the baskets there emerged the necks of half a dozen sealed wine bottles, while the boxes contained an assortment of multi-coloured ornaments from last year's Christmas tree.

"For you," the piping chorus repeated. Then confidentially, "The wine belongs to our *papacito*——"

I stared at the bottles, not knowing what to do with them. Obviously this was loot from a parental cupboard, fetched here for some unexplained purpose. As for the crystal balls and silver tinsel, they looked incongruous at any time except Christmas.

Rosalía's eyes searched mine. Like a miniature madonna she placed her arms protectively about the younger children.

"May we play with you?" she said.

A stab of pain went through me that I can feel to this day. Not only were the bottles and the tinsel wrong. Here was the gravest wrong of all: a family without a mother. In the security of our own happy lives my brothers and I had never grasped that homes could be shattered by death.

It went without saying that the four orphans joined our circle and took part in all our games. Rosalía and her younger sister shared the breath-taking thrill of a ride in Evelyn's flower-cart, with the baby brothers tucked safely between them.

The wine and the Christmas-tree ornaments, of course, did not remain in our keeping. Grasping the situation, our mother returned these stores across the street while the children's father was at work.

"Our *papacito* is happy," reported Rosalía one day, "because we come here so often. He says thank you."

Mama smiled. She reflected that the gentleman across the street might be even more grateful if he had known about his claret.

Paradoxically, it was at a birthday party in Rosalía's home, or rather, in consequence of it, that I nearly put an end to my life. At most Mexican festivities intended for children there is a *piñata* or pottery urn trimmed with tissue-paper to resemble some fantastic beast or bird, and filled with small trinkets and sweets. This *piñata* hangs from a rope, and blindfolded guests are expected to take a sound whack at it with a stick. When the urn breaks, a shower of goodies drops on everybody's head, not to mention large chunks of pottery as well.

Having attended many a *piñata* party, we were experts at

dodging the flying fragments yet at the same time garnering our share of the spilled nuts and hard candy. It was the latter that proved my undoing, for, on returning home from Rosalía's celebration, my pockets bulged with edibles. That night, on climbing into bed, I slipped a piece of hard candy in my mouth, planning to suck it as I went to sleep. Almost immediately the squarish confection lodged in my windpipe, cutting off my breath. I jumped from my bed and raced frantically round the room, looking for a glass of water, but on reaching the carafe and pouring out a drink I realized that I could not swallow. My need for air became desperate. I continued to race in circles, not knowing what to do.

Since the light had already been turned out, Sylvester and Arnim (with whom I still shared the nursery) failed to recognize my distress. We had a great respect for each other's inventive impulses; hence they reasoned that my antics were the opening phase of some new game I was thinking up. It was only when my behaviour became monotonous that they reached for the switch and found me gasping on the floor.

Either through the gesturing of my hands or the colour of my face they understood what had happened. Pulling me to my feet, they bobbed me back and forth between them, punching me from every side. A few seconds of this mistreatment brought results. I coughed with the last remnant of air in my œsophagus and spat out the obstruction in a wide arc.

Having rescued me, my brothers snorted in disgust.

"Very stupid," they said, stalking back to their respective beds.

A moment later, after the lights had been turned off again, I heard them spitting hard candy out of their own mouths.

18

MUSIC IN THE PARLOUR

IT WAS on returning from Europe that I actively entered the world of enchantment that is music. My brothers entered it with me, and for a time we were held equally in thrall, but they withdrew again—first Sylvester, a little later Arnim—after the novelty wore off and only the drudgery of daily practice remained.

We were conditioned from the start for a life in which rhythm and song played an important part. Almost every evening there were long musical sessions in the parlour, with Uncle Bichteler at the piano while Mama and Fräulein Trude sang duets. Since our parents were hospitable, callers came with increasing frequency to join in these sessions, which ended with a late *smörgåsbord*, dark Orizaba beer, and many a bottle of mellow Moselle wine.

The repertoire that dominated these evenings ranged from folk-songs through the incomparable *Lieder* of Schubert, Schumann, Brahms, Wolff, and Strauss. Our mother had a trained mezzo-soprano voice which lent itself to the intimacy of home recitals. Papa, on the other hand, could not carry a tune; but this never kept him from requesting at least one choral rendition of *Gaudeamus igitur* or some other student song of Heidelberg and Mittweida association. We children often thumbed through our father's *Kommersbuch*, which contained the texts of all his corps and college songs. The fat leather-bound volume was no bigger than a prayer book, though it differed in that the hobnails on the binding assured protection against beer-spattered table-tops during some exuberant student celebration or an equally damp ritual known as a *Salamander*.

Sometimes folk-music and classical songs were abandoned in favour of gipsy tunes, which were sung and played by ear. This led invariably to *csárdás* dancing, accompanied by heel-clicking, hand-clapping, and an occasional piercing whistle.

From the opposite wing of the house, where the bedrooms were situated, my brothers and I listened in rapt attention. Sometimes we crept out on the balustraded corridor that ran like an elongated balcony along the garden side of the house. Here we shivered in our night clothes while trying to catch some glimpse of the merry antics that held sway in the brightly lit music room.

The "Serenade" of Schubert was a particular favourite of ours. When our mother sang it we were held captive by an inexpressible sadness that was at the same time pure delight. A similar rapture that hovered close to tears was evoked in us by the Loewe version of a Scottish ballad, *Thomas the Rhymer*. Its opening lines were straight narrative:

Der Reimer Thomas lag am Bach,
am Kieselbach bei Huntley Schloss . . .
Da sah er eine blonde Frau—

(Rhyming Thomas lay beside the brook,
the pebbled brook of Huntley Castle . . .
There he beheld a woman fair)—

When it appeared that the blonde apparition was *die Elfenkönigin* (Queen of the Elves), who would hold the poet enslaved for seven or seven-times-seven years, no scepticism marred the listeners' pleasure. Even Papa, more at home among logarithms than arpeggios, took willing flight into the realm of fable.

If the *Lieder* lent enchantment to our nights, there was even greater delectation when Uncle Bichteler sat alone at the piano, for he was a virtuoso of the first magnitude. A pupil of Scharwenka and Leschetizky, he combined the former's depth (though not his harshness) with the latter's brilliance. I would lie sleepless for hours after the last note of Beethoven's *Appassionata* died down and silence fell across the garden. The next morning, when I looked at Uncle Bichteler seated at the breakfast table, I did not see in him an ordinary human being like ourselves. Despite his diffidence and youthful modesty (he was not yet thirty), a grave aloofness characterized him. Unquestionably he had the spiritual stigmata of genius, and it was to the credit of the environment in which he moved that his great qualities did not go unrecognized.

Our own piano lessons had started by this time. Twice a week a fussy, grey-haired lady by the name of Epigmenia López came to put us through our elementary paces. With admirable patience she familiarized us with black keys, white keys, sharps, flats, staves, bars, and crotchets. She expounded the difference between arpeggios and solfeggios, drilling our fingers in the former and our reedy voices in the latter. Finally, as she got us under way, Señorita López launched upon a daring project. She would coach us in a Spanish *seguidilla* for six hands, which we were to perform as a *tour de force* on Papa's birthday.

Our mother approved this scheme to the point of promptly ordering a carpenter to build a piano bench that would accommodate three budding artists. Although Papa's birthday was in June the *seguidilla* rehearsals started before Christmas, initiating an epoch of sheer torture. To be sure, at first we were agog over the novelty of the enterprise. Seated together on the long bench (chivalry dictated that I should be placed in the middle) we launched into our respective parts, only to bring shudders to our listeners. Unflagging in her optimism, Señorita López sentenced us anew to separate practice periods.

It happened that the top of our piano was covered with a collection of framed photographs in varied sizes, representing family members and a sprinkling of Habsburg faces. Oddly, there was also a picture of Queen Victoria, taken during her later years, it showed the little sovereign seated in an armchair, garbed in one of her billowing taffeta gowns loaded with *soutache* and *passementerie*. On her chest rested the Koh-i-noor diamond, while her short and pudgy fingers, studded with rings, spread out like so many small sausages.

Needless to say, during our practice periods my brothers and I found our gaze frequently drawn to the parade of silver frames marching before us in such neat array. But our interest was neither sentimental nor dynastic. As we practised our scales with ostensible concentration our eyes were fixed on the gentlemen in gold-braided uniforms and the ladies in décolleté gowns, with one single purpose in mind: we had discovered that by drumming vehemently on the keyboard we could set up a vibration that would cause the entire procession to collapse. And it took just under fifteen minutes to set the little army of pictures back in place. The process familiarized us with some historic personages of the day and delightfully shortened the practice hour.

However, for the *seguidilla* our stratagem proved damaging. Month after month went by without appreciable progress. We hammered out our separate parts acceptably enough, only to break down in the ensemble. Vainly did Señorita López exhort us to count aloud, singly or in relays, and to carry our individual motif by steadfast humming. We hummed, drowning out each other and the teacher as well.

Late in April the frenzied teacher bought some smelling-salts, which she carried in a compartment of her bulging handbag. As the lessons progressed we heard a recurring click and knew that the unhappy lady had snapped open her bag for a quick sniff to fortify her spirit. At each click we lost a beat, for the contents of the handbag interested us and we could not resist craning our necks for a hasty peek. Although Señorita López manifestly never left town, she carried all the equipment suitable for a distant journey. Besides gloves, handkerchief, galoshes, and tram-fare, the spacious pocket-book held pills, cold cream, face powder, paper, pencils, spectacles, pins, needles, scissors, stockings, string, headache powders, corn plasters, a bar of chocolate, and a medal of Saint Anthony of Padua to guard its owner against kidnapping or rape.

Unfortunately, the combination of the señorita's handbag and Mama's collection of photographs proved too much for the structural intricacies of our *seguidilla*. Long before Papa's birthday arrived our concert *à trois* was called off.

19

THE GERMAN SCHOOL

FOLLOWING THE example of other foregn groups in Mexico, the German-speaking colony had opened a school of its own. This was located at the end of Calle Colima on the wide avenue of Piety, or *La Piedad*. Completely secular in character, the school took on no religious shading from so pious an address. Its faculty was coldly intellectual, efficient, forbidding.

My brothers and I were enrolled in the *Colegio Alemán* (German School) immediately upon our return from Europe, the boys entering higher grades while I started at the bottom in a class called Octava. According to the Prussian system, all grades had Latin names on a diminishing numerical scale as they reached the top. Thus the class above mine would be Septima, followed by Sexta, Quinta, Quarta, Tertia, Secunda, and Prima. Students in their final year, before passing the *Abitur* or exit examinations (known in Austria-Hungary as *Matura*), were called *Primaner*, a name they bore with pride.

During our short residence in the Alpine turret on Novena Colima the daily trip to school could be accomplished on foot. We walked along tree-shaded pavements for nine blocks, skipping every line in the cement as we went. Half-way to our destination we met the Ulmer boys, Milton and Nené, the latter the one who had been victimized a year earlier by my kleptomaniac tendencies. Doted upon by their wealthy parents, these children were now in possession of a pair of black goats harnessed to a little wagon in which they rode to classes each day. A servant boy ran beside them and returned the vehicle after Milton and Nené surrendered the reins. Possession of the goat-cart gave the Ulmer lads a certain distinction for which we envied them wholeheartedly. At home our conversation dwelt with passion on the subject, although our parents appeared singularly unmoved. Once or twice Mama voiced her stand on goats on the score of their smell, a detail which our unfastidious young noses must have missed. But after a month of it we finally wore Papa down. One morning shortly before Christmas a crate arrived, with two bleating creatures cramped between the slats.

"*Santa María Purísima!*" cried Cruz, the cook. "*Chivos!*" ("Goats!")

She gathered up her skirts and scampered off in terror as the animals leaped from their wooden prison and promptly landed in the gardener Onéssimo's best flower-bed.

My brothers and I were jubilant. Not only had we achieved the status of the Ulmer children, but our beasts were long-haired and snow-white. If they had an odour we still did not perceive it. The goats walked straight into our hearts.

Unfortunately the fulfilment of our wish came at a time when we could no longer make the most of it. We had moved from Colima Street to the outskirts of town, where the *Rápidos* became our daily conveyance.

An enclosure had been built for our new pets, next to the mews. Here the goats flourished bouncingly, chewing great quantities of turnips, carrots, and the geranium creepers that ran up the wall. They also did away with most of their harness and nibbled at the laundry which Dolores hung inadvertently near their pen. Lastly, they gave trouble to the groom who tended Papa's horses, for they butted him and took a possessive attitude about the block of salt under the stable cribs.

With the fickleness of childhood we soon lost interest in the goats while, oddly, the attitude of our parents was reversed. The merits of goat milk and of the yogurt to be made from it were brought to their attention by our family doctor. In the Balkans, he expounded, the acidophilous curd product imparted longevity, as proven by the countless centenarians found in Bulgaria alone. From Budapest and the peasants of Solymár Mama recalled similar theories. In short, since our goats were fortunately husband and wife, the prospects of longevity for all of us were practically guaranteed.

The only flaw in this happy picture was Onéssimo, the gardener. Onéssimo was Japanese. He had come with the house, having worked as caretaker for our landlady, Madame Gaby. Mexico barred Oriental immigration, but loopholes in the law had permitted a sizeable influx of truck gardeners, cooks, and laundrymen from China and Nippon. These Asiatics worked hard, saved their money, and lived in voluntary want, dreaming only of eventual return—in old age—to their homelands.

Never did we have a more beautiful garden than under Onéssimo's devoted ministrations. He pruned the giant rubber tree that dominated the front lawn, shaping its branches into a solid awning under which Mama gave afternoon tea parties. But his forte was floriculture. Bougainvillea and rambler jasmine splashed our walls with colour, while the ineffable sweetness of heliotrope mingled with clove and violet scent to perfume the midday breeze. Colibris hovered above the blooms, beating invisible wings as they sipped their fill of nectar. Every size and shade of dragonfly, known in German by the poetic name of *Libelle*, danced like jewels in the sun. Amid all this loveliness Onéssimo laboured in the earth, saying nothing, eating his meals apart from the other servants, content with only an occasional exchange of courtesies.

If his attitude towards other matters appeared aloof, the Son of Heaven was nevertheless capable of sudden and tempestuous outbursts where vandalism against his handiwork was concerned. This is where the goats came in. For Jesús, the groom, was on occasion too engrossed with stable duties to keep an eye on the yogurt factory. As a result the *chivos* would come prancing forth and, before anyone could stop them, tear into one of Onéssimo's painstakingly laid-out flower mosaics.

For a time the gardener suffered in silence. But one day as a rose espalier came tumbling about his ears he could contain himself no longer. Jumping to his feet, he went after the goats and thenpolished off the negligent Jesús with a set of knuckle-dusters. This brought us to a parting of the ways. Though she fully appreciated the model gardener, Mama wanted no floral borders that involved the threat of homicide.

In less than a quarter of an hour the Japanese was packed. He came for his wages and bowed himself politely out the door. Crossing the garden, he turned back and surveyed the verdant scene that day and night had occupied his every thought.

"*O hi yo, hi yo!*" he called back. The phrase, he had often explained to us, meant hail and farewell. It sounded exactly like a state and river east of the Mississippi, which we had encountered in our geography lessons.

But Onéssimo was not the only embodiment of violence that coloured this period of our childhood. There was Herr Brink, a teacher at the German School. My fear of this man seems to have been so great that I cannot to-day remember what subject he taught, though his face, voice, and gestures remain vividly in my mind. Herr Brink was old, too old for his profession, and he could not have been in good health. His tall thin figure seemed to be all bones, his features were sharp, his grey hair stood in wisps that shot off at crazy angles, and his clothes hung on him as on a scarecrow. His voice was querulous, and he seemed permanently angry. Whether he had suffered torment at their hands, or because of some personal tragedy in his past, he hated children with a fierce and implacable fury. We trembled when Herr Brink entered the room, but the real agony came as one waited to see whom his terrible gaze would single out for recitation of tables. Fear naturally engendered failure in all but the most shock-proof pachyderms among his charges, so that no brilliant class ever emerged from his tutelage to bring him honour. Tuesdays, Thursdays, and Saturdays were "Brink-days," and they never went by without an ugly scene. It always started the same way: Herr Brink demanded quick, sharp answers to his queries. (This leads me to think that his subject was mathematics, and it may explain why even now the small attention required by a cheque-book stub can make me go limp.) At any rate, if a child hesitated or began to stammer, all hell broke loose.

"Come here!" the guttural voice commanded.

Often the hapless pupil was too terrified to move. At this Herr Brink flew into a rage. He rushed to the child and dragged him all the way to the blackboard. Here, without relaxing his monstrous grip, he croaked out his question once more and demanded instant response, all the while shaking his victim by the throat as though to squeeze out the words that would not come. How it happened that no pupil perished under this mistreatment can be explained only by the resilience of youth. Innumerable times I watched the dreadful struggle as some child, eyes bulging, cheeks growing purple, gasped out an answer with what seemed to be its last breath. And steadily my mortal panic increased that this might happen one day to me. That it did not was no indication of my merits as a student, for I learned nothing except fear in Herr Brink's classes. The fact that his cruel fingers did not close about my throat may be ascribed chiefly to the large number of pupils under his care, and to the development of particular grudges early in the term which caused him to single out certain enemies and go after them with cumulative sadism. Had he once touched me, I felt beyond all doubt, my heart would have stopped.

It seems extraordinary that this pathological torturer continued to hold his job for years, despite vigorous complaints made by ourselves and schoolmates to our respective parents. But it was precisely the savagery of Herr Brink's character that tinged our accusations with melodrama and made them unbelievable. If such a demon as we described were rampant in the school, Papa and Mama figured, the Board of Regents (there were no parent-teacher associations in those days) would soon hear of it and arrange for Herr Brink's salary to be paid to some one else.

In juxtaposition to the demoniacal Brink stood a fair young teacher of writing and composition, Herr Pleister, who won every child's unqualified adoration. He was boyish, smooth-shaven (Herr Brink had a fiercely bristling moustache), and gentle of disposition. Unfortunately this paragon of beauty and virtue did not stay with us long. There was a rumour that he planned to marry and must therefore seek a better-paying position abroad, where his fiancée awaited him. This caused considerable fluttering among the small girls in my class. We were resentful of any lady who might take Herr Pleister from us, and we stormed him with demands for a denial.

He did not clarify the point, but in response to our collective devotion he went to a photographer and sat for his picture, ordering three dozen postcard-size prints. On his last day at school he brought these to class, each picture beautifully autographed.

Alas, either through oversight or economy (he *was*, after all, looking for a more lucrative job), there were not enough photos to go round. We were thirty-seven, and he had only thirty-six. What was worse, the only child who did not manage to obtain the beloved teacher's portrait turned out to be myself. How it happened, I will never understand. As Herr Pleister spread the treasures on his desk there was a wild stampede from every corner of the room. I too joined the eager, screaming horde, my hands upraised in expectation. It was a plain case of individual failure. I simply had not pushed hard enough to get there on time.

20

A MEMORY OF CHRISTMAS

PHILOSOPHERS HAVE argued that if God did not exist He would have had to be invented. In equal measure this is true of Christmas.

Primitive peoples gathered together for rejoicing when the winter solstice heralded the return of spring, and ancient religions built their cult of sun-worship round this seasonal turning-point. Since Christianity's Messiah is computed to have appeared on earth in the midwinter of man's despair, his birth, like the returning sun, became the pivot of our surge towards light. The actual date of the Holy Child's arrival is uncertain, falling somewhere between the start of the Advent season and Epiphany, or Twelfth Night. "Epiphanous" means resplendent, as was Christ when He reappeared after the Resurrection, and that is what, at least once each year, all creatures long to be: enriched, transfigured, made splendid. Birds change their plumage, mammals don new opu lence of fur, reptiles shed withered skins, while we of the human family lay down the spent shell of our meanness to emerge in happier form. Here lies the divinity of purpose, the joyous note, the cosmic design: renewal—eternally, immortally! This is the special providence of Christmas.

The mystery and magic begin in childhood, with a web of fable and symbolism to cloak what is a far greater riddle: the flame of love burning in the human breast. Saint Nicholas, Bonhomme Noël, Christkind, King Wenceslaus, Befana, Santa Claus, the Magi—all can be explained in terms of parables. Yet who is to imprison in mere words the spirit behind these tender inventions of our fancy? And where is a key to that hidden music which rings inaudibly upon a starry night and takes the mind back to all the Christmas Eves that punctuate a lifetime, in ecstasy or pain? Recurrent, and too often rendered stereotype, it remains still the strangest of our feasts.

Of the ever varying, yet invariably similar, celebrations which my brothers and I look back to it would be difficult to single out the best and most special. We had known Christmas in Hungary, where Grossmama set a candle in each window before the household went to Midnight Mass. All through the dark hours Solymár roosters were kept carefully locked up so that no crowing might mar the instant of Christ's birth. Then, on returning home, the festive board waited amid garlands of tinsel, mounds of *Spekulatius* biscuits, marzipan, and the captivating aroma of a properly scored and crackling *Spanferkel* (roast sucking-pig). While this repast was washed down with aged Tokay wine every one waited for the *Karácsoni* (Christmas) Hussar, a towering figure in tight red trousers and with waxed moustachios, who went from house to house asking for more wax. What he collected, both in candle-grease and gifts, remained only temporarily his, since all such contributions ended in a village pool for orphans, the old people's home, and sundry occupants of the local gaol.

Papa's Huguenot background brought us in contact with French customs prevailing in the border town of Saarlouis. Here the tradition ruled, "From Saint Barbara's Day [December 4] to Epiphany [January 6] sing Noël!" Normally parsimonious to the point of avarice, peasants of the region now remembered the plight of bird life in bare winter fields. On the First Sunday of Advent great sheaves of wheat were hung above each farm door and garden gate, so that no winged creature need starve. Also, in tribute to the gentle beasts that had witnessed the stable scene in Bethlehem, all household animals received special attention; particularly must the cat be fed to capacity, since her mewing on Christmas Eve would bring bad luck throughout the coming year. Finally, for the delight of young and old, the *crèche* was set up in a grotto out of doors or on a rug before the hearth. Miniature figurines of the Holy Family, the Shepherds, and the Three Kings from the East composed Christendom's unforgettable drama against a papier-mâché manger and a moss-covered shed topped by a bright tinfoil star. The care of the *crèche* fell usually to some lone female relative of the family, preferably a maiden aunt who by tradition stitched altar cloths and vestments for the church. "She was left to dress the Saints," is a descriptive phrase applied to old maids not only in France but in most Latin countries.

During his student travel days our father had visited Italy, where he witnessed the Christmas fair in front of Milan's many-spired cathedral. Here the good witch Befana held sway, combining in her person the gift-bringing virtues of Saint Nicholas and the wistful pathos of the Wandering Jew. A corruption of *Epifania*, the name of La Befana referred to an old woman who was busy cleaning her house as the Wise Men of the East went by en route to Bethlehem. "Come with us," they said, "we are following a star!" But Befana put good housekeeping above everything else, and so she kept on with her dusting, while the Magi continued on their way. When she was good and ready, with all her cupboards spick and span, Befana looked for the travellers to return and tell her what they had seen. Alas, the Wise Men went home by a different road, and there the tidy Befana is still standing in her doorway, waiting—like Ahasuerus, the Jew who turned Christ from his threshold—to learn what she had missed. In atonement for an error which she never fully comprehended the old woman became a benevolent witch who annually tries to dispose of the possessions stored up in her house. But there is never an end. The more she gives away, the fuller her shelves appear, and with each passing year she grows more weary of dusting. It is the story of Martha and Mary in paraphrase, pointing out the antiquity of man's contempt for the domestic prig.

In Mexico no such allegory cloaked the Christmas legend. Quite simply and straightforwardly the celebration of the Nativity centred upon the Niúo Dios, or Infant God, whose birth was heralded at the Misa del Gallo (Rooster's Mass), held from midnight to pre-dawn. Prior to the 24th of December nightly *Posadas* were held, twelve in all, which took the form of house-to-house processions in commemoration of the Holy Family's search for shelter (*posada* means hostel or inn). Canticles were sung on these occasions, with responses alternating between the candle-bearing pilgrims and their successive hosts. In one respect these performances differed from the biblical original: while Joseph and Mary had been inhospitably rebuffed, only smiling faces greeted their modern counterparts. Opening wide his door, the Mexican host would burst into song:

Entren, santos peregrinos, entren
a este humilde rincón,
no de mi pobre morada, mi pobre morada,
sinó de mi corazón!

(Enter, saintly pilgrims, enter
this humble corner,
not of my paltry house, my paltry house,
but of my heart!)

Completing this stanza in slow, choral measure, he then clapped his hands and summoned a servant, to whom he gave orders in brisk polka tempo:

Andale, Lola, no te dilates
con la canasta de aguacates!

(Hurry, Lola, do not dawdle
over the basket of avocados!)

Nuts, cakes, and sweets were also marshalled musically, with the high note provided by the traditional Christmas salad of mixed tropical fruits.

Gifts were not exchanged, since this was a time of adoration. Not until the 6th of January, the Day of the Holy Kings, did children receive toys and other surprises in memory of the Magi and their offerings, while grown-ups were content with looking on. For weeks after the holiday celebrations little Mexican girls could be seen carrying their dolls about, still in cardboard-boxes and Christmas wrapping so as to preserve their newness.

For my brothers and me, even in a Spanish-speaking environment, the Feast of Feasts was steeped in Germanic custom. Early in December the front parlour was designated as the Christmas Room, and thenceforth locked off with a key. Christkind (the Christ Child) was busy in there with festive preparations, so we were told. How could this be, with double doors shut tight and windows darkened? Christkind moved on angel wings through space, and passed, spirit-fashion, through all barriers. He could not be stopped by stone walls or dark of night or the conditions of men. All through December, if one walked softly and but gave it thought, Christkind could be felt all around. Every stirring breeze might be the rustle of His wings.

December was a month of odours, too. Heavenly odours! Armed with Marishka's recipes, Mama invaded the kitchen and enlisted all available help for the baking of *Stollen*, *Springerli*, *Braune Kuchen*, and flat gingerbread men. Day after day square tin containers were filled to the top with delicacies that wafted a perfume of almonds, vanilla, marjoram, spiced orange and lemon rind, anise, and rosewater. At the same time that these edibles piled up in pantry and store-rooms there was a good deal of paper rustling and package hauling, which kept us in breathless suspense. Suddenly closets and cupboards that had always been accessible could not be opened, and there was no trace of Mama's keys. Some of my dolls—the more damaged, to be sure—disappeared, while Sylvester and Arnim missed parts of their toy railway. Altogether it was an unsettled and mystifying interval, when grown-ups seemed to be feverishly busy and no one had any time for us.

Mama tried to find tasks that would occupy our prying eyes and fingers, while keeping us from getting underfoot. She bought two photograph albums and set out a box of accumulated snapshots for the boys to sort and paste. "These will be your gifts to Onkel Bichteler and Tante Trude," she said. Next she put me to work on the petit-point background of some embroidered bedroom-slippers, which were to be finished by the cobbler "for Papa."

When we were done with our assignments there were still hours to kill. It paid to linger round the kitchen, where every now and then a whole tray of cakes came out a trifle overdone. These were divided evenly among us and dispatched with relish.

Also, there was Dolores, still with a stock of tales on tap. A special batch of legends fitted the Christmas season, though most of her stories fell into the perdurable King Lear pattern. Regardless of sub-plots, which she spun out with rare resourcefulness, Dolores liked to open on a dependable line: "*Éste era un rey, que tenía tres hijas*" ("There was this king, who had three daughters").

At times, of course, Dolores too failed us, since the pressure of holiday tasks encroached upon her idle hours. It was then that we fell back upon Loro, the parrot.

Loro spent his days in freedom on a garden perch, but at night he retired to his cage, which stood in the ironing-room just off the servants' hall. Here the household vied with one another for the bird's affection. Particularly after the evening meal, the maids hovered near the cage and gurgled sweet nothings into the parrot's ear, always keeping the cage well covered, for Loro learned best when shielded by a hood.

Such loving attention inevitably brought results. Our parrot talked and sang like no bird in the neighbourhood. At sun-down he blew 'taps' and fetched himself indoors, tooting the *Diana* of the Mexican army while padding along on his pigeon-toed little feet. He knew a special version:

Lorito, toca la Diana,
que mi jefe te lo mandó—
fué desde en la mañana
cuando la tropa marchó.
Lorito, tócala!
Lorito, tócala!
Turú, turú, turú, turú,
turú, turú, tu tu. . . .

(Little Loro, play the *Diana*,
for the chief has ordered you so—
it happened early this morning
when the troops prepared to go.
Lorito, play it now!
Lorito, play it now!
Turú, turú, etc.)

This song never went without a hitch, since this version was far too long. Accordingly Dolores or the cook sang loudly with the parrot so that he might not falter. Sometimes, when both accompanied him at the top of their lungs, Loro dropped out and cocked his head wisely to one side, enjoying their fervent duet. On other occasions he launched soulfully into the German folk song "*Am Brunnen vor dem Tore*," which emerged in Loro's own condensation: "*Am Tore! Am Tore!*" His style was *magno cum tremolo*, or what Uncle Bichteler called pure *Schmalz*, an expression derived from the mediocre musician's misuse of 'melting tones' or *Schmelz*. The change of vowels is important: *Schmalz* means lard.

It was my special delight to discover that Loro liked me above all others. This was no vain delusion. Fully grown parrots are dangerous to handle, their powerful beaks and claws being formidable. Though Loro was amiable enough to sit on anybody's wrist or finger, I alone could lift him bodily from his perch, stroking his wings and laying him on his back like a doll. The reason for this was no particular affinity, but simply the fact that I had never been hurt by an animal and was still too young to have learned fear of anything outside my dreams about the teacher, Herr Brink. I loved people and dumb creatures with indiscriminate abandon, which before long was to lead to a shattering disillusionment.

It happened during the hushed interval before Christmas week, when my best doll, Elsa, suddenly disappeared. (I learned later that she had gone to a doll hospital for a new eye mechanism, fresh wig, and general refurbishing.) During Elsa's absence a lesser doll, Dushka, rose in my seven-year-old affections until she almost rivalled the perennial favourite, Otto.

I was out in the goat-cart with my brothers, taking Dushka for an airing, when a swarthy woman in a shawl waved us to a stop. As Sylvester halted impatiently, the stranger's gaze fixed on me and on the curly-haired Dushka in my arms.

"Oh, what a pretty doll!" exclaimed the woman, stepping closer. Her mouth spread into a fawning, toothy smile, which

Mama would have called unladylike. Mama thought people should keep their gums and tonsils to themselves.

I did not like that vast oral hatch grinning at me, but my Dushka had been praised and I must make a gracious answer.

"She comes from Budapest," I said by way of explanation.

"My, my!" the woman gasped, with a great show of wonder. "How interesting—may I just hold her?"

Forthwith, before I realized what was happening, she snatched the doll from my hands and lifted it high in the air. For an instant she drooled some unintelligible phrases, then whirled about and dashed down the street. By the time Sylvester, Arnim, and the goats rallied to give chase the stranger had disappeared round a corner and through some twisted alley where we had little chance of picking up her trail. Even so, we cruised steadfastly up and down the neighbourhood, arguing that perhaps the woman was no thief; possibly she had merely borrowed my red-cheeked Dushka to amuse some sick child. If so, she might at any moment reappear. We ought to wait.

But such sophistry was useless. The face that had leered down on us was as old as history, and as unchanging. It was the face of knavery. We, and our ancestors before us, had seen it often enough lurking under the flap of a gipsy *patteran* that rumbled over the Solymár road. It was as well that we should learn early to reckon with the universal presence of evil.

For the moment, of course, my grief was immense. But, as providence would have it, the imminence of Christmas brought quick consolation. With each day the awaited feast drew nearer and our anticipation mounted to an almost unbearable pitch. At last the hall calendar, which had started as a fat tablet and had shed its pages with the waning year, thinned down to its last week. It was the 24th of December.

The day dawned sunny and crisp, typical of the highland dry season. To ease last-minute preparations about the house my brothers and I were given an early luncheon and sent into the town with Dolores for a last look at the Christmas market on the Alameda and the window displays of the big department stores, El Puerto de Liverpool, El Palacio de Hierro, and La Gran Sedería.

Just before dusk we returned home, and now the final half-hour had somehow to be lived through. The boys were freshly brushed, I wore my best taffeta sash over a dress of Swiss eyelet batiste, and the maids bristled in starched aprons. Speaking only in whispers, we sat on the back stairs that led to the servants' patio, alert for the sound of a breeze that might not be a breeze after all, but the flutter of wings. So vivid was our picture of the Christkind that materialization all but took place before our eyes. As for the wings, we heard them every time!

And then, in all that stillness, a fine silver bell tinkled out into the night—the Christmas bell. It was presumably rung by the Christkind himself, yet by the time we reached the threshold of the front parlour the small bell was always in our father's hand, while the Christ Child had escaped us on its infinite round of calls.

As for the scene into which we now stepped, how shall I describe its ecstasy? The electric lights were out, and in the centre of the room stood an enormous tree, reaching from floor to ceiling and aglow with a multitude of candles. The air was perfumed by the mingled aroma of hot wax and fresh pine, with a special incense produced by a small twig which Papa had deliberately burned.

We stared at the quivering points of flame that seemed to bring the tree to life. And now, from the music-room, we heard the opening bars of *Stille Nacht, Heilige Nacht*. With his right hand lifted briefly from the keyboard, Uncle Bichteler signalled us to begin. Our childish voices rose through the first stanza of the old, strangely compelling song. With the second verse our elders joined in, their eyes glistening with nostalgic flashes of what other Christmas scenes that lay behind them? On the third chorus Uncle Bichteler employed the pianissimo that was his special gift, as the words changed from music legend to prayer:

Gottes Sohn, o wie lacht
Lieb' aus Deinem göttlichen Mund,
Da uns schlägt die rettende Stund',
Christ, in Deiner Geburt—
Christ, in Deiner Geburt. . . .

(Son of God, oh how bright
Love shines from Thy holy face
As we wait the hour of grace,
Christ, when Thou art born—
Christ, when Thou art born. . . .)

As the last note faded away the chandelier came on and the room was flooded in white light. Now we were engulfed by an almost unbearable joy. For there, spread out under the tree, were treasures too manifold to encompass at one glance. Nothing was wrapped in paper or ribbons, since the full glory of a European Christmas lay in that bewitching first visual impact, the momentary mirage of *Schlaraffenland*, Kingdom of Heart's Desire, earthly Paradise. No need for suspense now. All of December had been suspense! This was the climax of fulfilment, consummation. Nor did material value achieve the true miracle. The sorcery of lights, song, and emotion combined to lift the most modest of gifts out of the commonplace. Only gradually did the general scene of fairyland crystallize into quite recognizable and familiar objects.

There were the books. All of us, young and grown, received books for Christmas. Though similar reading-matter might be available throughout the year, it was not the same. Books that had lain there in the gleaming candlelight, transfigured for an instant as though their bindings might be jewel-encrusted, were something to press to one's face with quick affection. The love-affair might not last through January's cool awakening, though most of the time it did.

And so it was with every other small delight that had been planned so carefully and lovingly, many weeks ahead. There was my doll Elsa, splendidly renovated and gowned in a dress of pink voile, stitched by Mama. The Christkind had ordered her to do this. Otto likewise sat once more under the tree, smartly attired in a *Kieler Matrosen* sailor-suit of authentic seaman's cloth. Also, to replace the kidnapped Dushka, a modern character-doll known in the toy trade as a *Käthe Kruse Puppe* made her first appearance. In the adult world this new type of lifelike doll aroused the most excessive enthusiasm, yet the little girls in our neighbourhood shared my preference for the unrealistic starry-eyed French *poupée* with porcelain cheeks, absurd rosebud lips, frilly dress, and an upswept bonnet of distinctly froufrou coquetry. It was the hat that first struck the eye. The size of the boxes in which French dolls were displayed in shop-windows actually was determined by the large picture brims of those delicious *chapeaux*, which framed even the least expensive cardboard face with an illusion of luxury. In short, such dolls did not look like people. They looked like *dolls*, which was what we wanted.

High on the list of remembered Christmas thrills was a pram of light wicker-scroll patterns over a brown chassis, topped by a folding hood of soft leather. This glorious vehicle had fringed curtains tied back with pompon tassels, as well as hinged nickel brackets like the gala victoria in which Mama had long ago enjoyed her Sunday outings. Furthermore, the pram was large enough to accommodate not only my whole doll family but on occasion to permit our dachshund Purzel, the tomcat Pancholín, or Loro, the parrot, to share the ride.

There were other outdoor toys as well, since we were an active lot. Apart from roller-skates, badminton equipment, and the appurtenances of a newly introduced game called baseball, we shared a current passion for *diavolo*. This was an Italian game of skill, requiring two sticks joined by a cord upon which one twirled a five-inch weighted spool. This spool could be thrown high into the air at other players, who caught it with their taut string and whirled it on in ever more daring parabolic curves. For several seasons there was a *diavolo* craze underlined by a predominance of bruised heads and cheekbones, as the descending spool often missed the string and landed on our upturned faces. It was an elegant if painful sport.

Climaxing all Christmas joys, finally, there was that delight of childhood—the miniature world of dolls'-house, marionette theatre, and toy railway. While the first of these held my special enthusiasm, Sylvester and Arnim threw themselves whole-heartedly into the operation of engines, coal tenders, *wagons-lits*, and related paraphernalia. But we shared the indescribable excitement of playing with the theatre. Here the love of gesticulation and drama which so strongly colours life in Latin countries stood us in good stead. All about us there was oratory, grandiloquence, a leaning towards the pompous.

Every year during my birthday month of November there were popular performances of the melodramatic masque *Don Juan Tenorio*, retelling the story of the immortal rake who trampled women's hearts like flowers in a meadow, only to meet finally his deserts in Satan's own trap. Among Don Juan's victims was the saintly Doña Inez, whom he carried off from a convent, and who prayed for him later as he fried crisply in the fires of Hell. In any case, during November in Mexico City, high and low, master and servant, attended the *Tenorio* masques, some to split their sides with laughter at the crude stage techniques, while others suffered acute palpitations as they lapped up the grisly plot. There were children's matinées, somewhat toned down, though still sufficiently lurid; in these the famed libertine refrained from tearing the leading lady's bodice, while his accusers—usually shouting "Rape!" or "Blasphemy!"—contented themselves with the mild retort that he had "insulted" them.

Since actors in Latin lands were notoriously lazy about learning their lines, the most important person in the theatre was inevitably the prompter, known in France as *le souffleur*, the whisperer, and in Spain as *el apuntador*, the writer of notes (for it sometimes took a paper pellet with instructions on it to rouse a performer from his siesta on the stage). With a prompter who took his job seriously the audience had the pleasure of hearing a play twice for the price of a single admission, since his voice buzzed on without pause while the actors trailed comfortably along until they spotted their cues. Often, owing to some quirk of acoustics, the audience caught on faster than the characters on stage, whereupon the lines were cheerfully relayed across the footlights and duly acknowledged with a charming bow, and the play resumed. Thus it was natural that most people, including my brothers and myself, knew the *Tenorio* almost by heart. We children loved nothing so much as staging the hoary drama in our cardboard theatre. One scene in particular delighted me, despite its fatuous banality, or perhaps because of it. This was a moment in the play when Doña Inez, long dead and lifted among the saints, reappeared to Don Juan as he walked in a garden. The device employed customarily was a backdrop of enormous dahlias and sunflowers, one of which opened like a porthole to allow the nun's face to bob into sight. This bit of macaronic stagecraft was promptly incorporated into one of our hand-made sets, with a thin silk thread operating the flap. Delegated to manipulate this thread, I never tired of my small function as the handler of stage effects.

We did not limit our productions to this example from the real theatre. There were endless plots to be taken from our Christmas books—tales about history and the world of the future for Sylvester, travel and adventure stories for Arnim, sagas and fairy-tales for me.

In the festive atmosphere of tinsel, candlelight, and cheer, the books lay quietly, biding their time. Their splendour was within; hence they could not compete with things of external allure. Even the midnight supper-table, heaped with viands and climaxed by the serving of *Waldmeister* punch, held us enraptured before we bothered to turn a single page. But the books waited. They took on life and spread their magic when the season of other magic had long fled.

21

BABIES AND BULLS

NEW YEAR'S EVE was St Sylvester's Feast and the birthday of my elder brother, a coincidence which accounted for his name. The triple significance of this date made it an occasion of special privilege, particularly with regard to late hours. We were allowed to stay up for the midnight *Bleigiessen* ritual, or lead-pouring ceremony, before seeing the New Year in.

The practice of soothsaying by means of fire and molten lead is very ancient. Through centuries of tradition it survived into modern times without change in form or equipment. The requirements were a glowing brazier, an iron spoon, some lead shavings, a basin of cold water, and a lively imagination. The procedure was simple: anyone who wished to know what the coming year might bring must place a bit of lead in a spoon and hold it over the coals until melted. Next, the liquid metal was dropped into the water, where, with fierce sizzling and bubbling, it solidified into a fantastic shape. The whole process, once the slow melting was accomplished, took only a split second. But the symbolic meanings to be sought in each metal formation kept tongues wagging for hours. Thus, on the particular New Year's Eve here described, our entire household burst into gales of laughter when Uncle Bichteler, a bachelor, fished his future from the water in the shape of a tiny gleaming cradle.

"A baby!" every one cried. "Well, well—how is he going to manage *that*?"

There was much taunting and prodding to learn if Uncle Bichteler had secret matrimonial plans. But early in February the prophecy explained itself. Our former governess, Tante Marta, arrived unexpectedly from Necaxa to await the birth of her first child. Because of the spaciousness and sunny exposure of his room, Uncle Bichteler was asked to move temporarily into the guest-room so that the visitor might enjoy the best possible accommodation. In short, a cradle impinged noticeably upon Uncle Bichteler's tranquil and well-ordered life.

For me the advent of Tante Marta was a matter of breathless agitation. In the foolish euphemism of the era I had been told that she was keeping an appointment with the stork. My brothers smirked at this, but my unenlightened ears took the news literally. For me the facts of life were still tied up in the bundle hanging from the long-legged bird's beak. Furthermore, the to-do about Uncle Bichteler's room (which had a skylight in the ceiling) caused me to make my own deductions. The stork would probably step right through this and drop the baby on the bed. It was an eminently suitable room, I decided.

Unfortunately the expected event was still several weeks off, which caused a severe strain on my patience. Since Tante Marta's bouncing health permitted daily outings and shopping trips to the town, I worried lest the infant arrive in her absence. Often I lingered on the threshold to Uncle Bichteler's chamber, wondering whether there might not be an unexpected speed-up in the stork's schedule. The suspense was terrific.

To ease the tension, as well as to keep me from getting underfoot, Mama arranged for my participation in a school production of *Snow White and the Seven Dwarfs*. It was immaterial to her what part I might be assigned, as long as I was kept busy. To every one's surprise, since I had never stood out among my fellow-schoolmates, I was cast for the leading rôle.

There were daily rehearsals during which I climbed on a platform and recited the somewhat inane line:

Schneewittchen heiss' ich,
mein Kleid ist schneeweiss—

(Snow White is my name,
for my dress is snow-white. . . .)

For some odd reason, which may well have been the first stirrings of literary criticism, this line embarrassed me. I tried every possible device to keep it from being understood: I mumbled, stuttered, choked, and dropped my tones to a *sotto voce*.

The members of the play committee were mystified. Every one knew me as a boisterous child of almost objectionable exuberance, yet there I stood, while the piping sounds that issued from my throat were pitiful to hear, if indeed they could be heard.

My brothers, who played dwarfs, fumed with mortification. They had preened themselves at my being chosen the prima donna of the show, but it was obvious that the fat rôle of Snow White was fast slipping from my grasp. By the end of the second rehearsal beautiful Irmgard Albert (later the wife of Baron von Erdmannsdorff, German Ambassador to Budapest) inherited the part.

Fortunately at about this time the long-heralded stork put in his appearance. Despite my watchfulness, however, I missed the interesting fellow. He came at night, while my brothers and I were asleep. It appeared certain, though, that he descended through the skylight in Uncle Bichteler's room, for here was our former governess lying in bed with a wee baby girl in her arms.

"Why are you in bed?" I inquired, frankly disgusted at such behaviour. "Why don't you bring the baby out into the garden?"

I was escorted from the room in haste. "Hush," some one said. "Tante Marta isn't feeling very well."

This only added to my displeasure. It was certainly a shame to wake up with a baby in one's bed and then not be able to rush out and show it to the neighbours. I demanded further explanations.

"What's the matter with her?"

Nobody had time for obstetrical discussions, so I was put off with a picturesque evasion which to a bright child of to-day would have been recognizable as such. As for me, I swallowed the clumsy fiction.

"The stork bit her in the leg," said Fräulein Trude, rushing past me with a batch of fresh towels.

I trotted briskly beside her. "*Why* did he bite her in the leg?"

Fräulein Trude disappeared into the room with the skylight and closed the door in my face. Her voice issued through the crack. "Because she wouldn't wake up, that's why!"

"Oh——"

I was impressed. To think that a stork had that much sense! No folderol about him. If he brought you a present you'd better look sharp or—snap!—one of your extremities was gone.

For the next fortnight my brothers and I could hardly contain our impatience. We wanted the new-born infant to be turned over to us for a triumphant ride in the goat-cart, while the neighbourhood stared with envy. But to our disappointment it now appeared that babies were fragile and unable to endure the sort of activities we had in mind. As a result, Sylvester and Arnim soon lost interest.

At the end of a week the christening was held and the infant received the name of Sári. Our mother and father stood as godparents.

The baby was bottle-fed, and her formula included a well-known American malted product. This tasted so good that I occasionally pilfered a portion under the pretext of determining whether it was too hot. The baby Sári soon caught on (she was very intelligent). When I reached for her bottle she clutched it firmly and raised an infernal howl.

She was a beautiful child, blue-eyed, with golden ringlets that framed her face like a halo. Her presence completely governed our household from back stairs to front parlour. If company came the little cherub was brought in to coo and gurgle prettily. Laundry day saw a mountain of napkins that took precedence over the family linen. Altogether, it because evident to me that helplessness wields an immeasurable power; the wee creature that called for so much service and attention asserted herself like an autocrat *par excellence.*

The ministrations that converged daily upon Sári strongly coloured my play. I experienced at this time a vehement renascence of mother love for my old and battered dolls, who, though they represented more advanced ages, were presently subjected to infant feedings and elaborate talcum routines. Otto in particular gave me trouble, for all at once I decided that he was wetting his bed; I spanked him soundly and hung up his sheets for make-believe drying, all the while wringing my hands and taking thermometer readings to keep track of half a dozen diseases that afflicted the rest of my brood. Altogether, I whipped myself into a highly enjoyable dither.

With the arrival of spring the baby Sári and her mother departed for Necaxa. A great emptiness was left behind. Uncle Bichteler returned to his skylight room, and the pattern of our lives became normal. It did not look as if the stork would call again.

I walked disconsolately about the house and finally sought comfort by confiding in Mama.

"How can we get another baby?" I asked.

She laughed and shook her head. "Haven't we a houseful of people already?" I could see that my plea would not be taken seriously.

Fräulein Trude gave me more hope. In Berlin, she said, children recited a little incantation when they wanted a brother or sister. It worked as a charm.

"Can I learn it?" I begged.

She nodded. The magic couplet could be memorized quickly. Then, the next time we walked through Chapultepec forest, I must pretend we were in the Grunewald and recite my lines to the wind.

It happened that on the following Sunday my brothers had

persuaded Papa to take them on a hike in which, after some entreaties, I was allowed to take part. We set out along the lonely Verónica highway that skirted the woods and led through a cattle-breeding reservation, where the fierce fighting bulls for Mexico City's arena of *el toreo* were raised and pastured. A deep ditch with water formed a natural barrier between the stud grounds and the tree-lined avenue. No fence was necessary, since the bulls were said to fear crossing the water.

For my brothers the sight of the prize beasts that pawed the ground as they turned a smouldering eye on passers-by was high adventure. When some animal showed particular ferocity, even to the point of edging up to the water and seemingly measuring the distance across, Sylvester and Arnim waved their caps and shouted with glee. Papa obviously shared their excitement.

I was somehow less enthusiastic. It seemed to me that the ditch was alarmingly narrow and that any bull with half a mind to do so could leap across it in comfort.

"Bulls don't leap," snorted my brothers. "They're much too heavy!"

But in the American kindergarten, years ago, I had learned an English rhyme about the cow that jumped over the moon. Admitting that this was poetic licence, I could not dismiss a vision of the Verónica bulls attempting the much smaller feat of skipping over that ditch. On the other hand, there was the threat of being excluded from future hiking expeditions if I did not control these alarms; hence I swallowed my fears and stalked valiantly along.

Stretched out to our left were the wide meadows dotted with the grazing herd, while on our right (we were facing Chapultepec Castle in the distance) the ground rose steeply to form one wall of the rocky elevation known as Las Lomas. Many years later this was to become the new residential section of Chapultepec Heights.

As we paused to study them the bulls moved majestically, yet —or so it seemed to me—with a distinctly springy gait. I slipped my hand into Papa's. He gave it a reassuring squeeze.

We walked on, then paused again to look. The animals ruminated peacefully, yet with an alert eye cocked always in the direction of the elevated road. These were not phlegmatic, cud-chewing kine, but high-strung creatures, spirited and tense. The very atmosphere about them seemed charged with menace.

Suddenly I looked back over the way we had come, and my heart skipped a beat. Some distance from us a large beast with wide-spread horns churned the ground at the water's rim, eyes glaring purposefully across.

"Papa!" I cried in panic. "That bull, he's coming after us!"

Father and the boys turned, but what they beheld was a familiar sight. A *toro* was just that stupid! He couldn't swim, so he just stood there stamping and snorting to relieve his bad temper. It was very funny.

Somehow, being by nature a coward, I was not reassured. To me the bull did not look stupid. He looked busy. His front feet were in the water, and he was plainly testing the depth of the ditch.

The elation of my brothers grew. "He'll never make it," they crowed. But Papa said we had better move on.

We moved on.

Behind us the bull emitted a low rumbling sound, as though in protest. We turned and saw that he had made no progress, but he seemed more agitated. The rumbling rose to a short bellow, which was repeated at quick intervals. I ventured an opinion.

"That bull is angry, isn't he, Papa?"

My brothers greeted this evidence of female timidity with great guffaws. But, holding on to our father's hand, I thought I could sense that we were walking faster. Even as we did so, there was a splash. I glanced over my shoulder and saw the bull floundering in the ditch. He had taken the plunge, and a moment later he was pawing at the steep incline on the opposite side. Our side.

Sylvester and Arnim were not laughing now, though manly dignity kept them from showing alarm. They marched at a brisk clip, conquering a natural impulse to break into a run. In this there was revealed an unspoken solidarity between them and our father, as all three preserved their composure in the face of unmistakable peril. I was the only one who gave way to loud hysterical outcries.

"Oh, Papa," I yelped, "he's coming! Let's run, please, let's run!"

"Don't worry," he tried to soothe me; "it's just a tame bull. See, now, he's climbing that bank quite slowly——"

My brothers took heart. "Sure," they maintained stoutly. "If he were really mad he would come galloping along!"

But I could see our father's eyes scanning the road, both in front of us and behind. It was deserted. Now his glance gauged the high unscalable cliff that rose on our right, barring all escape. Finally the trees caught his attention. They were the tall ancient giants, the "thousand-year-old *ahuehuetes* of the Montezumas," from which draped long fronds of Spanish moss, like flowing white beards. To climb one of these trees is difficult, for the trunk remains bare for at least fifteen feet, and the branches rise sharply upward, defying human reach. Still, Papa studied the *ahuehuetes*.

We heard an ominous shuffle now and knew that the bull had negotiated the crossing. By our accelerated pace we had put a considerable distance between him and ourselves. He looked actually quite small as he stood squarely in the middle of the road, seemingly pondering whether we were worth catching up with. After a few seconds he must have reached a decision. He started to amble towards us at a lazy pace.

The tenseness on our father's face relaxed. If the animal kept trudging along at this tempo we had a fair chance to reach Chapultepec and safety. From all indications this was not a bloodthirsty *toro*, but merely a venturesome one, whose curiosity drove him to investigate the other side of the ditch. We risked another backward glance. There! The fearsome creature was far behind, reduced to a mere fleck in the landscape. Our nerves had played us a bad trick. Sylvester and Arnim recovered sufficient jauntiness to whistle a thin tune. Papa lighted a cigarette.

I alone found it impossible to curb my terror. The fleck in the landscape was elastic. Whenever I turned back it seemed to swell in size, while my overwrought imagination caused me to hear the tattoo of hooves, growing louder, louder. . . .

Or *was* it imagination?

Presently we caught the echo of a definitely accelerated beat. The bull had broken from his slow jog into a trot. He looked larger now, and we could see his sharp horns glistening in the afternoon sun. There was also a snorting sound, followed by a short bellow, as the beast gained steadily on us.

The time for poise and male decorum was past. Again the hoofbeats changed in metre. We all had sufficient equestrian knowledge to recognize a full gallop by ear. In a split second Papa seized my brothers, each in turn, and hurled them like oversized soccer balls into the branches of the nearest tree. It was a desperate gamble, for their hands might have missed a safe hold, but there was no time to wait and make certain. Almost in the same instant I felt myself swung about my father's shoulders as, with superhuman effort, he hoisted himself—and me—up the trunk of a young poplar that chanced to struggle for a foothold amid the dominating Aztec giants.

During all this, needless to say, I was screaming at the top of my lungs. Unable to curb my panic, I made the age-old, useless, and characteristically feminine contribution to moments of crisis. I made noise. My shrill, bloodcurdling outcries chilled Papa to the bone, almost causing him to lose his grip. Yet in a way they —the cries—also saved the day. For we were alone, without help in sight, and beneath us the enraged bull tore up the brown earth. My brothers sat securely on their leafy perches, but Papa had had neither time nor strength to climb to a supporting branch. By sheer will-power he kept his leg and arm muscles locked about the tree-trunk, while I clung to his neck with a strangling, vice-like grip.

"Hold on, Minka," he exhorted me in choking tones. "Don't let go!"

I held on. But all the while my piercing screams rent the air, echoing upward to the top of the cliff, where a cavalcade of *charros* (Mexican cowboys) were heading home from their Sunday parade. At any moment our father's strength might have ebbed, causing the two of us to drop to certain injury or death. But the din raised by my young lungs proved an effective alarm. From all sides people now rushed to the edge of the cliff, spotting us down below. They hailed the *charros*, who in turn swung their lariats through space. It was only a matter of seconds before the bull was caught in a triple noose and held at bay while rescuers descended by additional ropes to give us aid. A moment later we had been lifted from our doubtful sanctuary and hoisted to the upper level, where a vendor of ices promptly offered a round of refreshments. Papa paid the *charros* and summoned a creaking hackney carriage to drive us home.

Mama received us with tea and apple-tarts. "Have you had any excitement?" she asked, expecting the customary report that followed our outings.

But Papa and the boys were strangely reticent. For once there was a tremendous narrative to unfold, yet they seemed loath to avail themselves of the opportunity. As for me, I could not pass it up.

"There was a bull," I burst forth, "*so big*! He came after us, and we had to climb trees, and——"

I paused and looked to the others for confirmation, but they were absorbed in their apple-tarts. Mama too waited expectantly for the usual chattering chorus. There was no chorus. At this her lips twitched in an indulgent smile as she patted my head.

"*Nohát!*" she said in Hungarian. "Fancy that!"

She had heard me extemporize before.

I went to bed that night crushed with disappointment. To think that so spectacular an adventure as had befallen us did not seem worth the telling! I found myself deploring my family's indifference to drama. I also wondered whether I should have to go through life, or to a ripe old age, without getting this story off my chest. The possibility was appalling.

Before dropping off to sleep I reflected that the day had been unsatisfactory on another count. At no time during the afternoon hike had I remembered to recite my magic couplets to the stork, though Fräulein Trude had rehearsed them with me most carefully. If I wanted a baby brother, I was to declaim in the woods:

> Klapperstorch, Du Guter,
> bring mir 'nen kleinen Bruder!

For a sister the formula ran:

> Klapperstorch, Du Bester,
> bring mir 'ne kleine Schwester!

I had memorized the second couplet (it was a sister I wanted) before setting out with Papa and the boys, but our encounter with the bull had blotted out all thoughts beyond the immediate need for safety. Indeed, in the panic that ensued it became quite obvious that for the moment our family was large enough. The speed with which Papa had shoved Sylvester and Arnim into their trees and then managed to rescue himself and me would not have sufficed for the disposal of yet another child.

Perhaps, I reflected drowsily, it was just as well that I had not augmented our circle.

22

PRELUDE TO REVOLUTION

SEPTEMBER 16, 1910, was the day set aside for Mexico to celebrate the centennial of its independence from Spain.

Great parades and pageants were held, with elaborate carnival floats moving down the main avenues of the capital, while delegations from leading foreign countries contributed diplomatic courtesies. The gifts that arrived from abroad reflected to some extent the national consciousness of their donors: from the United States came a statue of George Washington, from France a decorative fountain, from the German Empire a sculpture of Alexander von Humboldt, while China sent a forthright and quite useful clock-tower. Whatever the passing fate of nations, Time was eternal.

The centennial served also as a special jubilee for President Porfirio Díaz, who had held office since 1877 (seven terms) and was just being nominated for the eighth time. Opinions differed regarding the venerable Don Porfirio. English and American encyclopædias listed him as "one of the ablest and best of Mexican rulers," while political enemies called him a despot who governed with an iron hand and turned an ultra-conservative back on all social innovations and reforms. Certain it was that Díaz cosseted foreign industries, which threatened to turn Mexico into a happy hunting ground for international exploiters.

Whatever the merit of these contrasting views, Don Porfirio's luck had run out. The brilliant lights and fireworks of the Independence celebration ushered in the ageing president's sunset. With the folding away of garlands and bunting came the signal for revolt.

"What is a revolution?" we asked Papa, fixing on the ominous word that was suddenly on everybody's lips.

"It is a war between brothers," he explained, "a civil war fought inside a country rather than against an enemy beyond its border."

Mama looked significantly at Sylvester and Arnim, whose

frequent tussles called for tireless reproof. "It's the worst kind of fighting there is," she said, polishing off the point.

I heartily agreed. My brothers' recurring battles caused me sharp anguish, for I was congenitally unable to take sides. Loving both, I wanted both to win, so that there might be no defeat. In short, I wanted the impossible.

The boys preferred not to have me there when they settled an argument, because as an umpire I was a dismal failure. I wept loudly when they wrestled, which in turn was distracting and caused them to lose their holds. Usually they postponed the issue until by some ruse I could be cajoled out of the way. Sometimes they pooled their savings and sent me off to buy a stick of tasty *charamuzca* just so they might have peace for a stout boxing-match. If the affair ended in bleeding noses it was deemed a huge success.

My own conflicts with my brothers did not lead to blows. When they found me too exasperating Sylvester and Arnim disposed of me with the scornful chivalry reserved for small fry of my gender. They ignored me. As for my methods of vengeance, they were more cunning and base. Once, when Arnim displeased me through some trivial act, I crept to his bedside shelf and ripped through a picture in one of his favourite books, a story of travel in the Cameroons. Some time later I saw him gazing sorrowfully at the torn page and wondering how the accident could have occurred. He never suspected vandalism, nor did I find the fortitude to confess. But my punishment was the lasting realization that spite turns with bitterness upon itself, and a feud with those near us cuts deeper than the enmity of strangers.

It was such a feud upon which Mexico embarked at the end of the centennial year. The country was torn asunder by a conflict in which two classes stood engaged: the conservative, privileged rich, and the great mass of peons or dispossessed. The former held with Díaz, but the latter found as their champion an extraordinary idealist and dreamer, youngest member of a planter's family in the Laguna district of Coahuila, Francisco Indalecio Madero. At Parras, the native hamlet of the Madero clan, young Francisco had grown up on his father's estates in sheltered and scholarly seclusion. His brothers and sisters, thirteen of them, had been educated abroad and, returning home, had enlarged their patrimony by adding great vineyards that soon gave forth the luscious Parras grape. From planters the Maderos turned into manufacturers of wines and liqueurs; their former cotton-gins were replaced by distilleries that earned quick renown. An enterprising Scotsman named Richardson, who married the Madero heiress, Pilar, gave further impetus to the business by acquainting his new brothers-in-law with the fine points of whisky-making. The Coahuila climate did not prove favourable to the Caledonian product, but an acceptable brandy emerged after some experimentation and was bottled under the label of Cognac Madero. Our household's knowledge of Cognac Madero derived from the simple fact that Papa succumbed to Richardson's eloquence and became a stockholder in the firm.

It was a matter of concern to the wealthy Maderos that in their midst dwelled a socialistic apostle who did not believe in money. Though he had grown up in luxury, Francisco's heart beat only for the poor. He had travelled much about his own country and had seen its backwardness and sloth. A few flourishing industries, mines, cattle-ranches, and haciendas did not hide the widespread squalor and misery of the nameless Indian.

Francisco brooded about these things and lectured his brothers endlessly. He entered the village chapel in Parras where the Santo Madero (the Holy Splinter) from the Cross was kept, and preached a new doctrine of humanitarianism from the chancel. But a mystic impracticality coloured all his schemes. His formula for social regeneration consisted of a simple slogan: taking from the 'haves' and giving to the 'have-nots,' or robbing the rich to feed the poor. If followed to its logical conclusion, Francisco's plan would leave eventually no rich to take from, while there would still remain the ubiquitous poor. Indeed, the destruction of wealth as prescribed by the Parras Samaritan would merely have augmented the ranks of the needy by adding fresh numbers of impoverished rich. In any case, young Francisco met with slight support. The state of Coahuila valued its prosperous citizens who provided employment and revenue; hence there was no enthusiasm for Francisco's share-the-wealth preachments.

Within his own family circle there was patient indulgence rather than hostility for the would-be reformer. His friends thought it best not to take Francisco seriously. They left him alone with his theories and his books.

He turned hopefully to the Church, only to find that ecclesiastic policy favoured conventional lines rather than militant revolt against established order. In the matter of philanthropy, the Sermon on the Mount said, "Blessed are the meek. . . ." Then why rob people of blessedness by changing their economic status and making them less meek? The Church passed its collection plate and doled out stipends to its orphanages and old people's homes. This and the spreading of God's word among the heathen, along with administration of the Sacraments to the faithful, encompassed the mission of Christianity.

For Francisco I. Madero it was not enough. Disappointed, he turned from orthodox religion and sought the solution to mankind's problems in mystic philosophies. Growing a beard, like a Tibetan monk, he took up spiritualism and held séances during the night. It was said that he employed an illiterate villager for a medium while toying with ouija boards, planchette, black screens, and other paraphernalia required by this strange necromancy.

How much of the Madero legend was truth or deliberate myth it would be difficult now to determine. But the one factor that came to his aid and set the Revolution rolling was not a thing of ectoplasm or astral whimsy. It was an earthy peasant in the north, Doroteo Arango, known to the world as Pancho Villa.

Born in 1877 at Rio Grande in Durango, Villa had spent a miserable childhood among the starving hill-people of Chihuahua, where resentment against the Díaz dictatorship was at a boiling-point. On reaching adolescence he had become the ringleader of a band of desperadoes who looted feudal estates and, Robin Hood fashion, divided their booty among growing hordes of followers. Before long a price had been put on the outlaw's head, and Mexico's feared mounted police, the *Rurales*, were on his trail.

Madero knew of Villa only through the newspapers. He had read about this intrepid bandit, whose war-cry was "Land for the Indians!" In his seclusion the intellectual reformer measured his own stature against that of the wild *caudillo*. Madero dealt in ideas, while Villa was a man of action. Madero hoped to fight greed and social injustice by philosophic argument. Villa could not even read, let alone compose a conscience-stirring manifesto, but his six-shooter spoke loudly enough. In short, each man had what the other lacked. They must get together.

It was a simple matter to write a message and dispatch it northward by secret courier. But there remained the perplexing question whether the *caudillo* could be made to understand what was wanted of him. If no one in Villa's entourage could decipher the letter Madero's offer of political and financial partnership would go unanswered and a great opportunity might be for ever lost.

As luck would have it, there was among Pancho Villa's followers a highly educated young man named Felipe Ángeles, a former cadet in the Chapultepec Military Academy and member of a prominent Mexican family. The presence of this extraordinary character in the rebel ranks was an enigma to shocked members of his class. Ángeles never explained. Nor did he don picturesque bandit costume of tilted sombrero, bright sash, and kerchief about the throat; instead he wore a sober military uniform of khaki drab and the campaign hat of a Texas Ranger. He was Villa's liaison officer. Correct in conduct and bearing, he rode beside the outlaw chieftain, lending an incongruous respectability to the latter's bloody and often barbarous exploits.

It was Felipe Ángeles who read the message from Madero and who replied "Yes, we will join your cause!"

23

EARTHQUAKE

WHILE THE revolt spread in the remote rural areas there was no sign of unrest in the cities. Life in the capital proceeded along its accustomed course, with only an occasional rumour of disorders among agrarian elements up north. Actually, two years of inconclusive action passed before the Revolution got properly under way.

For the casual citizen the reports of occasional disorders carried no political implication; they were regarded as the routine uprisings and plunderings that went on in zones not under adequate police control. No country in the world could patrol every inch of its territory against the depredations of its 'bad men'; hence there were bound to be unsavoury incidents in provinces where vigilance was lax.

Now and then newspapers carried a report concerning troop movements against bands of marauders known as *Maderistas* and *Villistas*, but such reports caused only mild excitement. Sensation-seeking servants lent interest to these tales by supplying atrocity stories culled from local police gazettes. Thus Pancho Villa soon took on an almost fictional quality, joining the ranks of popular ogres against whom orderly society the world over waged ceaseless battle. Ogres were universal and therefore commonplace. People took them in their stride.

On the other hand there were those who feared the notorious bandit and hoped he could be kept within the bounds of his native state. Every locality had, after all, its own quota of evildoers, without need for importations from a neighbouring province. Mexico City, for one, had long been haunted by a murderous renegade known as "The Strangler" or "El Tigre de Santa Julia," who roamed through the Santa Julia suburb and garroted his victims with a strand of brownish beads. As this elusive madman's crimes continued unchecked, a souvenir trade sprang up among alert merchants. Cheap shops displayed hideous Santa Julia necklaces for the titillation of the morbid.

"In commerce there's not much room for taste," said Uncle Bichteler, who lacked the profit instinct.

Papa was early in 1912 confronted by a decision which hinged completely on profit: he had been offered a position as head of a Canadian utilities company at Monterrey, in the state of Nuevo León. There was talk of our transfer to the northern city.

Our mother showed distinct reluctance when the matter was broached in family council. She loved a metropolitan atmosphere, having lived in Budapest, Vienna, Berlin. Besides, Monterrey was *Villista* country, wasn't it?

"We should be in constant danger!" she protested.

Papa laughed. "No, no! Monterrey is a fine, progressive city, far to the east of Villa's stamping grounds. And anyway, the rebel movement is heading south."

"You mean," gasped Mama, "this—this revolution talk is to be taken seriously?"

He nodded. "A plan is afoot to oust Don Porfirio from office."

To Mama this seemed blasphemy. Reared under a monarchy, she had a deep respect for established order. Let there be freedom of thought, she argued, provided there is no conflict with accepted law.

"Laws can outgrow their acceptability," Papa pointed out.

Unable to disagree with him, our mother took a sentimental tack. "But Don Porfirio is a true gentleman—and he has been president for more than thirty years!"

"That's just it. Like his laws, *he* may have outgrown his acceptability. General Díaz is an old man who thinks in terms of a generation ago, whereas Mexico has moved forward in these thirty years."

Ten centuries of royalist thinking stirred in our mother's Hungarian soul. "In Europe we don't dismiss our kings and emperors simply because their hair turns grey!"

"No," said Papa, "but it might not be a bad idea if we did."

The subject of our moving to Monterrey was dropped at this juncture, but it came up again at breakfast the next day.

"FRANCISCO I. MADERO MARCHES ON CAPITAL!" was the headline in the morning paper, and by noon there were reports of Federal troops engaging the rebels in combat only seventy miles away. At the dinner-table our mother seemed less adamant.

"This Monterrey," she asked in a tone deliberately casual, "what sort of climate does it have?"

"Sub-tropical," said Papa, "with accent on the tropical. It's rather hotter than what we are accustomed to."

Mama actually minimized the implied drawback. "Oh, I don't know—the summers in Budapest can be *something*!"

"European heat-waves are a joke," our father insisted, "compared to what American temperatures do to a thermometer." He wanted her to harbour no illusions regarding the lowland areas to the north.

Mama knew he was right. Mexico City could be counted among the world's exceptionally favoured spots. Situated in the lofty Vale of Anáhuac, with its clear, limpid air of Alpine freshness, it boasted a "white man's climate" in the fullest sense of the term. But there was gunfire now converging upon the capital and groups of malcontents had begun rioting in the streets. Temperatures did not matter where the safety of home and family was at stake.

"Perhaps one could get used to the heat," Mama conceded thoughtfully.

That evening, forces beyond human control ended all vacillation. As we prepared for bed a violent earthquake shook Mexico City, destroying numerous buildings and burying people in the debris. We ran outside into the garden, terrified by the eerie phenomenon. But frantic servants shooed us back again to the safety of reinforced doorways.

"Walls tumble and the earth opens up," they warned, "but the frame of a door will hold."

With this they went down on their knees and intoned loud prayers for heavenly aid, while the ground beneath us rocked in titanic convulsions. It was the peculiar silence of the seismic attack that lent an indescribable sense of awe to our experience. Although human cries mingled with a muffled subterranean rumble that seemed to originate in the bowels of the earth, there was an unreal quality about all sound, as though the tympanum of the ear had been plugged and we were listening through a wall of glass. There was no stir of breeze, no dancing leaf, no flutter of bird or insect, for all surface motion appeared engulfed in a deeper movement that swelled and pulsated from the planet's core. Our dog Purzel stalked dizzily about for a few paces and then cowered on his belly in whimpering bewilderment. Loro, the parrot, toppled from his perch, while my brothers and I watched swaying chandeliers and felt a pang of nausea. Through it all there was that hushed stillness, as of a grim pantomime.

The cataclysm lasted less than three minutes, yet the destruction disclosed at dawn was appalling. Near the centre of the town homes and public buildings had been wrecked, while here and there thick asphalt paving opened in a yawning crevasse. Elsewhere whole city blocks had shifted their levels, sinking twelve inches or more into the sponge of swamp soil upon which the capital was built.

Digging itself out of the disaster, Mexico City temporarily forgot Madero, Villa, and the threatening siege. As ambulances picked their way through rubble-blocked streets, charitable organizations appealed for food and volunteers to bring relief into the stricken areas.

Our own neighbourhood did not emerge unscarred. A second-floor wall in the home next door had crumpled, while the skylight in Uncle Bichteler's room crashed down together with a goodly portion of ceiling and roof. Storks could visit us now by the score, had we but half a mind for such concerns.

In surveying the damage Papa found irrefutable answer to a problem that had of late absorbed him. The world over, cities were introducing piped gas for industrial and home use. It had been his dream to bring this advancement to Mexico's capital, but the project was not feasible. In volcanic subsoil even the slightest quake would rip open the mains and cause uncontrollable fires. But Monterrey, only five hundred metres above sea-level, with a terrain that was solid and sound—there was a challenge!

Mama appeared to be all for it. "I think Monterrey would be lovely," she said.

That same week she began to pack.

24

THE PURLOINED SNUFF-BOX

BEFORE LEAVING Mexico City our mother paid a farewell visit to her best friend, a lady named Antonia Cereghino. As on countless previous occasions, I was dressed in a white frock with a pink sash and taken with her.

Doña Antonia did not live in a house but—a rare thing at that time—in a town apartment. She was a handsome woman of indeterminate age, well educated, elegant, vivacious, and seemingly in very comfortable circumstances. Her position in society was rendered piquant by the fact that she had been divorced from her husband, an Italian art-collector. Divorce was almost unheard of in the Mexico of that day.

What remains indelibly in my mind, however, was the opulence of Doña Antonia's apartment. Always on arrival my attention focused on the splendour about me. First there were the Aubusson carpets, delicate in colouring and exquisite to walk upon; Doña Antonia, who wore a hostess gown with a ruffled train, swished across the tinted floor-tapestry as over a flowery meadow. Next, there were the pictures that hung in gilt frames from the walls or stood on painters' easels in every corner. Most of the canvases were oils, with a few lithographs and water-colours among them, as well as some fine miniatures on porcelain. These last stood about on tables cluttered with statuettes and knick-knacks, such as filled Mama's parlour at home.

It was almost four years since I had been punished for purloining from my small friend, Nené. Following that disgraceful episode there had been moments of temptation which I could not have resisted except for sharp parental vigilance. Beyond doubt I was at heart a felon, held in check only by pedagogic restraints. This alone could explain the fact that my youthful propensity for assimilating alien property was thoroughgoing and sincere; I snatched up everything that charmed my round and covetous eyes, apparently, as modern advertising phrases it, because I loved "nice things." My hands reached out indiscriminately for toys, edibles, kittens, handy coins that might fit my fat painted pig bank, or the fancier gewgaws off ladies' dressing-tables.

This vice, however reprehensible, was not without its tinge of magnanimity, as on the occasion when my brother Sylvester's stamp collection seemed to me altogether unimpressive beside the album belonging to Carlos, the boy next-door. The latter received periodic donations from his godfather, General Reyes, whose correspondence extended over many countries of the world. Moreover, Carlos was careful about trading even his duplicates, except in a worthy exchange, which kept his collection at a deservedly high level.

I resolved to remedy this situation. With cheerful aplomb I abstracted four Congo Yellows and a rare Transvaal Blue from the unsuspecting lad's treasure, in the hope of thus improving the balance between 'haves' and 'have-nots.' The manœuvre garnered no applause for me because Sylvester, an individual burdened by scruples, returned the philatelic trophies with an apology for my childish prank. Childish prank, fiddlesticks! I was in dead earnest.

Proof of this became apparent in my stealthy exploration of the Cereghino boudoir. While Mama and her hostess chatted happily in the front parlour I stood goggle-eyed before Doña Antonia's mirrored dressing-table. There, in dazzling disarray, lay every sort of trinket to tempt the feminine heart—and mine was utterly of this order. I saw rings, bangles, necklaces, brooches, ornamental combs, perfume flasks, powder receptacles, and—wonder of wonders—an exquisitely carved miniature snuff-box with two lids. For some inexplicable reason this snuff-box captivated my fancy. I pounced upon the trinket, slipping it into my dress for future inspection.

Having concealed my plunder, I returned brazenly to Doña Antonia's parlour, gorging myself there on the good lady's tea and nut layer-cake. On the way home with Mama I drew forth my booty, inventing an astonishing narrative of how I had come by it some days ago in a lottery at school.

"How strange," said Mama. "A very similar box sat to-day on Doña Antonia's dressing-table. I saw it when I stopped to remove my veil."

This unnerved me somewhat. But Mama seemed casual as she fingered the trinket.

"Oh, look," she cried suddenly, "there's a Russian inscription on it! Shall I read it to you?"

I was startled. We had learned from early childhood that

Magyars and Muscovites were traditional enemies; they had no traffic together and were fiercely loath to speak each other's tongues. Countless times we had heard Solymár arguments end with the refrain: "Everything evil comes from Russia!" Yet here was our own mother laying sudden claim to a knowledge of Slavic script. What was more, I could not recall seeing any writing on the snuff-box; the scrollwork on it seemed to me purely ornamental.

"What does it say—in—in Russian?" I asked, with definite misgivings.

Mama narrowed her eyes, evidently engrossed in translating. Then she read slowly: "The *smallest* donkey in the world!" and snapped open a lid. There, inside the box, bedded on a tuft of cotton, lay an infinitesimal quadruped with a pair of disgracefully protruding ears. "Donkeys are very stupid," added Mama as an afterthought.

I gazed in rapt delight, hugely pleased with my loot. All misgivings had vanished. I could hardly wait to show this wonderful acquisition to my brothers and playmates. The sad truth that stolen goods could not be flaunted at random before one's friends had not yet dawned upon me; indeed, in the face of such a disadvantage, pilferage would lose its chief attraction. The essence of possession was in my case ostentation. Whatever I poached I displayed in short order, often before the flabbergasted owners themselves.

But Mama had not finished with me.

"I want you to listen," she went on quietly, "to what your little box says on the other side." Her voice rose a shade as she read this time: "The *biggest* donkey in the world!" And again she added what seemed an afterthought: "Donkeys are so stupid—so very stupid. . . ." With this the second lid was opened and held before my astounded eyes. Inside I saw no tuft of cotton, but only a brightly polished mirror. It reflected my own face.

Not until years later did I learn that our mother knew no Russian whatsoever and that the arabesques engraved on Doña Antonia's snuff-box had been no inscription after all. Only on reaching maturity did I grasp how heavily my vice had weighed upon Mama's spirit and that she could not bear to make of it a direct verbal issue. Rather than bring it into the open for the ugly thing it was, she had preferred to give no name to my misdemeanour. Instead, she had planted the small trick box, hoping that its originality of shape and design would arouse my covetousness. Had the ruse not worked at Doña Antonia's apartment it would have been repeated over and over, until I eventually caught myself in the waiting trap.

No punishment followed. I had merely been given to understand, discreetly and without public pillory, that my disgrace was known and would never be tolerated. It behoved me to make amends, unless I wanted to go through life with those long donkey ears.

The trifling episode struck deeply and wrought a lasting cure. It also left a subtle torment to haunt me through the years. Was Doña Antonia's dressing-table the first spot selected for my plotted downfall, or had the little snuff-box trailed me through numerous derelictions before catching my greedy eye? In retrospect it was equally humiliating to contemplate either my prompt compliance with Mama's calculated design, or the certainty of prolonged surveillance while I cheerfully went about doing wrong.

The former cast a reflection upon my intelligence; the latter delivered a body-blow to poise.

25

JOURNEY TO MONTERREY

FRÄULEIN TRUDE did not accompany us to Monterrey. Early in the summer she had met an American oil expert who beguiled her into wedlock under the derricks of Port Arthur, Texas. He was a busy man, with little time for folderols, hence the autumn wedding did not entail the ceremony and frills that had marked the departure of our first governess. Nevertheless, Fräulein Trude made a pretty bride and we were sad to see her go.

A short time later, in the autumn of 1912, our own household broke up and vanished into crates, to be shipped northward. We set out for the state of Nuevo León by railway, and for the first time made the acquaintance of an American Pullman car.

My brothers and I had slept on trains before, but only in the *wagons-lits* of Europe, with their individual bedrooms off a side passageway. The Pullman system of upper and lower berths, protected only by a length of buttoned curtain, appealed to us as highly chummy. We felt a close kinship with the other travellers in our particular car and could hardly wait for nightfall, when every one presumably paraded down the aisle in slippers and nightshirt. Nowhere in Europe had we shared so cosy a community boudoir. The trip promised to be very sociable indeed.

Actually, once we had been tucked into bed, the prim decorum of Pullman life proved disappointing. Though we peered expectantly from behind our draperies of poisonous green wool, we detected among our fellow passengers no *esprit de corps*. There was no frolicking or horseplay in the aisles. There was not even conversation. With solemn mien, ladies and gentlemen climbed into their respective lairs, fully dressed, to undergo grotesque contortions that would divest them of their clothes. Those who succeeded could presently be heard snoring in deep contentment. All preserved a masterful decorum. Convention could not have been better served if, in place of flimsy curtains, there had been a wall of stone.

Some 167 miles north of Mexico City, at an altitude of almost six thousand feet, lay ancient Querétaro, where sightseers could leave the train for a visit to the memorial chapel erected on the site of the Emperor Maximilian's execution on the Cerro de las Campanas (Hill of the Bells). To many onlookers the Gothic chapel, built with Habsburg family funds, appeared an anachronism. Its architectural style did not belong in this primitive setting. Only the arch and the grille-work of Colonial Spain could fuse with Indian planes and rectangles to form a pattern intrinsically Mexican. There was no room here for the Goth.

"Like his chapel," mused our mother, "poor Maximilian did not belong!"

From Querétaro the northward journey continued steadily downhill towards the warm fruit country of San Luís Potosí. We slept through much of this, but were up early the next morning to see the rolling tablelands of Coahuila. Again the ground rose, not to the heights of Mexico City, but to a pleasantly cool elevation as Coahuila's capital, Saltillo, sprawled on a plateau approximately five thousand feet above the sea. Now there remained a quick descent of three thousand five hundred feet before the city of King's Mountain, Monterrey, came into view.

Approaching at sunset from the south-west, we came upon a theatrical stage backdrop of high mountain ranges that enclosed the town on three sides. Only to the north was the horizon clear, leading downward for the last drop of altitude along the way to Laredo and the Rio Grande. To the east loomed the Cerro de la Silla, or Saddle Mountain, its outline resembling not just any saddle but specifically the high-pommelled type used by the Mexican *ranchero*. That this particular geological shape should occur, not haphazardly in Tibet, Tartary, or Hindustan, but in the homeland of the lasso-wielding *charro* (who himself designed the knob that held his lariat) permitted a metaphysical speculation. The Saddle Mountain could not be simple coincidence. A Mexican Jehovah, feeling very Mexican, must have put it there.

Flanking the Cerro de la Silla and joining it to the vast cordillera that formed the spinal column of the Americas was the lofty Sierra Madre, which soared to a chill height of more than eight thousand feet. This serrated range served as a mighty link in the mountain chain that began with the Canadian and American Rockies, continuing through the Sierra Nevada and Sierra Gorda, to sweep southward across the Guatemala highlands towards Peru and the Chilean Andes.

Although situated two hundred miles north of the Tropic of Cancer, Monterrey had an almost equatorial climate. In October it was still summer, with solar rays going full blast. Even at night the accumulated heat seemed to bounce back from walls and pavements, enveloping the city like a giant feather-bed. Never had we felt such warmth as this.

"What can it be like in July or August?" asked Mama with grave misgivings.

We drove from the station in a horse-drawn surrey adorned with a gay fringe of twisted cording, and piloted by an eager and loquacious driver. These *coches*, or carriages, afforded the only available taxi service, but they were more than adequate. Miraculously they were able to manœuvre in the older section of the town, where streets were narrow and tortuous, permitting only one-way traffic and even this at considerable hazard. Another delightful aspect of *coche* riding was the fact that the driver's seat was shared by a passenger in the intimate "*Tú y yo*" ("you-and-I") fashion of French parlour benches or sentimental love-seats, in which each beheld the other *en face*. This made for rapid camaraderie. In no time at all the jovial driver insinuated himself so thoroughly into the good graces of his fare that brief journeys expanded into prolonged rambles at the end of which, often as not, the *cochero* might burst out exuberantly: "Ours was a beautiful conversation, señor! For this I do not wish to charge. . . ."

Needless to say, he counted on vehement contradictions and a handsome tip, both of which were usually forthcoming.

We spent our first night in the annexe of the Hotel Continental on the Plaza Hidalgo, in the centre of which stood a heavy cast-iron statue of the liberator priest, Miguel Hidalgo y Costilla. The hotel was built in French Colonial style, with long balconies of lacy grille-work running the full width of its façade. Near by, over the waving fronds of the palm-trees, we could see the square Spanish outlines of the Municipal Palace, with thick pillared arches shading its four sides. Beyond this lay another and larger public garden known as the Plaza Zaragoza at the eastern end of which rose the graceful cathedral.

There were minor *plazas* scattered all over town, each with its church, its flowered pathways for strolling lovers, and its bandstand. On successive nights of the week, we soon learned, a police or military band played at a previously specified *plaza*. People read about this in the papers and flocked eagerly to the appointed rendezvous. In keeping with strict Spanish tradition the sexes walked separately in opposite directions, the ladies tripping demurely on the inside, while a host of admiring swains crowded the outer rim. This seeming restraint actually facilitated the blooming of romance, as lovers' eyes met tenderly on each successive round. It might even have encouraged promiscuous flirtation, since every one was on display for every one else's approval, and no swain could jealously guard his chosen maid from the bold ogling of other admirers nor keep an eye on her furtive coquetry.

As we retired for the night the balmy air that floated through our trellised balcony brought with it strains of distant music which, repeated from a different direction on each succeeding evening, presently revealed to us the personality of Monterrey. Here was the singing soul of a provincial town. This music we heard had nothing to do with the sophisticated blare of metropolitan night-life; it was gentle, tender, often touched with an overtone of melancholy. It was also imperfect, as the police bandmaster was known to be tone-deaf and the leader of the military brasses was said to fall frequent victim to the cup that cheers. Yet both wielded their batons with an ardour that surmounted sour notes and garbled tempos. Hit or miss, their semiclassic repertoire of Chaminade, Albéniz, and Granados, invigorated by an occasional dash of bullfight melodies, enriched the nocturnal hours and banished loneliness!

Though the music might have lulled us to sleep, the heat kept us awake. It hung about us, this unfamiliar febrile air, embracing, tactile, damply palpable. We lay on beds that had neither quilts nor blankets, but merely a sheet (and this was warm) for covering. My brothers and I found the experience wondrous indeed! Never before had we slept only between sheets. Even the hottest Hungarian summer called for proper covering at night. Yet here we seemed to be part of the atmosphere, suspended in warmth as it were, and drifting off to slumber on a current of thermal breezes.

Actually, Monterrey temperatures were not excessive, when compared to the earth's true torrid zones. While in winter the thermometer seldom dropped below sixty degrees Fahrenheit, the summer peak hovered about ninety. Our sensitivity was simply due to the fact that we had lived, up to now, in genuinely temperate climates. Particularly was this true of Mexico City, with its heady air and brilliant but often heatless sun. For us children the first taste of a tropic night was deeply satisfying. We stretched and revelled in it like biscuits in a friendly oven.

On the following morning Papa and Mama set out in search of a house. By noon they had found it, on a street called Matamoros, towards the west end of town, facing the small Cerra del Obispado

(Bishopric Hill) and the towering Sierra de la Mitra (The Bishop's Mitre). These majestic mountain formations completed the third backdrop, or wing, of Monterrey's spectacular stage-setting.

The house on Calle Matamoros looked grim from the outside. It was built flush with the pavement, in severe Romanesque style, with tall grilled windows, a narrow portal, and a solidly beamed carriage entrance to one side. On the door was an iron knocker in the form of a woman's hand, neatly cuffed at the wrist. Affixed to the wall was a bright tile, with the number, 250.

Owing to my sorry weakness in the field of mathematics, I have always preferred round, even numbers. At sight of them, particurarly compound sums that end in zero, I relax in relief. In later years the tendency to seek easy arithmetical sailing would lead me to puerile expedients, such as the writing of cheques and money-orders always in round sums that simplified the book-keeping on my counterfoils. It went without saying, therefore, that the Matamoros address pleased me immensely. I knew I would like this house.

On entering, a charming surprise greeted us, for the grimly mediæval exterior gave way to a vista of pure delight. At the end of a cool vestibule that was beautifully tiled, a tall gate of elaborate grille-work opened on a sunny patio paved in flat terra-cotta bricks. In the centre of the patio a mosaic fountain splashed cheerfully, while a colonnade of Corinthian arches framed the scene on three sides. Completing the quadrangle was a vine-covered wall that separated the courtyard from the carriage-way and stables lying to the rear.

Around the fountain stood glazed flower-pots, in assorted colours and sizes, with begonias, geraniums, and white jasmine in full bloom. There were also large flower-beds cut out of the brick paving, from which shrubs and small trees sprouted in incredible profusion. A pomegranate bush rose above a young banana palm that dipped its fronds towards a cluster of impressive elephant ears. A fig-tree, unsuited to Mexico City's altitude, reached here a thriving height, its gnarled trunk and dull foliage evoking a vision of Greece. An olive sapling, unable to bear fruit in these latitudes, stood forlorn and spindly amid the perfumed opulence. Hibiscus and camellia blossoms mingled above our heads, while San Diego and bougainvillea creepers sent tendrils of pink and purple bells dripping down the grey stone columns.

Above this rhapsody of colour there hovered an unforgettable scent—the drugging fragrance of jasmine. It was the compelling odour, the very essence, of Monterrey. I had learned early to respond to the flower cachet of a place: the sight of poppies swept my childish memory back to the fields of Hungary, Parma violets evoked the shadows of Berlin's Grunewald, a single spiced carnation recreated the floating gardens of Xochimilco, heliotrope spelled San Miguel Chapultepec, and ecstasy pierced the heart at the mere thought of roses in Tacuba. With such bonds as these to bind one's senses to the earth, it would be desolate indeed to find no garden in heaven.

One thing about the Matamoros house disturbed me. It was the name of the street, which meant "Killer of Moors," and derived from a now-forgotten Christian defender of Granada against the Infidel. Spanish descendants of this unknown battler had adopted the description as their surname, bringing it later to the New World, where its bloodthirsty connotation paled into respectability. The gentleman honoured by our street was pictured in Mexican history-books as an innocuous civil servant in high stock and flowing cape. Nothing about his prim exterior bespoke the slaughter of Moors or, indeed, the massacre of a single fly.

Even so, the name cast a chill upon me. I dreamed about Señor Matamoros off and on for years. He and his savagely descriptive patronymic haunted the house that held so much perfection.

26

NEW FACES

TOGETHER WITH our furniture, which arrived by freight train from the capital, we had brought Papa's automobile and horses, Mama's canary, the dogs, a cat, and Loro, the parrot. Only the goats had been left behind; together with harness and much-used cart they had been given to the Gonzales children on Calle Gelati.

"Goats in the tropics?" Mama closed the subject. "I should say not!"

Another sorrow attendant upon our transfer to Monterrey was that the Mexico City servants had not come along. Travel in those days was not a commonplace matter, especially among Indians. They clung to their soil, believing that nothing but evil would await them in another clime. Thus we were faced with a complete change in household personnel.

Heading the new staff was a cook named Luciana Landeros, tall, bronze-complexioned, and devout. Ostensibly she was a widow, though this, we soon learned, did not prevent her from having babies now and then.

"But, Luciana, how immoral!" Mama reproved on each occasion.

At this the cook looked injured. She was still a married woman, wasn't she? Even though, alas, her husband had been defunct these sixteen years. . . .

There was no gainsaying that. Technically Luciana could not return to the state of a virgin, hence she refused to live like one. In any case, her culinary prowess was such that our mother deemed it wise to leave Luciana's private life strictly alone. Save for brief absences in the interest of propagation, the fruitful female ruled our kitchen with expert finesse.

For a *mozo*, a large, burly Indian named Petronilo had been engaged. Belying the usual languor of his race, Petronilo was a dynamo in action. He rose before dawn to tend the stables and saddle the horses for the daily ride. He scrubbed the second courtyard at the rear of the house and hustled the maids to start breakfast.

"We can stop looking for a groom," said our father. "This fellow won't leave anything for him to do."

In truth, Petronilo would not have tolerated another male about the place. With his encompassing presence he ruled the back-stairs region, browbeating every one into submission. Even the self-possessed Luciana quickened her pace under his prodding. If she but stole a moment during afternoon hours for a brief siesta he chided: "And is it not time, Doña Luciana, to boil down some guava paste for the children?"

Actually it was not our happiness so much as his sweet tooth that prompted the suggestion, for Petronilo had an insatiable appetite for sweets. He furnished a striking demonstration of the energizing factor in sugar. His vitality was boundless.

This was not the case with our chambermaids, of whom a changing series marched through the house in rapid succession. Their main trouble was youth and its inevitable amorous complications. Love is the servant girl's Waterloo. In the case of Monterrey domestics, most of whom were comely in appearance and fiery of temperament, the hazard seemed especially great. They appeared to be ceaselessly enmeshed in erotic dilemmas of the most dramatic character.

Virginia López was the least reprehensible and also the prettiest. Just over twenty, she had smooth olive-toned skin, almond-shaped eyes, perfect teeth, and a figure that made callers say "Ah!" Uncle Bichteler referred to her only as the "Aztec Venus," while Papa pointed out that this showpiece belonged in the front part of the house rather than out of view behind a barrage of mops and brooms.

"We can use her as a parlour- and serving-maid," Mama agreed. "It won't cost so much to get an assistant for the bedroom and scullery work."

She avoided using the word *criada*, which was going out of fashion. Household servants, formerly born as serfs on the estates of their masters, had been known as *criados* (from the verb *criar*, which means to rear or raise) under the ancient patriarchal system. With the decline of feudal patterns, under which aged retainers gained such authority at times that they bullied their owners with a mixture of tyranny and devotion, the term came into disuse. Modern Spanish favoured *sirvienta* to denote a female helper, though the advent of unionism would soon render even this appellation distasteful. The time was coming when, in factory or home, a worker would classify herself as an *empleada* or—particularly when answering the telephone—as "the señorita who is here."

At the moment of our discovering the need of a second maid, however, it was Luciana who spoke the obsolete word *criada*, saying that she had just the person for the job. Among her assorted offspring there was a fifteen-year-old daughter, Virginia, a husky adolescent big enough to lift a horse.

Our mother protested that we could not have two girls with the same Christian name.

"But that is nothing," said Luciana. "Every one calls my daughter La Chamaca [The Brat]!"

This was hardly reassuring. Mexicans used three graphic ways to describe a girl: she could be an aristocratic *niña*, a plain and commonplace *muchacha*, or a grubby vixen known as a *chamaca*. By dubbing her daughter the last of these, Luciana furnished a pretty clear idea of what to expect. At the same time her pleading was so insistent that our mother weakened and gave in. The next time Luciana went home to her village she was to bring the Chamaca back with her.

Less than a week later The Brat descended upon us.

She was big-faced, pug-nosed, loose-jointed, and as tall as our houseman, Petronilo. She had frizzy brown hair, a pasty complexion, and small porcine eyes that shifted constantly from side to side. Because of her heavy-footed gait Uncle Bichteler at once labelled her Das Trampeltier. Added to all other attributes, La Chamaca was possessed of a booming voice that echoed through the corridors like the call of a distressed moose.

Luciana had spoken truthfully when she stated that her daughter was big enough to lift a horse, but this accurate description did not commit the Chamaca to any feats of strength. Whatever her muscular potentialities, the girl displayed a prodigious laziness. Daily at washing-up time there were battles in the kitchen, during which spoons, pans, and crockery flew indiscriminately through space as the aroused Luciana disciplined her child. The Chamaca for her part ducked expertly and burst into great guffaws at her mother's poor aim.

For my brothers and me these antics were a treat. We took a lively interest in the mother-and-daughter feud, rejoicing that no truce appeared in sight. Week after week Mama threatened to dismiss both the cook and her intractable offspring, only to be assured with vows and supplications that one more thrashing would bring the Chamaca to heel.

"She is strong as a bull," Luciana boasted. "After I whip her good she'll fetch and carry like three maids! You'll see!"

She whipped her "good," but there was no change. The Brat loped about the house, dodging work like the plague and keeping us entertained with her unquenchable high spirits. It must be admitted that Sylvester, Arnim, and I grew quite fond of her. We had never known anyone so full of resourcefulness and downright mischief. The fact that the Chamaca had been singled out by her own mother to serve as a back-stairs slavey who was to perform the lowlier tasks scorned by the other servants seemed to us a huge joke. We could see plainly that no one would ever make this wench do anything. Like a steamroller, she let insult and injury spend themselves against the stolid cuirass of her body. The house might cave in, but the Chamaca would emerge unscathed and still laughing.

27

MOSAIC IN THE FOUNTAIN

IT WAS through Petronilo that I happened to be steered quite accidentally in the direction of biological enlightenment.

Among our pets was a new terrier bitch whose middle had of late become enlarged. She was slow about romping with us now, and, when we cajoled or prodded her beyond even a dog's patience, she snapped. I complained to Petronilo about this.

A grave look came over his face. "Can't you see," he said reprovingly, "that she is heavy with the puppies she is carrying?"

Puppies! So that was it. Immediately I scanned Paloma from stem to stern, only to shake my head in bewilderment. There was no denying that the dog had lost her waistline, but I could perceive no puppies.

"She carries them inside her belly," Petronilo explained with the same earnestness that characterized all his actions, "in a special pouch."

This was indeed a revelation. I did not feel quite sure that the manservant knew what he was talking about, since he was Indian and illiterate. I resolved to check elsewhere.

We had company for lunch that day, and I could hardly wait for a lull in the grown-ups' conversation. At last, between the bouillon and the fish, I laid down my spoon and excitedly addressed the table.

"You know what?" I exclaimed in voluble tones that would have startled the dramatics coach who once eliminated me from the cast of *Snow White* on account of my inaudible mumbling.

"No," said Mama unsuspectingly, "what?"

When joining their elders at meals children of that day were not encouraged to take part in the conversation. But with guests at the board the prevailing atmosphere seemed genial, so I took full advantage of it. Eagerly I repeated Petronilo's preposterous story about Paloma and her concealed pouch.

"He says it's a pocket," I added uncertainly, "where she keeps the puppies——"

Silence fell across the table. Then Mama spoke quickly: "You're a little mixed up, dear. Shall we talk about that later?"

On the following day the subject of Paloma's delicate condition was broached again, though in what seemed to me a cursory manner. Without very detailed clarification Mama skipped from dog anatomy to human beings, stating that small boys and girls originated in a similarly handy fashion, and that the legend of the stork was only a euphemism.

"Does that mean it's a lie?" I wanted to know, for the matter of indiscriminate fabrication was a sore point in my life. I had been disciplined too often for stretching truth to weave a fascinating tale.

Mama's regard for ancient sagas and folk beliefs was deep. "No," she said meditatively, "it's the start of something called literature."

She went on to explain that there was an epic poem of Norse origin, one of the *Edda*, in which a god named Hoener is personified in various bird forms—a swan, a stork, a phœnix. This Hoener, the Long-legged One, Lord of the Ooze and the Marshes, stalked through the primordial mud of Creation ("moving in Chaos," was the actual text) until his brooding eye caught sight of a proper nesting-place for the hatching of the egg of the world.

"Before mankind arrived at scientific explanations," Mama concluded, "fables and parables answered every question. Until children are old enough to understand science, fables and parables continue to be employed, and they still hold the same answers, even though cloaked in imagery."

It was all rather blurred and sketchy. But out of the mingling of allegory and fact there emerged for me a firm conviction that the literary point of view towards life's mysteries was far more enticing than that of the laboratory analyst. I accepted the plain evidence of Paloma's predicament, yet put it out of my mind as quickly as possible. The long-legged divinity stalking through the marsh of Eddic legend offered a far more imaginative satisfaction.

As a result of Mama's disclosures, however, my esteem for Petrolino had greatly increased.

"It is so," I conceded on seeing him that same day. "You were right about Paloma."

He gave a snort of displeasure at my admitted doubts. "But certainly it is so! Paloma, she is *embarazada*."

Here was a new word for my vocabulary. To be embarrassed is, in Spanish, to be encumbered or pregnant. English-speaking tourists, particularly of male gender, often arouse considerable hilarity by putting their trust in literal translation and declaring themselves *embarazados* when they are merely ill at ease.

Another word, leading to more serious misunderstanding, is *picadillo*, the Spanish name for hash. Many an adventurous traveller, on spying a tavern sign with the promised bargain—"*Picadillo, 30 Centavos*"—may have grown disenchanted at sight of a sinless serving of chopped meat.

Apart from colourful linguistic turns, there were other facets to Petronilo's personality, such as his ability to see "things behind things."

There was the matter of the fountain.

From the day when we first entered the house on Matamoros Street there was a mystery about the fountain. Though its outer rim showed a bright pattern of mosaic traceries, the inner basin had long darkened under a hard coating of lichen-stained calcium. The spray of crystal-clear water which shot upward from the centre spout fell back into this shadowy pool and reflected its murky hue.

"It is an old fountain," said Petronilo disapprovingly. "I am going to clean it."

With this he marched off to the Santa Catarina river-bed at the foot of the Loma, a low fringe of mountain that skirted the Sierra Madre. Burrowing among the rocks, he found just what he wanted: a piece of porous lava stone.

Half an hour later he was home again, ready for action. He rolled up his trousers of white Indian homespun far above his knees, kicked off his cow-hide sandals, cocked his sombrero at an enterprising angle, and stepped into the pool.

For days he remained at his self-chosen task. Having emptied all water from the bowl, he crouched on his knees and patiently rubbed the lava stone over the slimy, bottle-green surface. Three times a day Luciana brought him a mug of steaming coffee, a batch of *tortillas* folded in a napkin, and a bit of *choriza* sausage mixed with a paste of red beans. He ate in silence, still sitting on his haunches. Then he licked his fingers clean, picked up the pumice, and continued to rub.

"Whatever is he after?" asked our mother in bewilderment. "That fountain is as clean as it will ever be, allowing for the stains of age!"

Petronilo sensed her doubts. "There is a design, señora," he declared solemnly, "at the bottom of the fountain; there must be —there always is."

No one believed him. "Nonsense, Petronilo! You'll find nothing but plain concrete."

He shook his head vehemently. "No concrete. It is an old fountain," he persisted. "I will find the design."

We got used to his obstinacy. For days the monotonous rhythm of his rasping strokes disturbed the siesta hour and furnished a hardly less welcome obbligato during dinner. Yet we found ourselves presently wandering straight from the breakfast-table to the patio for a check-up on the manservant's progress. It was hard labour, this self-imposed undertaking that Petronilo sandwiched in between his routine chores, and it was thankless too, since no reward awaited him. Mosaic in the fountain. Would he find it? Suddenly we were all in this with him. Would Petronilo arrive at his design? *Was* there indeed a design?

At bedtime I began to solicit divine complicity by putting the matter firmly up to God. "Please don't let Petronilo work so hard and find nothing. Make him a pattern, quick!"

The Almighty responded nobly. After a week of effort Petronilo came loping down the corridor in his bare feet, shouting, "Señora! Señora! It is as I have said—I penetrate to the design—please come and see!"

He turned back and waved his vast sombrero in mute signals towards the patio.

Mama put down her needlework. "Yes, Petronilo, I shall come and see. Wait—we'll *all* come and see."

With this she summoned the household together. A moment later we gathered about the fountain to gaze upon a marvellous sight. For there, dimly as yet, but unmistakable in colour and line, an exquisite mosaic arabesque had come into view. Its stylized *motif* centred in an octagonal star, from which delicate scrolls curled outward to the rim of the bowl.

As we broke into a chorus of praise Petronilo grew bashful. Minimizing his efforts, he muttered deprecatingly, "It needs more rubbing."

"It needs a good dousing of *amole* juice, if you ask me," said Luciana, who kept her pantry spotless by daily application of this miracle root, which, boiled in water, released a potent sap that foamed like soap and bleached away dirt with the ferocity of lye. It also took the paint off walls and furniture, having left Luciana's kitchen table a naked expanse of raw oak.

"*Amole* juice, bah!" scoffed the manservant, making it plain that he took little stock in woman's advice.

With this he tacitly dismissed all of us and set once more about his task. But now things happened quickly. The last filmy incrustations gave way under renewed attack, until a thorough rinsing left every inch of stone flawless and clean. Now the fountain was swept and left empty for three days in the hot sun. And lastly, with a trace of unction, Petronilo requested two reales (twenty-five centavos) for the purchase of half a dozen over-ripe mangoes.

After this we saw him, comfortably balanced on the rim of the fountain, devouring the succulent fruit while his strong toes firmly grasped the slithery skins and swished them back and forth in expert swoops. Wherever the turpentine oil of the mango came into contact with the hot, porous stone, it was instantly absorbed, imparting to the multicoloured fragments of mosaic a truly amazing depth of pigment. Before our eyes the fountain had been transformed into a work of art.

To cap its perfection, Uncle Bichteler obtained an assortment of goldfish, a turtle, and a beautiful conch shell. Henceforth, as the clear jets of water tumbled into the basin, we beheld a miniature marine world of dancing rainbow colours. To complete the thrill, my brothers and I would lift the conch shell to our ears and listen to its strangely hollow voice.

"That's the ocean you hear," we were told, as children everywhere in the world are told. "Listen carefully, and you'll hear the sound of the waves!"

We listened, and it was indeed the sound of the waves. No one forgets the voice of an ocean. Its echo lives on, even in a conch shell that has lain stranded on dry land through geologic æons surpassing calculation.

As for Petronilo, who had afforded us so signal a demonstration of "the thing behind the thing," he was rewarded with a pair of new trousers to replace the ones he had worn threadbare at his job of buffing. He also received a leather wallet with a crisp five-peso note.

"What will you do with your money, Petronilo?" I asked him eagerly.

He grew shy once more and shook his head, unwilling to tell. But we came upon him a short while later, squatting in the toolshed before an enormous crate of mangoes (the peso bought a lot in those days). They were fine, golden, red-cheeked mangoes, ripened to a turn. Their skins, not yet sufficiently deteriorated, were valueless as polishing agents, wherefore the Indian tossed them placidly over his shoulder while he munched the juicy pulp.

"I have a suspicion," said Papa, "that Petronilo's motives may not have been purely artistic."

Withal every one was pleased. Every one, that is, except Luciana. She liked the fountain well enough; it was quite pretty, what with the majolica flower-pots set in their proper places round the rim. But she had her doubts from a sanitary angle.

"Nothing is ever really clean," said Luciana, "unless it has been sloshed in *amole*."

28

MYNHEER THOMA

THERE WAS again the problem of our education.

Owing to the complications involved in a change of residence from one city to another our parents had not as yet found time to look into the Monterrey schooling situation. Thus for a pleasant interval my brothers and I cheerfully fended for ourselves.

On our first day in the house on Matamoros Street we struck up a quick friendship with three young Spaniards next door, Manuel, José, and Servando, who answered to the respective nicknames of Manolo, Pepe, and Cholo. They were the children of a corporation lawyer, Don José Garrido, who was associated with the Monterrey Steel Works, of which in later years our father became Director-General. This firm, known as the Compañia Fundidora de Fierro y Acero, Sociedad Anónima, was one of Nuevo León's proudest industries. Its smelting plant, rolling-mills, and blast-furnace lay on the outskirts of the city at the foot of the Saddle Mountain.

Naturally my brothers and I knew nothing about the Garrido family's social prominence. We did perceive, however, that the three young brothers were extraordinarily well mannered. As our ages corresponded happily, Cholo became my logical partner in any games where a girl might be tolerated. Still, I considered Cholo small fry because he wore a French schoolboy overall or smock that buttoned down the back and covered the otherwise manly cut of his clothes. He looked neat and charming in this outfit, but juvenile—decidedly juvenile. I was all the more gratified to discover that the fair-haired Pepe and the darkly handsome Manolo did not scorn my company. When we played robbers, tag, or hide-and-seek, these two chased me with flattering abandon.

I also enjoyed the companionship of my new friend María Strozzi. This eight-year-old girl with the distinguished Florentine name was the daughter of a widowed seamstress who lived in a little house across the street. There were other children in the Strozzi household, but María alone had time to play with me.

She was attractive, with light brown hair, blue eyes, and a perfect complexion. She was also intense and highly imaginative, which made her a resourceful playmate. We both had dolls'-houses, but with a difference. Mine was a permanent structure with several stories and furnishings of considerable elaborateness. María had only a collapsible box with oddly assorted miniature pieces which never remained in place, since they must be stored away in a drawer each night. Yet somehow the nondescript equipment that made up María's dolls'-house was infinitely more fun than my more perfect pieces. The reason for its magic lay perhaps in the fact that we were kept eternally busy sorting the shabby collection and giving it new shape each time we played. Nor did this happen invariably in the same spot, for the cramped Strozzi house afforded little extra space. María's dolls'-house took form, now on the stairs, now on a patch of rug in the small parlour, but always it was a miracle of delight. Against this background we acted marionette shows of our own composition, using a cardboard-box or packing-case for stage and proscenium, while parts of an old scarf provided the curtain. Our actors were coloured cut-outs from fashion magazines discarded by María's mother. Dialogue and plot were patterned after the French Pathé films we attended on the occasion of children's matinées at the Teatro Variedades, in Zaragoza Street, or based on hair-raising yarns from that inexhaustible source, the neighbouring servants.

For my part I could have continued this existence indefinitely, playing make-believe games each day, running barefoot over the scrubbed tiles of the patio, climbing the pomegranate tree to gorge myself on its luscious fruit, inventing stories with María Strozzi, or simply listening to Petronilo's wondrous philosophies. But our parents were of a different mind.

"This can't go on," said Mama. "Minka is illiterate, and even the boys are forgetting everything they ever learned!"

Father agreed and promised to look into the school situation. He made inquiries and, after a tour of the city, returned with none too encouraging a picture. Like the rest of Mexico, the state of Nuevo León had public schools, but these were intended strictly for the poor and under-privileged. Families of comfortable means were expected to take no advantage of such free facilities but to send their children to private institutions. These were primarily convents for girls and Jesuit colleges for boys.

Our mother's nonconformist spirit balked at such a choice.

It was not that she had any objection to orthodoxy; indeed, she herself would never have turned Protestant. But her mind rebelled against the practice of harnessing the young to any fixed creed.

Father did not cavil at this reasoning. But it left the problem of our schooling still unsolved.

"Why don't you try a tutor?" said Uncle Bichteler, holding up *El Porvenir*, the morning paper. "The Dutch Consulate lists a teacher here who is looking for work."

It was thus that Mynheer Leo Thoma entered our lives.

Mynheer Thoma was grey, round-shouldered, and nondescript, but his qualifications were out of the ordinary, for he had mastered several tongues and had a degree in science from the University of Leyden. After a short conference Papa rejoiced in having found so adequate a man. The question was, what to do about the disparity in age between my brothers and me. Would it be wise to key the lessons down to the level of the slowest pupil or should the opposite course be taken? After brief discussion it was decided that the boys' requirements came first, since they faced greater future responsibilities than a mere girl. I must follow along in their shadow as best I could. For me it was plainly a question of sink or swim.

All things considered, the arrangement proved satisfactory. Mynheer Thoma revealed himself as a learned man with a strong sense of duty. He gave of his knowledge without stint, arriving each morning punctually at eight, aglow with pedagogical enthusiasm. At sight of our mother he bowed ceremoniously. Next he drew forth a frayed handkerchief, faintly scented with 4711 Cologne, and polished a pair of gold-rimmed spectacles before adjusting them on his nose.

"Ah!" was his greeting, as he fixed a stern eye on each of us in turn. "Now let us see about the Spartans and Athenians!"

Under the ægis of Mynheer Thoma the Spartans and Athenians figured very prominently in our lives. He had a passion for the antique world under the glory that was Hellas. So relentless and thorough was the drill in classical history that I can still, blindfolded, draw the Peloponnesus, three-fingered Thrace, fair Ilium, and the boot of Italy rising in the west. For Mynheer knew the Mare Nostrum of the ancients as well as he knew every fold of his carefully tied cravat.

As might have been expected, I could not hold my own. The boys were already doing algebra while I had yet to learn multiplication tables; they studied the phases of the moon before I could recite the names of the continents and oceans that made up our own earth.

By way of compromise Mynheer Thoma put me to work memorizing reams of poetry, so that he might be free to initiate Sylvester and Arnim into the mysteries of the logarithm. Similarly, while he and the boys digressed into the field of elementary astronomy, I was allowed to turn the pages of a handsomely illustrated geography manual. Here I came unexpectedly upon the clear and reasonable pattern of the United States. Never had I seen a more pleasing map! At first glance it looked almost geometric in structure, like a chess-board, and far easier to remember than the gnarled shapes of Europe, Asia, or even South America. Then there were beautiful names like Pennsylvania, Georgia, Oregon (reminiscent of the royal Spanish line of Aragón), and Kentucky (which I read with the stress on "Kent"). All these delighted the ear, even when pronounced in Mynheer Thoma's Netherlands accent. Decidedly I liked this place called the United States.

29

RANCH LIFE

FOR ALMOST a year we remained in the excellent schoolmaster's charge. During that time my brothers were extraordinarily well grounded in academic subjects far beyond their age requirements, so that the loss of school had been more than made up.

The same could not be said for me. I had straggled along on the fringe, picking up bits of information here and there, but missing a great deal more. Among the benefits that accrued to me, however, was one for which I would be permanently grateful. Through the ceaseless repetition of poetic stanzas I acquired an almost photographic memory. After a while I no longer memorized. I simply remembered.

However, circumstances now arose which caused us to lose our tutor and to suffer a new break in our education. A notice arrived from the Netherlands Consulate, informing Mynheer Thoma that a state pension awaited him if he returned at once to Holland. There was no choice but to let him go. Bowing ceremoniously, Mynheer Thoma stepped out of our lives.

Summer had arrived meanwhile, and Papa decided on a holiday for us before the problem of our future schooling needed to be faced. We were to spend the hot months on a ranch some nineteen miles from Monterrey. The estate in question belonged to the Light and Power Company and was operated at a handsome profit. Part of its acreage was planted with cotton, corn, and sugar-cane, while the major section served as grazing land for cattle, horses, and other livestock. As general manager of the firm, our father made frequent visits to *la hacienda*, residing in a comfortable ranch-house under the care of a Chinese houseboy, who did double duty as serving-maid and cook.

For my brothers and me there was no greater thrill than to be taken along on these trips. On learning that we were to spend the entire summer living like *rancheros*, riding gaudy Mexican saddles (Papa favoured English harness in town), and watching the three great harvests brought in, our cup of happiness overflowed.

On a sunny morning in June we set out from the house on Matamoros Street, taking along the dogs, the cat, and Loro. We drove in the noisy Protos (to make a proper impression automobiles had to be noisy in those days) and were followed by a mule-cart packed high with provender.

At the ranch all was in readiness. The Chinese in charge had hung mosquito-netting over all the beds, he had swept the rooms, freshened the low porch with a watering-can, and set up a table for lunch.

Next morning Papa and Mama returned to Monterrey, leaving us in charge of Uncle Bichteler, who loved ranch life and had volunteered to supervise our summer holiday. Since my brothers and I spent all our time out-of-doors, his only concern would be to round us up before dark and send us to bed at a reasonable hour. Reasonableness, however, was with Uncle Bichteler a variable concept, for he was an æsthete enslaved by music and totally indifferent to clocks. Each evening he spent long hours at the archaic ranch piano, while we sprawled on the veranda floor and listened to the magic that poured from his fingers. It did not matter to Uncle Bichteler that a few keys stuck and the pedals were out of order.

"Mozart used no pedal at all," he reminded himself, "and the most weather-beaten or neglected instrument of our day is better than the spinets and clavichords of Haydn's time."

With this he caressed the battered keyboard as though it belonged to the magnificent ebony Bechstein he had left at home. A true musician, we began to grasp, could perform miracles on the poorest instrument.

Mostly he played Beethoven: the simple early sonatas which were really sonatinas, and thematic segments from the symphonies, particularly the Sixth, or *Pastorale*. But there were days when he soared to special heights, as he struck the bold opening measures of the *Sonate für das Hammerklavier* or plunged into the glorious Opus 111 (*Sonate Furor*). This last, with its powerful chromatic climax followed by the tender and exquisite Arietta, left me invariably shaken. Listening to this majestic work of the composer's third and richest period, when the titanic Beethoven lived imprisoned in deafness, I grew dimly aware of the mystery of genius. Here was music of such greatness that interpreter and listener found themselves almost equally involved in its performance. Not until years later, after Uncle Bichteler had died, did I learn that only an artist of unusual skill can play Opus 111, since its technical intricacies are too much for the mediocre musician. But by the same token the splendour of the musical phrase was such that even the uninitiated listener could respond to its impassioned sweep. Here indeed was the test of a masterpiece!

The combination cook-and-manservant who looked after our needs at the ranch answered to the name of Enlique Lee.

Enlique was a young moon-faced Cantonese with an angelic disposition. Like most of his compatriots in Mexico, he had come across the border from California, bringing with him a rudimentary knowledge of North American foods and fads.

While in the United States he had learned enough English to change his original name of Li Hwang to Cholly (Charley), only to discover that innumerable fellow-Asiatics had made the same choice. The reason for this was the enormous and world-wide popularity of the British farce *Charley's Aunt*, coupled with the growing renown of an Anglo-American comedian named Chaplin. Even in remote Mongolian villages provincial audiences applauded the lady from "Brazil, where the nuts come from," and the little fellow of the cane and moustache. Our cook proved no exception.

Still, he was an individualist, and it irked him to find so many Chinese abroad named Cholly. He cast about, therefore, and picked himself the more distinguished Henly (Henry), after an up-and-coming Detroit motor-car manufacturer. He further anglicized his surname to Lee, inverting the order in Western fashion.

As Henly Lee he crossed the Rio Grande, only to meet with the necessity of further alteration. The Spanish tongue contained no aspirates; hence in Mexico Henry became the Latin version Enrique or, in the cook's version, Enlique.

He had many commendable traits. One of them, perhaps the most outstanding, was his ability to bake a chocolate-pie. We did not know this godlike dish, being accustomed to Continental desserts such as puddings, *petits fours*, and strudels. Enlique's pies ran the gamut of flavours: butterscotch, mince, lemon, coconut cream, apple, and all the berry possibilities. Plus chocolate. Inevitably this awakened in us a lively enthusiasm for the unknown republic to the north. What a satisfactory place it must be! Based on the cook's descriptions, we visualized a land of untold plenty, where lucky children thrived on a diet of honey, caramel frosting, and a divine creation known as an ice-cream cone.

To offset his success in the sweets department, Enlique next introduced us to a type of bread (he called it American) which drew forth our unanimous protest. It was oblong, box-shaped, soft, quite without crust, and of an indescribably flabby texture.

"Art gum," was Uncle Bichteler's opinion.

"It's like biting into a bale of cotton," the ranch hands said.

In every other respect Enlique was a jewel beyond price. When our shoes or riding-boots needed polishing he rubbed them lovingly to a high gloss. If the Chamaca, whom Mama dispatched to the *hacienda* as general housemaid, tore the mosquito-netting while clumsily making our beds Enlique produced a sewing-kit and deftly repaired the damage. If the violence of a tropical storm wakened us at night he hastened to the kitchen and brewed a kettle of hot cocoa to soothe us back to sleep. But, best of all, when his working hours were done, he took off his apron and obeyed our pleas to sit on the porch in the cool of evening and tell us about China.

It was then that we came to know the real Li Hwang, who seemed to be no servant at all, but a delightful companion. He had just passed his twenty-fourth birthday and his father in Canton wished him to come home to marry the girl selected for him during childhood.

"Are you going?" we asked apprehensively.

"A man must marry," he said.

We did not agree. As long as Enlique Lee had us to live with, what need was there for him to take a wife? My brothers and I had come to love Enlique, quite as much as we loved big Petronilo back in Monterrey.

"Why must a man marry?" we challenged him.

His answer carried all the philosophy of the Orient. "A man must have sons to bear his name and to bury him when he dies. My father is old, but he has me to lean upon. Yet I have no one to do those things for me. It is time to go home."

We were impressed, as we envisioned a lonely man in China moving serenely towards death. The simple passing of the years held no finality for this old man. Across the ocean chasm he had a son, to whom his spirit could cry out in the full certainty of being heard. Without written or oral communication Li Hwang's father knew that in the ripeness of time his son would come home.

Our own father must have known about it too, for Enlique's housekeeping grew increasingly expensive. It was not that the almond-eyed cook juggled his budget funds; Enlique was scrupulously honest after his fashion. But, bearing in mind that he had a costly ocean passage to plan for, he traded with a greengrocer of his acquaintance who handed out commissions with his sales. Naturally these commissions came ultimately out of the customer's pocket, but from Enlique's standpoint it was all completely ethical and above-board.

The fruit-growers and market-gardeners round Monterrey were in the majority Chinese, and most of them too answered to the name of Cholly. They went from house to house with a huge pole slung coolie-fashion across their shoulders, heavy baskets of produce dangling at opposite ends. Almost every street had its own particular Cholly (Chali, the Mexicans called him) who never trespassed into a competitor's territory. But there was also the market-place in the centre of the town, where more prosperous dealers had their stalls. Here operated Enlique's friend and fellow-countryman, a lean individual named Malgalito.

Malgalito had been a hard-working house-to-house pedlar in his younger days, but by dint of skimping and saving he had been able to hire an assistant, who did his planting and carrying for him. Acquiring a tiny stall in the Mercado Colón, Malgalito nowadays sat contentedly behind the counter, watching the stream of customers file by. Gone and forgotten were the hours of drudgery, the peregrinations from door to door, the back-breaking burdens that had cut a permanent ridge across his shoulders. He had even lost his coolie walk, that peculiar swaying trot, always on the run to keep ahead of exhaustion. And, to fit his new estate, he too had exchanged an alien name for one more fitting. Aware that in Spanish the endings 'o' and 'a' usually determined masculine and feminine gender, he came up with his own improvisation on Marguerite.

Our cook, Enlique, drove to town each week to fetch supplies. On these trips he inevitably stopped to pass the time of day with Malgalito, and the two friends shared a spot of *tequila*. Nothing was so conducive to smooth business relationships as a convivial drink, Malgalito had long ago discovered.

The long hot ride back to the ranch always sobered Enlique up, but it soon became apparent that our housekeeping expenses were increasing sharply by reason of these sessions.

"A man must marry," he explained, when he was confronted with his dereliction. "I must make much money to go back to China!"

"Instead of China," Uncle Bichteler pointed out, "you'll end up in gaol with your good friend Malgalito, don't you understand?"

At this the cook became unstrung. He retired to his kitchen, where he let a batch of biscuits burn to a crisp. That night, while Uncle Bichteler played Chopin, my brothers and I sat on the veranda and speculated on the unhappy Enlique's fate. Would old Li Hwang in far-off Canton die and be buried by strangers, now that his son's supplementary earnings were threatened? Would the girl chosen for Enlique jilt him and accept another? Most important of all, were the cook's feelings hurt to the point where he would lose interest in the manufacture of chocolate-pies?

A difficult week went by. Gloomily Enlique puttered among his pots and pans while the Chamaca waited on table and half-heartedly buffed our riding-boots. No longer did the ranch kitchen beguile our noses with divine odours. There were no flowers in the vase above the sink. The herb-garden in its box on the window-ledge looked unwatered. Twice the mosquito-netting ripped above Uncle Bichteler's bed, but Enlique's handy sewing-kit did not appear. With the Chamaca's aid some random stitches were taken, only to disclose their inefficiency when Uncle Bichteler emerged from his room the following morning with itching bumps and a malarial complexion. One and all, we were made to share in Enlique's Oriental gloom.

And then, as abruptly as it had descended, the cook's melancholia lifted. In some recess of his soul Enlique unearthed a fragment of Confucian philosophy to dispel the black mood. With cheery glibness he quoted: "Tarry with marriage. He who begets children in old age receives the present of second youth."

The clouds parted and his beaming Mongolian smile broke through. China could wait. Li Hwang senior, measured by the longevity of his ancestors, was good for another decade at least. And as for the maid who pined for an early wedding, let her seek another groom. Enlique would go home in his own time, certain always of fair lotus-blossoms to be had for the picking.

That week-end the cook produced his finest dinner. Our parents planned to be with us for Sunday, bringing a few guests. This put Enlique on his mettle. He ordered a fine turkey in the near-by village of San Nicolás de las Garzas (Saint Nicholas of the Cranes), or San Nico, for short. This bird from San Nico was to be the main prop of a feast patterned after an American holiday called Thanksgiving. Once a year, Enlique explained to us, those wonderful Americans showed their gratitude to God by sitting down to a huge dinner of mashed potatoes, yams, buttered beans, pickled peaches, cranberries, gravy, mince-pie, and the classic fowl. Enlique did not state whether the size of the meal bore any relation to the degree of thankfulness involved. But he heartily approved the custom.

The turkey, known to us by the Aztec term *guajolote* or the Spanish *pavo*, arrived in a large crate and was released among Enlique's assorted barnyard creatures. To the terror of ducks, geese, and guinea-fowl, the great bird strutted haughtily, gurgling his war-cry and spreading his tail-feathers into a wide fan.

"He looks athletic," Uncle Bichteler commented. "Won't he be tough?"

Enlique smiled sagely. "One gives him a drink of *tequila*. The muscles relax, and he is not so tough!"

"In that case," said Uncle Bichteler with feeling, "let's make it something better than *tequila*!" He unlocked the liqueur cabinet and reached for the Napoleon brandy.

The following morning we awoke to see the turkey tottering happily among the petunia beds. He oscillated back and forth, raising his wings in limp gestures of flight and emitting a shrill chirp. Once or twice he leaned back cautiously and sat down on his proudly spread tail. Beyond a doubt, the chopping-block would hold no terrors for the relaxed and manifestly tenderized turkey of San Nico.

The dinner was a notable success. As we sampled each tasty mouthful our admiration for American dishes grew.

"We must have this often," said Uncle Bichteler fervently.

"I'm afraid it will be expensive," Papa reflected.

Mama waved gaily across the table. "Nonsense, dear. The turkey is a native bird, served in *mole* sauce every day. It costs no more than chicken——"

"I was thinking," said our father, "of the Napoleon brandy."

30

MUSICAL NOTES

ALTHOUGH THE departure of Mynheer Thoma had put an end to our schooling, my brothers and I continued for a while with our music lessons. Our first Monterrey teacher was a portly gentleman named José Villaseñor, who played in a local orchestra and barely managed to support a wife and half a dozen children with his gains.

Señor Villaseñor was great fun. He opened and terminated each lesson by seating himself at the piano and regaling us with the merriest polka or march-tune of the day. He also knew a variety of musical tricks, all based on the 'chopstick' principle. But what he did best was to smoke Uncle Bichteler's cigars, blowing rings over our heads in fancy elliptic patterns.

We learned more parlour tricks than preludes under the guidance of this genial mentor, with the result that Mama soon called a halt. Our next teacher was a young society woman, Anita Degetau, who was quite talented and gave lessons as a pastime. She did not come to our house as was the custom with other teachers; instead, we trotted twice a week to her beautiful home at the north end of the town, where she was usually to be found in some flowing and picturesque house-robe. Trailing gracefully before us, she led the way to a large salon, where the open Steinway waited in the far corner, flanked by elegant furnishings, fine porcelain vases, and an array of ancestral portraits.

Musically, this period was fruitful enough, but we derived from it an added benefit. Señorita Degetau was an inveterate reader, who could not resist a chance to implant her enthusiasm in the young. Each time we came she had another book for us to carry home and devour with zest, for she imparted a quality of breathless suspense to the adventure of reading.

It was while we were in the hands of Señorita Degetau that my brothers made their final break with the piano. Up to now there had never been anything which Sylvester and Arnim did not do better than I. Whether at games or school work, in all things we followed one another according to age. This pattern governed even our appropriation of toys or other gifts that could be shared in common; automatically, though we were not instructed to do so, Arnim and I stood back at Christmas-time, waiting for Sylvester to make his choice. Only after he had taken possession did we, each in turn, reach for our own.

The same psychological hurdle confronted us now in music, until—inexplicably—I advanced with sudden strides that left my brothers far behind. It couldn't be! It upset the proper order of things! The ease with which I memorized and performed the same assignments, over which both boys laboured and strained, caused them abruptly to rebel.

"We don't like piano-playing," they declared defiantly. "It's girl stuff!"

Our mother was horrified. To her Magyar soul life without music was unthinkable. But Papa took it philosophically.

"The world is full of unemployed and hungry musicians," he said. "But there aren't enough good engineers to go round."

Mama sought comfort by pinning her hopes on me. Perhaps my talent would be great enough to make up for the boys' defection. In any case, I must be placed in the hands of Mexico's best teacher, Daniel Zambrano. This meant that Uncle Bichteler would coach me throughout the summer on the ranch, so as to prepare me for an autumn audition.

Daniel Zambrano was an artist of renown, who had returned only recently from years of study abroad. Like Uncle Bichteler, he was a pupil of the Prussian-Polish composer Xaver Scharwenka at the Conservatory of Leipzig, where he had prepared for a concert career.

In music there is many a slip 'twixt practice and performance. Uncle Bichteler found the concert platform less rewarding than the composer's ivory tower. A virtuoso's achievement, at least in that era before mechanical recordings, belonged to the fleeting present. The finest recital, once it was over, could not be recaptured; the performing artist was doomed to oblivion unless his next concert equalled or surpassed the first. Nor did illness or the infirmities of increasing age ease the strain. He must continue surpassing himself each time he appeared in public, or his star would sink. The composer, on the other hand, had deeper and more lasting satisfaction in store. He could write one masterpiece (always assuming that he *could* write a masterpiece!) and sun himself in its success for the rest of his days. Painters, poets, and composers could grow witless and incompetent with age, but their works remain for ever young. Performers perish each time the curtain falls; only the creative artist lives to be interpreted, over and over, even after death.

Daniel Zambrano likewise found the concert stage a difficult hazard. Though possessed of rare musicianship, he was acutely shy in public. This agonizing trait blighted his professional appearances, for Daniel Zambrano never played as well on-stage as he did in the privacy of his own study. Monterrey music-lovers bore witness to this fact; the young pianist, fresh from abroad, had held his opening recital at the Teatro Independencia, only to break down with an attack of nerves before he was half-way through his programme. After recovering from the ordeal he resolved to give up concert work in favour of teaching.

It was a wise choice. The son of a banker, Daniel was indifferent to money and could afford to choose his pupils. Even those who successfully passed his auditions were weeded out periodically if they did not live up to their first promise. His fame as a teacher had spread rapidly, confirming the musician's truism: "Great performers cannot teach; great teachers cannot perform."

Our summer at the *hacienda*, then, became for me a period of preparation. While my brothers rode over the fields on horseback and helped round up cattle, or watched the cotton-picking and the sugar-harvest, I spent long hours with Uncle Bichteler at the dilapidated ranch piano.

As a pedagogue Uncle Bichteler left much to be desired. Highly gifted himself, he had no patience with ineptitude. The piano held no secrets for him; hence he looked for the same facility in others. One particular failing of mine was torment to his sensitive ear; at the stroke of the hour, when my practice period ended, I flew from the keyboard without bothering to complete whatever musical phrase my fingers had been struggling through. These unresolved notes dangling in mid-air drove Uncle Bichteler to distraction.

"*Never* do that!" he stormed, as near to anger as I ever knew him to come. "Musically it's the unforgivable sin!"

I agreed. But what was I to do about it?

"Solve the harmonic structure," he commanded sternly, "by finding a chord to fit the note you want to stop on. Until you learn to do this you'll be only a piano player, never a pianist."

To illustrate his point he let his fingers glide over the keys in a series of dominant, sub-dominant, and seventh chords, giving me my first lesson in abstract harmony. As his white hands moved from one chromatic arabesque to another it became evident to me that the true artist could be interrupted at any point without inviting chaos. "It's very simple," said Uncle Bichteler. "Once you understand harmony you can do without a score, and you'll be able to make your own music."

It was hard work, but not without a lasting reward. For, as my familiarity with musical structure increased, I gained in confidence and inventiveness. Soon I was able to pick out folk-tunes, many of which had been known for generations without reaching publication. I also concocted an occasional ditty of my own. But what I yearned most to achieve was mastery of the gusty French *Le Tourbillon*, which Uncle Bichteler recalled, by ear, from his student days. Whenever he felt in a beer-tavern mood he regaled us with this noisy yet completely fascinating bit of banality.

Through the years I searched for a copy of *Le Tourbillon*, but the mazurka-like waltz with its fast rolling bass and electrifying rhythm was long out of print, its author lost in oblivion. Laboriously then, for Uncle Bichteler was no longer alive to help me, I jotted down the measures that emerged from the blur of childhood memory. Though fragmentary, they evoked an aura of early twentieth-century cavortings, gas-light gaiety, and the petticoat swish of Parisian dance-halls.

31

SECULAR SCHOOL

WE RETURNED to town early in September, ruddy-faced, brown, and boisterous. After one look at us Mama exclaimed, "They've become peasants! They need a thorough scrubbing!"

She was right. We had enthusiastically adopted the easy primitivism of ranch life. True, Uncle Bichteler's presence had proved of some disciplinary value, causing us to retain at least a vestige of table manners and rudimentary grooming. But it was evident to our parents that such essentials as the brushing of teeth or the combing of hair had been reduced to the inescapable minimum. We had practically lived and slept in riding-breeches, skipping ablutions whenever possible, and confining costume changes to the occasional flourish of a fresh handkerchief.

Despite such reprehensible flaunting of hygienic rules my brothers and I were in excellent health. The daily ranch diet of coarse foods, including the perennial *tortillas*, *frijoles*, barbecues, and vegetable stews, agreed with us. Between meals we had cut down long stalks of sugar-cane for sucking, chewing, and exultant spitting. In short, though we had shunned the tube of tooth-paste that lay conspicuously on the bathroom shelf, our teeth were strong and white from constant gnawing at *palo dulce* (liquorice root), piñon kernels, melon seeds, and raw peanuts.

Also, despite our gluttony, we were wiry and thin, for the constant activity of the *hacienda* had kept us in the best of trim. Long hours of riding, often bareback, had alternated with daily visits to the sugar-mill at the southern tip of the ranch. Here we had watched the giant copper cauldrons that steamed with lazy bubbles of brown sorghum. We had many friends among the plantation workers, not only because our arrival broke the monotony of their day, but because we helped to tidy up the pouring-room by licking the syrupy overflow off the cooling *piloncillo* (brown sugar) moulds.

Altogether ours had been a happy and rewarding summer, though scarcely an intellectual one. Academically speaking, we had vegetated. Our young heads were as smugly free of ideas as a cabbage.

"Once and for all," Mama said doggedly, "something must be done about a proper school!"

Sharing her desperation, Papa consulted the Austrian Consul-General, Don Roberto Bremer, and returned with a partial solution. Señor Bremer's own sons, six or seven of them, attended the Colegio Marista, a religious institution operated by the good Fathers of the Order of Mary. Our neighbourhood chums, the Garrido boys, were enrolled in the same school.

It was not what our mother and father wanted, but they bowed to necessity. Although the Colegio Marista took boarders, Sylvester and Arnim started as day pupils. They went off to classes each morning with Manolo, Pepe, and Cholo. As I remember, Sylvester had been entered in Manolo's class, Arnim in Pepe's, while Cholo belonged to a lower form.

I took great pride in my brothers at this stage, owing to an aura of privilege and distinction that went with being a Marista boy. For one thing, their appearance necessarily underwent a change. From the unkempt savages I had known on the ranch only a short while ago, they had been transformed into sleek little gentlemen in long trousers. I was further intrigued by their new associates, two of whom awakened in me a pre-adolescent impulse towards coquetry. The lads in question were Eduardo Bremer, eldest son of the consul, and Constantino de Tárnava, whose father was head of the Milmo bank.

It must be set down as proof of innate fickleness or, perhaps, of a prodigally expansive heart, that I found it difficult to choose between my heroes. Without scruple, I idolized them both. Needless to say, neither Eduardo nor Constantino had the slightest use for me. Well launched into their 'teens, they cultivated a bogus maturity and behaved like blasé men of the world. They frequented the evening promenades around Plaza Zaragoza, or, on Sunday mornings, waited on the Cathedral steps to ogle the curvaceous señoritas (alas, I was too young for curves!) emerging from Mass.

Ironically, Constantino's younger brother, Luís, a fair and blue-eyed lad of my own age, looked upon me with touching favour. But Luís was patently a child, as unexciting as my neighbourhood playmate, Cholo. I wasted no time on anyone so infantile.

Monterrey had three convent schools to serve the educational needs of three separate social strata. These schools were conducted by the religious orders of the Sacred Heart, Saint Joseph, and Saint Mary-of-the-Poor, respectively. Local people knew them as El Sagrado Corazón, San José, and María Auxiliadora.

The first of these enjoyed distinctly aristocratic rating, for it was part of the famous French Sacré-Cœur and boasted a parent house in Paris. Its black-robed members wore snowy coifs edged with starched ruching of such width that their profiles were hidden from view. They called themselves *las Damas* (the Ladies) rather than plain nuns, and were seldom seen on Monterrey streets, since they had lay sisters trained to run their errands. The convent itself was situated on the corner of Calle Padre Mier and the cross-street of Doctor Cos, about two blocks from the cathedral. It went without saying that the high-born *Damas* received into their charge only the daughters of the city's self-styled élite, which meant mainly (though not always) children of wealth.

The second convent was precisely that: the second convent. Its nuns, known as the "Josephines," resided in a grim, medieval structure on a slope near the Santa Catarina River. At times, when a sudden flood struck, every one feared that the *Josefinas* would be washed away. But the good sisters invariably sat out the danger behind their solid walls, where they went on expounding multiplication tables, catechism, biblical history, and a smattering of grammar to pig-tailed hopefuls from the middle classes. At Saint Joseph's no bonnet blinkers were worn; the coifs were close-fitting in the classic manner, with a straight white band across the forehead (specifications for the *Damas* required that this band be black). On the whole, the habit of the *Josefinas* was quite becoming, with its flowing veil and prim white bib that lent an air of innocence even to ageing faces. Also, the order was not strictly cloistered. Unlike the Sacré-Cœur sisterhood, the *Josefinas* were anything but aloof. One could see them several times a week, bustling along in pairs like busy madonnas, making their rounds through the market, bakery, and altar supply shops. They looked healthy, pink-cheeked, and merry as chipmunks on a rampage. The pupils in their charge reflected this bounce and vigour. Wearing dark-blue uniforms with Peter Pan collars of white piqué, these children were a winsome and appealing sight. But it was still the second convent.

Through all my years in Monterrey I never really found the building that housed the brown sisters of Nuestra Señora María Auxiliadora. These nuns were of so humble a caste that they did not even rate the standard black of conventual garb. Their robes were coffee-coloured, shoddy, and quite unrelieved by white touches. When they walked the frayed hems of their Mother Hubbards dragged in the dust and flapped about their feet, as modesty forbade the lifting of religious skirts, while lack of time or sheer fatigue must have prevented all but the most essential repairs. The Auxiliadoras, it appeared, were on the streets both day and night. Theirs was no fashionable top-drawer boarding-school, nor even a self-sustaining middle-class institution; the brown sisters were beggars who lived off charity to keep a nursery and elementary school for orphans and the poorest of the poor.

Of the three convents, I was destined to know only the Sacré-Cœur, where my parents eventually enrolled me as a pupil. But before this there came the episode of the Colegio Central.

The Colegio Central Para Niñas was a secular school for girls, just opposite the British Consulate, in the heart of the town. It had been founded by two spinster ladies of unknown antecedents but commendable pioneering spirit, for this was a day when, among Latins, women in business were regarded with suspicion.

The Colegio Central came to the attention of my parents as they weighed the pros and cons of placing me in the hands of the French nuns. At no time had our mother and father deviated from their preference for a non-sectarian, and certainly non-parochial, education. They had relented in the case of my brothers because the Marist Academy was in our vicinity and the boys could come home during the lunch-hour, thus breaking the monastic routine. Furthermore, Sylvester and Arnim were old enough to have developed a definite personality pattern, and they did not lean towards introspection or emotional excess. With regard to me, Papa in particular had misgivings. I was easily swayed by outside influences, especially if they appealed to my extravagant imagination.

"Religious ecstasy would be just her dish!" said Papa. He employed the word *ekstasis* in its Greek meaning of "trance, mystic convulsion."

Mama agreed. She would almost rather have sent me off with the Chamaca, who still spent part of each day at one of the Government schools. Here bricklayers' and servants' children of both sexes capped a minimum of classroom work with long hours of rowdy outdoor play.

The rumour got about regarding our parents' indecision in the matter of my education. This led to a call from the headmistress of the Colegio Central, who came to extol the virtues of her school. She stressed the advantages of short hours, secular teaching, and—what pleased Papa especially—a daily period of *deporte* (sports). The upshot was that by early October I was registered as a pupil at the Colegio Central.

My curriculum was crowded with interest, much of which derived from the feature called 'sports.' There was no gymnasium, to be sure, but as a concession to modern physical culture we were made to march in formation across a courtyard, swinging dumb-bells, Indian clubs, soft fabric-covered balls, or on occasion merely our clenched fists. Such 'exercises' alternated with much 'jumping of rope,' singly or doubly, in an intricate technique worthy of the ballet. All the girls loved this *brincar la riata*. With petticoats flying they leaped into action, forward, backward, over two ropes twirled in opposite directions, and finally at a fast pace called *mole* or "hot pepper."

Our academic curriculum was tailored along patriotic lines, dealing mainly with Mexican history and folk-lore. Up to this time I had been exposed to little of either, my knowledge of the country's past being confined to the Maximilian interlude, while hearsay alone supplied what I absorbed of legend or belles-lettres. But now I found myself immersed in the violent story of a land once known as Anáhuac, where Aztecs, Toltecs, Chichimecs, Otomis, Yaquis, and untold other tribes with equally fierce names and tempers had left their mark in fire and blood. All this, of course, touched only the past. Of Mexico's current travail no notice was taken at the Colegio Central. Prosperous, industrial Monterrey lay—up to now, at least—outside the area of political strife. We knew from newspaper reports that President Porfirio Díaz had long toppled from power, and that he had found refuge in that haven of exiles, France. We had also heard that during the Decena Trágica, a ten-day-long bombardment of Mexico City, the fine clock-tower sent by the Chinese Government as a Centennial present (the one truly useful gift!) had been shattered. But beyond this the Revolution was ignored at Monterrey.

Living in the past, the Colegio Central put its main emphasis on memory work. For hours we read aloud in chorus, covering the vast enterprises of Cristóbal Colón, voyager and discoverer of the Americas, without the annoyance of oral interrogation. While our daily stint was rattled off, the teacher sat serenely at her desk, engrossed in tatting or crochet work. She seldom looked up or missed a stitch unless her ear caught a break in our rhythm. This was sometimes induced by the fascinating pictures interspersed throughout our history text, depicting scenes from Indian life, such as the distillation of *pulque*, or a corpse being nonchalantly tossed off the lee side of a pyramid. We lingered over these fascinating illustrations until there was an admonishing rap to bid us resume reading.

The extraordinary fluency of speech characterizing all Hispanic peoples may well be attributed to this parrot system of education. Certain it is that at the Colegio Central oratory flourished as we skipped from viceregal nomenclature to such Aztec tongue-twisters as Cuauhtemoc, Xochitl, Atzcapotzalco, Tetlepanquetzal, or Netzahualcoyotl—respectively a prince, a maiden, a place, a hero, and a poet-king.

Once a week copybooks were passed round and the *exámenes* were on. With sighs and much chewing of penholders we scribbled down what our small heads retained from the ill-digested mass of reading. Promptly, then, on Friday mornings came the report-cards.

Memory conjures up three additional aspects, all of them trivial, of my sojourn at the Colegio Central. The first of these was a crochet craze that hit the entire school as a direct result of the hobby to which faculty members were addicted. Suddenly all but the smallest pupils were bent on fashioning round bonnets or skull-caps made from an imported yarn of unwieldy thickness. This yarn, trade-marked "Carola," was sold by Levantine merchants in lower Morelos Street at scandalously high prices. Several Arab girls in the school were, in fact, the first to sport the new fashion, thereby advertising the parental merchandise. For some inexplicable reason these aquiline-profiled children of Semitic stock were looked down upon, but such were the peculiar charms of Carola yarns that the crocheting epidemic soon got out of hand. Among the older girls, more accomplished with their needles, rivalry arose as each came to class bedecked with her woolly creation. Younger children (myself among them), who had never handled a crochet-hook, were out of luck. Some few succeeded in persuading their mothers to manufacture or purchase the head-gear in question. But others, again myself among them, met with no co-operation whatever.

In this, it must be admitted, Mama showed rare good taste, for the Carola caps were hideous beyond description. Owing to the thickness of the yarn—like macaroni, Mama said—the finished product grew to enormous size. It looked like nothing so much as an inverted calabash or half a watermelon. Also there was the matter of colour; always two contrasting shades were employed, and each girl prided herself in achieving some especially lurid clash of colours, such as pea-green and magenta, or saffron and blue. Yet despite these horrors I longed for a Carola atrocity. The tyrant of fashion had enslaved me before the age of ten. However, Mama remained adamant. I was marched off to school each day in a broad-brimmed sailor hat with streamers down my back. It was very humiliating.

Another freak caprice that suddenly took the Colegio Central by storm was even more absurd. White stockings and black ankle-strap shoes were popular with children at that time, but one morning a sophisticated little girl named Dolores Castillo arrived in class with black stockings and white shoes. In some other child this might have passed unnoticed. But Dolores was a haughty, bored young minx, whose every action aroused the most intense interest. Not only did her page-boy bob curl *under*, while other girls wore home-made corkscrew ringlets that shot out Zulu-fashion on all sides, but her slender legs encased in the long dark hose looked twice as dainty and fragile. Instantly the school was divided in two camps: the enraptured new black-leggers, and a minority of die-hard whites. As in the case of the bonnets, I was left on the side-lines, for, alas, I wore socks. Also—supreme onus! —my hair was tied in pig-tail braids, the sort that I had longed for once, at Solymár.

The third incident connected with my short term at the school became responsible for its shortness. In all fairness it must be stated that the Colegio Central was not necessarily implicated in the discovery, made by my mother, that I was infested with head-lice. But the discovery severed my relations with that institution.

"It's those Arab girls!" said Mama, with deplorable intolerance. IT might very well have been the Chamaca or my faithful friend Petronilo.

But the practical results were the same. While my locks suffered immersion in a basin of petrol, a formal letter gave notice to the school that conditions had arisen which prevented my further attendance. Meanwhile, my hair profited handsomely through the gasoline bath. Not only did the lice drop off as loathsome cadavers, but my head emerged in a halo of shimmering gold.

"We should have done this long ago," mused Mama, whose constant lament was that blondes turned mousy between shampoos.

32

WHILE ROME BURNS

In view of the incompleted school term, Father decided that my leisure had best be spent in learning how to swim. There was no telling, he maintained, when one might be faced with shipwreck, or just a spill while sitting in a rowing-boat. Nor did he admit that living in an inland city far from the sea was an excuse for not knowing how to hold one's head above water.

In keeping with his belief he rose early each morning and took my brothers to the *alberca*, a body of water fed by fresh springs in the very centre of the town. A bath-house had been built round this natural pool, with diving-boards, a trapeze, and a spectators' gallery at street level. The place bustled with energy and athletic prowess. I had no taste for it.

After some ineffectual whimpering I found myself one day in a *maillot* suit beside Sylvester and Arnim at the shallow end of the pool. Papa counted to three, and we all stepped off into glacial water. It was a shattering experience. I bawled.

"You must kick!" Papa admonished. "And move your arms, like this!" He splashed and performed elegantly for my benefit, but all in vain. I continued bawling.

My brothers hauled me out and dropped my chilled form on the sun-warmed ledge, then hurled themselves back into the pool, gurgling and cavorting in preposterous fashion.

"It's not cold," they crowed, though I could see their teeth chatter.

To my disgust, Papa and a number of wet strangers agreed with them. This was sheer duplicity. For the record, the crystal-clear water of Monterrey's *alberca* measured (and still measures) 20 degrees Centigrade, which is cold. In fact, as the British Consul affirmed one morning after withdrawing a bluish toe, "damn' cold."

No amount of shivering, however, altered our daily programme of "a plunge before breakfast." Bright and early we lined up at the shallow end (this was a concession to my inexperience, as the others all would have preferred diving) and, hand in hand, hopped into the miserable pool. By now I had stopped howling, since this in no way diminished my plight. Instead, out of desperation, I kicked and churned the waters in an effort to keep warm. But I could not swim.

Papa grew troubled about this. The boys had given him no difficulty. They responded to discipline and could, when necessary, be dealt with roughly. But towards me Papa was not stern. Either because I was the youngest or, more likely, because I was a girl, he found himself unable to punish or even reprove me. The most he achieved, when some misdeed of mine pained or angered him, was to frown. Papa's "serious" look, I called it, when I knew myself to be in disgrace.

My inability to swim gave rise to many a "serious" look. While Sylvester and Arnim had mastered this art by dint of being tossed into deep water and forced to strike for the shore, I retired invariably to my ledge. Sun-drenched and secure, I waited here for the others to be done with their Spartan antics.

"Why not get Minka some water-wings?" proposed our mother, in order to put an end to the deadlock.

Papa disapproved of such makeshifts. But he hit upon a canny idea. If I learned to swim, and crossed the deepest part of the pool, he would give me one hundred silver pesos.

Mama looked shocked. "Must we resort to bribery?" she asked. "Since when do children receive payment for what is meant to do them good?"

Father grinned sheepishly, admitting his shameful indulgence towards me. But he did not withdraw the offer.

As it happened, I knew next to nothing about money. A shiny copper in the pocket of my pinafore was to me a symbol of affluence. So long as I did not lack the humble wherewithal to buy a stick of *charamuzca* from the candy-pedlar on the corner, I felt eminently solvent. But one hundred of anything (including bottle-caps or cigar-bands) looked big to me. There was no holding me now.

The next morning it was marvellous to behold the way I gulped, puffed, and struggled to keep afloat. A few days later I ventured towards the deeper section of the pool, where the water reached to my shoulders, my chin, and finally over the top of my head. All through this, of course, my brothers hovered near, urging me on and all but turning cartwheels so as to whip up my courage. For they were as dazzled by the thought of the prize money as though they could hear it jingling in their own pockets.

It was hard going. But by the end of a week I mastered a

primitive sort of locomotion, which got me, dog-fashion, under way.

"That's it!" the boys cheered. "Keep on kicking!"

By now I had an audience of sympathetic spectators. Swimmers, bath-house attendants, the barber, the masseuse, and even a policeman or two held their breath as I steered finally towards the centre of the pool. Now I was far beyond my depth, for the shadow of the high diving-board fell just where the water looked darkest. I paddled on, aware that only a few feet away Papa swam silently beside me. I could hear whistling and applause from the upper gallery, where spectators had gathered to watch the last lap. It seemed to be quite a show, and I was unquestionably its heroine.

"Well, well," I thought, and stopped kicking. "One hundred pesos—easy!"

Whereupon I sank.

A wild commotion was set up as, on all sides, diving figures left their perches and joined my father in fishing me up from the deep. I went down not three but half a dozen times in the ensuing mêlée before some one at last had hold of my middle, propelling me like a rubber ball to shore. Once on dry land I recovered quickly, though I had had a severe fright.

"Too bad," I heard a medley of voices, "she didn't win her prize!"

"What happened?" Papa asked sadly. "What made you go wrong so near your goal?"

I did not know exactly. But somewhere in my consciousness lurked a realization that my failure sprang from that brief instant of self-contemplation when I had seen myself as the centre of attention. I had become drugged with sudden importance, and my ego had begun to preen itself in anticipation of glory. Previous to that moment all my powers of concentration had been fixed in single-mindedness upon the task before me. *I was swimming.* Then my ears caught the applause I had not yet earned, and, instead of ignoring it, I had listened. It was thus that I lost mastery of myself and went down.

Of course, I could not have explained any of this, yet I knew it was true. I also felt that what had happened to me was vaguely discreditable, and so I preferred not to talk about it.

A week later the test was repeated. This time I sternly kept my head, disregarding the siren-song of a joyous and cheering gallery. I negotiated the length of the pool with never a faltering stroke.

The money went into an account for me at the Milmo bank, and I still had only coppers to buy *charamuzcas.*

33

VISIT TO PARRAS

"I have to go to Parras," said Papa one day. He referred to his annual trip to the Madero plantations at Parras, Coahuila, in which he had a small financial interest. To my delight, he added, "I think I'll take Minka along."

We went by train to Saltillo, capital of Coahuila, where—as luck would have it—we ran smack into the religious fiesta of El Cristo Rey. This celebration was traditionally held in the town square, within sight of the Cathedral, the Municipal Palace, the Casino, and the gaol. Pilgrims attended from far and near, arriving on trucks, hay-wagons, or mule-back, as well as on foot. At the height of the festive proceedings a sea of humanity ebbed and flowed through the winding streets until the town threatened to burst at its seams. All was gaiety and noise. Fruit vendors hawked their produce while above glowing braziers the aroma of sizzling *enchiladas* perfumed the breeze. Round-eyed Indian children stood about in an agony of indecision, weighing the merits of an edible sugar cow against the puppet-maker's loose-jointed *títeres* that danced and performed extraordinary tricks at the pull of a string. In the end their innocent gluttony won, with subsequent pangs of regret when the confectioner's titbit had melted down their gullets while the marionettes still dangled enticingly from the Punch-and-Judy stall.

In Saltillo we were met by Doña Pilar Madero and her husband, Mr Richardson. They had arrived in their brightly lacquered Renault, just in time for the torchbearers' procession and the evening fireworks, which we planned to observe from the Casino terrace. The Revolution? In Saltillo, too, no one seemed to have time for it.

With the fall of darkness a glow of Bengal lights announced the climax of the festivities. The stridor of human voices which had filled the air throughout the day seemed to redouble with the detonation of hundreds of Roman candles. The ensuing racket was ear-splitting.

"*Ay, qué bonito!*" cheered the crowd. "How pretty!"

Continuously the explosion of rockets rent the night, splashing the sky with a blaze of pyrotechnics, while here and there sputtering catherine-wheels contributed their luminous glow.

It was now, at the height of the jubilation, that the good pilgrims bethought themselves of Him who was being honoured in this gala manner. Stampeding through the church portals, they fetched the holy statue of El Cristo Rey from its murky altar niche and mounted it on a platform supplied with rollers. Next, chanting a pious canticle, they joyously pushed the statue out into the square.

"*Viva Cristo Rey!*" cried the spectators, happy to see the revered image abroad to enjoy its own fiesta.

I was swept off my feet by the general exhilaration. At the top of my voice I sang the first tune that popped into my head, which was the roundelay of the *Santos Peregrinos.* It was a fine song, albeit intended for Christmas.

Doña Pilar too was singing, though I could distinguish neither words nor tune. She had one of those hooting sopranos that emerged through pursed lips and shook in the upper register.

"Wooo—oo—oo!" sang Doña Pilar. Her brassy treble melted away in the prevailing uproar.

It was well past midnight when Mr Richardson coughed discreetly and called to mind the long drive back to Parras.

"But no," said his wife, "we cannot go until to-morrow!"

"To-morrow?"

"Yes. There is a dawn service at the Cathedral. Remember, we promised Don Clemente to attend and pray for rain."

Don Clemente was the despotic but efficient major-domo on the Madero estates. His wishes and pronouncements were law, not only to his employers but to other landholders of the region. Paradoxically, for me the name of this authoritarian character was associated with the well-known jingle describing a crowd-following toady:

Adónde vá Clemente?
Adónde vá la gente. . . .

(Which way is Clemente going?
The way everybody goes. . . .)

Far from fitting the above description, the formidable overseer issued orders like a Tsar. The crops had been poor, and the vines were withering on their stocks. Don Clemente needed rain, and, by God, somebody was going to pray for it.

Though the city was crowded, rooms were made available for us at the Gran Hotel Coahuila, a dilapidated rookery that had seen better days. We slept fitfully under badly ripped mosquito *pabellones* (canopies) which, far from affording protection, served as insect traps.

By 4.30 A.M. Doña Pilar was back on her feet, handsomely arrayed in black silk, gloves, and shawl, with a high comb in her hair. While her husband, Papa, and I dozed on into mid-morning, she bustled off to church and dealt single-handed with the Parras irrigation problem.

"I offered up a full litany to San Isidro, the Water Patron," she confided to us at breakfast. "If that doesn't help, nothing will!"

By ten o'clock we stood on the street, waiting for the Renault to drive up. It was some twenty minutes later that Jacinto, the chauffeur, arrived with unhappy news.

"El carro está descompuesto—no quiere andar!" ("The car is decomposed—it does not wish to run!")

Jacinto accompanied his disclosure with graphic gestures. He had been a muleteer in younger days and he knew about the stubbornness of pack-animals. When a Mexican donkey did not wish to run you were up against it. The Renault, Jacinto intimated, was equally hopeless.

Fortunately both Mr Richardson and Papa were of mechanical bent. Their combined tinkering put the Renault in order, and, shortly after lunch, we continued on our way.

The road leading from Saltillo was macadamized for a distance of some forty miles. Beyond this there lay open desert, dry, dust-laden, and furrowed by centuries of ox-cart travel. Over this arid terrain we jolted and bounced at a merry clip, accompanied (though scarcely aided) by Jacinto's deafening klaxon. To Doña Pilar's chauffeur the function of an automobile horn lay not so much in its warning power as its irresistible expression of the joy of life. Certainly the wilderness through which we careered at a whizzing tempo presented no conflicting traffic. But Jacinto was happy. How else was he to proclaim this state of his emotions if not with intermittent blasts of his horn?

As the afternoon waned our eyes were dazzled by the desert sunset that plunged the horizon into a vast sea of flame. Under its crimson glow the oasis of the rich Madero empire sprang suddenly into view, sprawling beyond the little Indian village of El Rosario. Doña Pilar pointed to the neatly walled cemetery.

"Here is our family burial ground. And there is the votive chapel where we keep the Santo Madero, the splinter of the True Cross, from which our name is derived."

A short drive beyond El Rosario brought us to Doña Pilar's home. It was one of eight spacious manor-houses, built almost exactly alike and set back from an avenue of towering poplars. From the appearance of the formal landscape, with its flowering and grassy borders, one would not have guessed that there was a lack of water.

"There are deep springs at this spot," Mr Richardson explained, "but they do not reach to the vineyards."

The whole setting was one of strange contradictions. To begin with, the ancient houses—built from the same blueprint—seemed to scream modern mass-production. Yet their design, the furnishings, and the character of the life within those thick stone walls all bespoke a survival of sheerest feudalism. Sameness of pattern and structure was here not an æsthetic blunder, but the deliberate embodiment of family solidarity. On this soil lived the Madero clan in self-sufficient and splendid isolation.

It was from here that the humanitarian Francisco had torn himself loose, to bid farewell to patriarchal grandeeism. Leaving wealth and privilege behind, he was at this very moment fighting the poor man's battle in the vanguard of the Revolution.

In the family circle they did not speak of Francisco except to lament his misguided actions. For at Parras the clock stood still and the old ways survived. To walk under the portico of Doña Pilar's house was to enter a mediæval world of slightly tarnished pomp, of stateliness by candlelight.

At dinner that evening the Madero brothers gathered about the festive board. There was Don Evaristo, who bore the name of the father of the clan. Beside him sat his beautiful wife and their blonde daughters, Jesusita and Abelina (the younger children, Catalina and Yolanda, were still of nursery age and not in evidence). Don José and Don Ernesto, wearing chaps and silver spurs, strutted about and aired a favourite Parras boast.

"Our fruit harvests would put California out of business, if only we could get water into Coahuila!"

"I prayed for rain," announced Doña Pilar, her face set in unshakable composure. With San Isidro's intercession the liquidation of California's grape and citrus industry was all but an accomplished fact.

Later that night the gentlemen went for a stroll in the moonlight, past the *bodega* with its wine-press and huge storage vaults.

Here and there they stopped to sample a keg or to observe the workmen steaming their bodies prior to taking over the late shift at the vats. Needless to say, the ripe and succulent muscatel grape was trampled—in immemorial fashion—with bare feet.

Back at the main house the womenfolk gathered in Doña Pilar's Louis-Quinze drawing-room. Here, to the accompaniment of an all but tuneless dulcimer, the undaunted dowager gave a song recital. With sustained and raucous hoots she rendered the *Ballad of the Marqués de Aguayo.*

Although disguised as a love-song, the *Ballad of the Marqués de Aguayo* was a ghost-story of blood-curdling overtones. It concerned a Spanish knight who, during viceregal times, had settled with his pretty bride on the lands that to-day made up the Madero domain. Wealth and a retinue of servants surrounded the young Marquesa, but she pined for the lover from whose arms she had been torn by her parents' desire for a rich (even if ageing and cruel) son-in-law. Then, one day (*Stanza II*), a new equerry entered the service of the Marqués. He was handsome, bold, and noticeably attentive to the Marquesa. The lady's spirits picked up. The alert husband grew suspicious. He plotted a journey to Saltillo (over the very road we had just travelled with the ebullient Jacinto) and arranged for a change of horses at intervals along the way. Then, at dusk, he spoke elaborate farewells and ostensibly set out. But after dark he returned and trapped the lovers, who had, of course, kept their secret tryst. From here on the tale grew gory and spine-chilling. With his poniard the Marqués fell upon his rival, killing him instantly. Next, he chopped off his wife's fair head and tossed it from a turret window, after which he mounted a charger and tore into the night. But the end was not yet (*Stanza III*), for a new frenzy now seized the murderer. As he sped on, pursued by an avenging conscience, the urge to blot out every trace of his deed drove him to further bloodshed. Each time he paused along the route to exchange horses he thrust his dagger through the waiting groom's breast, leaving behind him a trail of death. At dawn the rider and his last mount reached the outskirts of Saltillo, but both collapsed with lungs bursting from the mad chase. Such was the *Ballad of the Marqués de Aguayo.*

Except for the epilogue.

Ever since the harrowing legend had become part of the region's folk-lore it was said that the vast Aguayo estates were haunted. When the Madero clan, descended from the Marquesa's kin, came into the inheritance they found a ready-made ghost on the premises. To this day a wailing woman in white was said to trail on moonlit nights over the parapet of whichever manor-house harboured a thwarted romance.

Doña Pilar finished her song on this lugubrious note, just as the men returned from their inspection tour. As they filed in, one by one, followed by the overseer and his assistant, the pall left by our hostess's grim recital lifted somewhat. I, for one, was grateful to hear burly laughter and voices warmed by recently tasted vintages.

"Now for a nightcap from a different land," said Mr Richardson, opening a cabinet and setting out a bottle of Scotch.

He rang a bell, and a servant entered with a tray of exquisitely etched glasses, each an heirloom of priceless quality. While the drinks were passed round Don Evaristo cleared his throat prior to offering a toast. But he was halted by a shriek and the splintering of glass. The servant, threading his way through the crowded room, had accidentally knocked a goblet out of Doña Pilar's hand.

It was no minor catastrophe. The costly Venetian piece, part of a crystal service that was used only on rare occasions, was irreplaceable. But Doña Pilar, after her initial shriek, kept her composure. Smiling at her husband and speaking "the English," she cried out, with a little squeal, "Oh—my veesky!"

The gloom that had threatened was lifted. As the men pressed about the gallant hostess to proffer their own glasses, the servant swept out the debris. A small fortune had for an instant lain shattered on the floor. Doña Pilar's eyelids closed momentarily in sharp awareness, then reopened, bland and serene. Her hand brushed lightly through the air as she reached for a new drink. The broken treasure was treasure no more. It was a piffling mound of rubbish.

"And now, my little chicks"—Doña Pilar turned from the adult guests to her circle of nephews and nieces (she had no children of her own)—"off to bed, *adelante*, *adelante*!"

Her gentle mandate included me too, for I was to sleep in the guest wing of the Evaristo house with Jesusita, Abelina, and their already slumbering baby sisters.

Salustia, Doña Pilar's own ancient *pilmama*, or one-time wet-nurse, shooed us out of the parlour into the long corridor. Here we were each given an old-fashioned candlestick with handle and saucer. Thus equipped, we trotted obediently along the columned loggia that led to the mansion next-door.

I did not sleep well that night, for my dreams were enlivened by an eerie white spook that fluttered and stirred in the moonlit frame of the tall window. It looked like a badly frightened spook, too, what with the sound of the Marqués de Aguayo's horse beating at its spectral heels.

And once, for a fleeting instant, I thought I saw the vengeful knight himself. He was clad in sixteenth-century doublet and hose, though his face appeared to be that of Don Clemente, the major-domo.

34

I ENTER THE CONVENT

THE PARRAS trip became the deciding factor in my parents' decision to enrol me at the Sacré-Cœur convent. The reason was not only Doña Pilar's urgent counsel in this regard, but the fact that the Evaristo children—who were beautifully reared—attended this French school.

We drove to the convent on a Saturday afternoon, with Mama and Papa dressed in their severest clothes. I too was attired in keeping with the gravity of the occasion; my navy-blue frock with its sailor collar lacked all frivolous touches. At the last moment the Chamaca, who brushed my hair, obeyed an inspired impulse and replaced the ribbons with a neat hair-slide.

Never shall I forget the smallest detail of that day, or the years that followed, in the monastic atmosphere. For to enter the convent was to embark upon a new existence in a strange and secret world.

To begin with, the building itself fascinated me. It was a Spanish Colonial structure not unlike the *bodega* at Parras which Papa had just inspected. There was the same centre quadrangle surrounded by a colonnade in whose shadows a vast store of wine kegs could conceivably be kept. But here the resemblance ended, for the outside walls of the convent presented a contradiction to its architectural design. For some forgotten reason the old stone walls were painted a bright chrome yellow, while the shutters and main portal boasted an extrovert and cheerful green. This colour scheme was incongruously reminiscent of Castle Schönbrunn on the outskirts of Vienna, upon whose venerable façade a Biedermeier emperor's fancy had run riot. Here was a nunnery with overtones by Offenbach and Franz Schubert.

At the sound of an iron knocker we were admitted by the sister doorkeeper whom I would later know as "Madre Cortina." In Spanish, *cortina* means curtain, which admirably suited a religious concierge in her function as an intermediary between the secrecy of the convent's inner life and the profane outside world.

It happened, however, that this was the nun's real patronymic, its fitness being entirely fortuitous.

Having passed through the main portal, we found ourselves in a vestibule with no other opening save a latticed panel that swung noiselessly under a stained-glass arch. In a low whisper the doorkeeper asked our names, whereupon Papa presented his card.

"But yes," she cried in seeming recognition, "you have an appointment with our Mère-Générale!"

With this, she speedily escorted us through the latticed panel and down a long arcade. As our steps resounded over the stone-flagged floor my attention was caught by the silent movements of the cowled figure beside us; Madre Cortina walked on padded, slippered feet. This soundlessness sharpened my hearing. I found myself growing tensely alert.

After admitting us to a reception parlour the sister doorkeeper bowed and scurried off to fetch the Mother-General. In the interval that followed, my parents settled themselves upon a stiff sofa that faced a gilt-framed oleograph of Jesus (in flowing scarlet robe) at Gethsemane. There were votive candles burning in the corners of the room, and in the exact centre of the bare floor stood a table with a book on it. I opened this book and found it to be a photograph album with pictures of school alumnæ in white communion dresses and veils.

"Look," I gasped, holding the volume up for Mama's inspection, "how pretty!"

Mama looked, but she seemed displeased with the saintly maids in their edifying poses.

"Don't ever let me catch you rolling your eyes like that!" she warned, pointing to a seraphic creature whose hands were folded piously under an upturned chin. How did Mama know that I was already fancying myself in that particular attitude? She seemed to guess that I could hardly wait to practise lifting my lashes demurely heavenward.

Her cool tone brought me back to earth. I turned for solace in Papa's direction, but there was no comfort in his eyes. Only now a sudden realization struck home: both my mother and father had been overtaken by regret. They were too worldly for a setting such as this. The bleak parlour, the sombre oleograph on the wall, the faded album that had captivated my immature taste, all seemed to oppress them. I could see that they were pushing themselves into doing something which they did not fundamentally want to do.

Even as this discovery began to weigh down my spirits the

door opened and a tall, angular figure swept into the room. I was at first reminded of a portrait of the fifteenth-century monk Savonarola, though, of course, this white-coiffed, black-veiled personage was a nun.

"Mère Isabelle de Campou, our Mother-General," announced the sister doorkeeper from the threshold, retiring forthwith.

My mother and father rose, while I stepped forward and dropped a curtsy. At this, the Mother-General burst into a blast of Gallic eloquence. "*Ah, mes amis, mes amis, mes amis*," she buzzed in a hissing crescendo, "this is absolutely *splendide*!" One thing was certain, she was no master of Spanish.

After greeting my parents Mère de Campou turned to me with an effervescence that seemed out of keeping with her grave eyes in their dark hollows, and the sharp bony nose. This nose, I observed, was slightly off centre, its tip being deflected towards the right side of an exceedingly virile face. The whole thin yet powerful silhouette of the Mother-General rather overwhelmed me. I sensed here an indomitable will, backed by boundless energy. Something of that will registered with me now as the nun's fingers closed over mine, with a faint and subtly forcing lift, to convey that this hand must be kissed. I recognized the gesture, bred into Hungarians by centuries of formalism. It was with pride that I acknowledged it.

A sage smile spread over the Savonarola countenance. The Mother-General and I were going to get on together.

The ensuing conference with my parents was supposedly carried on in Spanish. But Mère de Campou's deficiency with regard to this tongue was such that the discussion soon bogged down. Papa suggested going on in French. At this the nun grew voluble with joy, releasing a flow of fabulous eloquence. Her vocabulary was magnificent and explosive.

It developed in the course of these dialectics that Papa's position with the Electric Power Company was no secret to the conventual authorities, for the Mother-General repeatedly raised her fearsome eyebrows and sputtered, "Tsk, tsk, tsk—such prices we pay for the kilowatts!"

She also touched lightly on plans for a new cloister to be built against the slope of the Obispado mountain.

"The view is something *extraordinaire*!" was her lyrical endorsement of the site. "Already many prominent persons have made generous donations. . . ." But (and a shadow fell on the Mother-General's face as she came to the crux of the matter) of what use was a fine new building on a mountain-side if city traffic did not go in that direction? A special inter-urban line with a spur leading right up to the projected convent's portal—"would it not solve the question in a manner *admirable*?"

Papa allowed that it would. At the moment, however, he was more interested in the school's present location, its curriculum, tuition fees, and other minutiæ that were to affect his daughter's life.

"Tut, tut, tut, tut, tut," exclaimed the nun in a descending chromatic scale. "*Ça s'arrangera!*" With a flick of the hand she dismissed such tiresome details.

I had never before heard anyone say "Tut, tut, tut, tut, tut!" Nor did my parents appear altogether at ease or able to make a suitable retort. But Mère de Campou was a past-mistress at winding up an awkward situation. Almost effortlessly she obtained the signatures that placed me under the tutelage of the Sacré-Cœur. Though I could sense throughout the negotiations that my parents were inwardly straining to withdraw from their half-hearted purpose, the Mother-General obviously never entertained the slightest doubt regarding the outcome. It was a genteel, masked duel, performed in impeccable style.

"Our girls have identification numbers," said Mère de Campou at one point in the proceedings. She pressed a firm finger against my collar-bone. "Yours will be sixty-nine."

I was startled that she had not consulted any sort of tabulation or notebook; the number had popped from the tip of her tongue. I also noticed a peculiar medicinal odour on the nun's breath. She was sucking a cough-drop.

"There are specifications with regard to the uniform," she elucidated further, drawing a key from her pocket and opening a near-by cupboard. "We have here a correctly dressed *poupée* to serve as a model."

With this she produced a doll, about fourteen inches in height, clad in the regulation pleated black skirt with shoulder straps that flared at the top and contrasted sharply with the white blouse of ribbed piqué.

"You will observe that there are three double tucks across the front of the blouse. It must be exactly so—three double tucks."

A faint smile flitted across Mama's lips, and I knew what it meant. To Mama nothing in the world ever had to be "exactly so"; she could always think of half a dozen other ways. I was immediately alarmed. Obsessed with childhood's fierce urge to conform, I worried lest liberties be taken with my blouse, making me look different from the other children. It was my passionate desire to be turned out exactly like the *poupée* in Mère de Campou's hands.

Happily it was the Mother-General who solved the problem by announcing that uniforms were ordered in the convent's own tailor's shop. If measurements were taken now everything would be ready within forty-eight hours.

Again Mama raised a question. "This cloth," she inquired, fingering the doll's stiff skirt, "it's heavy wool. Do the girls wear the same thing in spring and early summer?"

Mère de Campou was taken aback. Climate, I vaguely grasped, had no place in the religious life. The nuns themselves wore their voluminous habits and veils year in, year out, with never a concession to temperature. The students, however, need not dispense with comfort.

"But *certainement*," was the quick reply, "a tropical worsted may be ordered for later in the season. It will, of course, take a little more time." The convent seamstress, it was evident, had only one kind of material on hand. To satisfy Mama's irregular demand, a bolt of lighter-weight cloth would have to be obtained.

A dossier of further essentials filled the next twenty minutes. Black stockings and shoes were obligatory; the shoes might be kid or calf for every day, patent leather for dress. Then there was the long black veil of sturdy net bordered with lace, for church wear. And now a serious matter came up, as the Mother-General addressed herself to me: "Are you confirmed? And have you received First Communion?"

I stared blankly, while Mama answered. "Oh, not yet! She is not yet ten. We thought——"

There was a slight tightening of Mère de Campou's lips as she explained the Sacré-Cœur policy of leading children to the Sacrament at the age of eight, if not earlier. It was plain that my defection in this regard would be attended to.

"We will talk about the Communion dress when the time comes," the Mother-General passed over the matter. "Meanwhile there is need of a white uniform with all white accessories for Sundays and special Feast Days. For this outfit the veil is circular instead of square, and silk rather than cotton."

I was beginning to feel like a bride preparing her trousseau. Never had my personal wardrobe entailed such punctilious consideration. Needless to say, I basked in all this limelight which endowed me with such unaccustomed importance.

The subject of clothes having been disposed of, Mère de

Campou talked about other needs. "All our pupils have their own table cutlery, each piece engraved with name and number."

I saw Mama jotting things down in her morocco memorandum-book.

"A napkin ring," the nun continued the inventory, "a silver drinking-cup——"

The list seemed to go on indefinitely, including such items as a missal, a rosary, a chain and medallion with the likeness of my patron saint.

At this point we ran into another snag. I had been born on November 1, which was All Saints' Day and entitled me not to one patron alone, but to the combined favour of the heavenly host. That is, all the beatified company of saints would make my welfare their special concern if, according to ecclesiastic canon, I had been properly named *Santos*. Alas, I was not. As had been manifested years ago in Solymár, my parents' liberalism rejected such orthodox compulsions.

"What a lost opportunity!" deplored the Mother-General. "By invoking the Holy Virgin, the double name of María de los Santos would have been as good as a dispensation from Purgatory."

Mama raised a slight objection. "It seems so arbitrary to prescribe a rigid choice of name for each day of the year. There are changes in fashion."

Papa supported her. "Most early Christian names are too complex for modern use—Theodosia, Melchisedech, Polycarp!"

"What about Leap Year?" Mama asked unexpectedly. "Is there a saint for February the twenty-ninth?"

Mère de Campou preferred to ignore this question, either because it struck her as flippant, or because theologians were not yet in agreement on the matter. Father further obscured things by asking, "Since canonization continues through the centuries, what happens when the saints outnumber the days of the year?"

"They already do," said the Mother-General severely. "We honour them simultaneously, sometimes two and three at one time."

I sighed with relief. Mama and Papa had learned something they obviously had not known, namely, that there was no ceiling on saints, and these venerable beings cheerfully doubled up when there was a shortage in days assigned to them. But I remained heavy-hearted with regard to my name. María de los Santos—to think that so fair and sonorous an appendage was my birthright! I profoundly regretted its loss. In secret I resolved to lay claim to it none the less, calling myself María de los Santos among strangers and during soliloquies held in the privacy of my room. By so doing I might yet establish some sort of rapport with the angels and archangels who, after all, were in duty bound to take me in their charge.

The matter of my medallion, however, remained unsolved. No jeweller on earth had ever struck off a composite image of God's company of saints.

35

MONASTIC ROUTINES

My FIRST day of convent life began the following Monday at "eight minus five." This was the way Mère de Campou put it in her precise French.

I was lodged in a dormitory on the second floor, with some twenty-odd children of my own age. Like myself, they were mostly fourth-formers. Other girls of different age groups lived in similar halls that ran the length of the building. All dormitories were divided into small cubicles, with heavy muslin curtains separating each narrow white bed from its neighbour. There were chairs at the foot of the beds, but no other pieces of furniture. Special wardrobe rooms held clothes cupboards and shelves for our belongings. Beyond these lay the community wash-room and baths.

While unpacking my small trunk I learned a preliminary lesson on the subject of monastic caste. A young nun with red hands and short stubby fingernails came to assist me in my cubicle. Her friendliness was weighted with humility.

"I am Sister Elena," she said. "If you need something please come to me. I have the night watch on Mondays, Wednesdays, and Fridays."

The fact that she spoke of herself as Sister and not Mother or Mère Elena puzzled me, as did her outward appearance. Beyond a doubt here was a nun of lesser category than Isabelle de Campou or even Madre Cortina in the porter's lodge. Her coif was starched but not fluted into a ripple of pleats such as framed the gaunt face of the Mother-General. Nor did she have a silver chain and crucifix about her neck. But what really disconcerted me was the strange manner in which Sister Elena wore her habit, for the black top-skirt was folded up from the hem and pinned back against a waistband round the nun's middle. This exposed a considerable frontage of coarse blue denim petticoat while the rear, where the upper skirt bunched downward to the floor, looked like the folded wings of some oversized beetle.

"Why do you wear your dress like that?" I had to ask.

The nun flushed. "I am a lay sister, serving my novitiate," she explained. "I scrub floors and do other work that is hard on clothes."

This made me think. "But if *you* scrub floors, what do the servants do?"

Her lashes fluttered as she closed her eyes and smiled. "We lay sisters are the servants, my child. We remain servants until we take our vows, and fresh novices fill our place."

There was much more to be learned from Sister Elena, particularly regarding the freedom of choice still enjoyed by an apprentice nun. If, before taking her vows, she tired of menial chores and the severities of a cloistered regimen, there was nothing to stop her from returning to the outer world. Even her hair remained intact, for it was not cut off until the instant of irrevocable consecration.

I was avid for further revelations, but a bell clanged loudly, and Sister Elena warned: "That's the call to assembly. Hurry, or you'll be late!"

She propelled me gently from my cubicle, though not before running a brush over my hair and flicking imaginary particles of dust from my blouse and skirt. My scalp hurt from the unaccustomed tight braiding prescribed by convent rule, but I felt eminently proper and neat.

The stairway teemed with children headed for the assembly-hall, a large L-shaped wing, at the apex of which the Mother-General waited on a dais with a lectern before it. From this vantage point she could survey both arms of the great L, carefully scrutinizing each pupil that walked in, the younger ones coming through the short wing, while the senior girls used the main door.

At the sight of Mère de Campou I could not repress a smile of recognition, but the Mother-General gave no sign of response. She stood very erect and tall, peering with owlish eyes over a pair of gold-rimmed spectacles that sat low on her nose. On Saturday, in the little reception-room, she had worn no spectacles.

It became apparent to me almost at once that the assembly-hall was used for the morning study period, since there were desks placed in pairs along both sides of each wing. These desks did not resemble ordinary schoolroom fixtures, nor had they been fastened to the flooring. They were high, four-legged tables of light oak, with chairs pushed under them. Each table-top lifted, desk-fashion, to disclose a capacious hollow for books and other paraphernalia.

Automatically the long file of students passed down the centre aisles and, with a minimum of confusion, each girl found her appointed place. I alone was left floundering about, since no desk had yet been assigned to me. For an instant I was gripped by a feeling of panic. The well-ordered procession of children became suddenly distorted into a stampeding horde, in the midst of which I was hopelessly lost. To make matters worse, I could perceive the owlish orbs of Isabelle de Campou fixed like gimlets upon me. At this point some one nudged my elbow and I heard a whisper: "What's your number?"

I turned and looked up at a big olive-skinned girl with nicely shaped white teeth. "My n-n-number?" I stammered, nonplussed. "I don't know—I haven't any number."

The big girl giggled. "We all do, silly! Wait—I'll look inside your collar."

Even as she reached for the neck-band of my blouse I remembered Saturday's interview. "It's sixty-nine!" I breathed excitedly.

"Then your desk is over there on the left; those are the uneven ones."

My confidence had been restored. A moment later I spotted seventy-one, before which stood a dark-haired girl of about my own age, named Amparo Garza. The desk beside her, along the inner wall, was empty. With an air of casualness I took possession of it. As I did so my eyes travelled towards the dais where stood the Mother-General. And now something unforeseen happened; Mère de Campou's spectacles dropped from her nose on to the lectern as she bobbed her head in vigorous approbation. The smile that lighted her bony face was cast unmistakably in my direction, and its glow wove a momentary aura about me, causing curious heads to turn. No longer was I just a newcomer; I was an *approved* newcomer. A minute earlier the collective stares of some two hundred eyes might have disconcerted me and led to a flood of tears. But now, with a desk and chair of my own, as well as the Mother-General's unspoken approval, my ghosts were laid.

In the row immediately ahead a girl with curly yellow hair whispered, "I am María Rivero. What's your name?"

I had scarcely answered when other introductions were hissed from behind me and across the aisle: Rosalía Muguerza, Margarita Canseco, Carmen Odriozola, Luz Gonzales, and an indeterminate number ending in Martínez, Villareal, Treviño, and Zambrano. Several rows away I could see the big girl who had befriended me. Her name, I learned, was Aida Arredondo. And beyond her, side by side, sat Jesusita and Abelina Madero.

By now the assembly-hall had filled, and two nuns who brought up the rear silently closed the latticed doors. Along the outer walls of the L all windows were opened wide, admitting street noises and the moist but mild winter air. It was impossible, however, to see anything of the outside world beyond ankles and feet of passers-by or a strip of sky above, for the entire centre portion of each aperture was screened with Venetian slats. Unlike the doors, these shutters were rigid and could not be thrown ajar. The blur of sounds, movement, flower-scents, vendors' cries, and broken rays of light that filtered into our hidden world had a profound effect upon me throughout my convent life. My perceptions seemed to become sharpened by the very things I could not see, for they reached me only through my sense of smell and hearing.

The convent had its own sounds, all of them muted so as not to jar the claustral calm. The nuns never raised their voices to utter a command or reproof. Instead, they flicked a clapper from their pockets, and with it tapped out whatever signal was required. This clapper consisted of two tiny wooden blocks, no bigger than a match-box, connected by hinges and made to resemble a miniature prayer-book. To accent this resemblance many nuns pasted holy pictures on the inside of their clappers. Since the function of the wooden gadget was strictly disciplinary, the images of the saints took quite a beating throughout an average day of school. For the clapper clicked but faintly when we were summoned to prayer, yet it could drum out an angry tattoo if aroused by some show of childish misconduct.

Needless to say, the Mother-General's clapper surpassed all others in eloquence. From the opening of the morning assembly to the observance of vespers in the convent chapel her fingers operated the contraption with true virtuosity. In her hands it cajoled, praised, or scolded, leaving never the slightest doubt as to its staccato meaning.

"Click!" went the clapper now, calling us to silence. The Mother-General herself led the matin orisons: ". . . Sainte Marie, Mère de Dieu, prie pour nous pécheurs——"

Although Papa's origin was French, and I had heard the language in early childhood, it fell upon my ears as something new. I found myself unable to join in the prayer, and my heart sank.

Fear gripped me, lest I be left out of the magic circle and banned from the vast solidarity about me. I felt lonely.

The voices had paused for breath, then resumed with the Pater Noster. This was recited with the same nasal intonation: "Notre Père, qui es au ciel——"

My situation was unbearable. Resolutely I followed the lip movements of my nearest neighbour and imitated the sounds issuing from her throat. With even slight concentration it was possible for me to leap, as it were, upon each of her syllables, getting a firm hold on its tail. Thus I seemingly synchronized my facial contortions with those about me, yet actually trailing the merest fraction of a beat behind.

After prayers the Mother-General delivered a short speech, ostensibly in Spanish, though all her idioms and her intonations were hopelessly French. She began with an outline of the day's curriculum, but soon lapsed into a curtain lecture on incivility. A number of art students, it appeared, had laughed out loud when their teacher, Mother Piccard, fell over an easel. Not only did such rudeness show poor breeding, but it touched on blasphemy when directed against the religious cloth. Tactfully, Mère de Campou mentioned no names. She advised the guilty ones to appear in her private study during morning recess, at "ten hours minus fifteen," to offer Mother Piccard their apologies. This would in no sense redress the wrong, nor were bad marks in deportment nullified thereby. But life in the Sacré-Cœur demanded strict observance of the amenities, and the offended Mother Piccard rightly refused to return to her classes before being given full satisfaction.

This matter being disposed of, Mère de Campou fumbled for the pocket in her voluminous skirts and brought forth her clapper. With a double click she issued a brief order: "Pinafores!"

At this a commotion was set up as all desk tops opened and each pupil donned a black and white checked garment that had lain neatly folded among the books. I thought the pinafores quite lovely; they had ruffled shoulders trimmed with white bands of Swiss embroidery which made the smaller children look like butterflies. On adolescents the effect was somewhat overwhelming.

During the donning of the school aprons I experienced an added thrill. A peep into the open desks about me revealed what appeared to be common practice; each girl within my range of vision had built a miniature altar in the centre space between her books and writing-blocks. In some cases there was no more than the tiny figurine of a patron saint with bits of paper lace or tinfoil for a frame. But other desks contained small vases of glass or porcelain, with a few blossoms or a sprig of fern kept alive in less than an inch of water. Still others boasted cardboard shrines surrounded by tinted sea-shells and diminutive candlesticks with tapers, such as might belong on birthday cakes. One girl named María de Lourdes had a replica of the famed Grotto, complete to its smallest detail, expertly anchored between her French grammar and the ruled notebook in which she practised her writing; in addition to the Virgin on her rock of papier-mâché there was a kneeling Bernadette under a festoon of tumbling Lilliput roses.

I was entranced. No sooner had the study period begun than I whispered furtively with my nearest neighbour and pumped her regarding the source of such treasure.

She eyed me with astonishment. "Didn't you bring anything from home?"

This put me on my mettle. I couldn't bear to expose either myself or my family by admission that we had no holy icons or other pietistic props. As a matter of fact, my memory fixed suddenly upon the votive picture of Maria Einsiedeln, a reproduction of which had been given me years ago by Grossmama.

"Oh, sure," I whispered back, composed. "I just haven't unpacked."

For the next quarter of an hour I took a mental inventory of the toys and knick-knacks in my room at home. Already several baubles suggested themselves as adornment for my desk altar, among these a dainty slipper of Dresden china stuffed with a velvet pincushion. By ripping out the pincushion I should have a handy receptacle for a sprig of pink San Diego vine or even a cluster of dwarf jasmine. The question of a patron saint would have to be settled by compromise; I intended setting up my chromo of Maria Einsiedeln.

36

THE CHRISTIAN MARTYRS

THE SACRÉ-CŒUR, or Society of the Sacred Heart, had been founded in 1800 at Amiens by Madeleine Sophie Barat (later canonized as St Madeleine Sophie) under the direction of a Jesuit priest, Joseph Désiré Varin. The purpose of the order was to "educate young ladies of the higher classes." With a network of more than 150 branches spread across the world, and a staff of no fewer than 6750 consecrated members, its spiritual mission carried with it an inescapable blend of French culture and French living patterns.

This was apparent at every stage of our daily routine. Except for Spanish composition and reading, all classes were taught in the tongue of the school's founder. Likewise during 'break' the children played hopscotch, skipped, or rolled croquet balls, keeping score in French.

There were two 'breaks' of about twenty minutes during the early part of the day. The first was at mid-morning, when every child received a cordial of excellent bitters or a glass of sherry; at the same time a tray of cream wafers was passed round, which were furtively split and licked from the inside where the fondant was the tastiest. We thoroughly enjoyed this mildly alcoholic spree, which gave us a grown-up, worldly feeling.

The second recess came at noon when we lined up for an orderly march into the refectory. Here, while an excellent meal was served by humble lay sisters who performed all catering tasks, a nun read aloud from the *Tales of the Christian Martyrs*.

The tales of the Christian martyrs were terrible, but the food was very good. Convent kitchens, indeed, call for superlatives, owing to the urge for perfection with which a nun applies herself to even the most trivial task. A large budget is no requisite. An apple cored and sliced becomes a work of art. A glazed carrot can be made to melt on the tongue like some priceless confection. Our Sacré-Cœur menus, in short, were memorable. Nowhere in the world have I eaten such fluffy pink Spanish rice garnished with sweet melon rind or slabs of banana browned in butter. There were succulent stews and ragouts with gravies of impeccable texture and flavour. In deference to Mexican custom a daily platter of *frijoles* appeared, either *fritos*, *refritos*, or *re-refritos*, depending on how much crisping the mashed bean could take. As for salads, desserts, and the final cup of foaming cinnamon cocoa—language fails me.

Two factors turned the simplest of these meals into epicurean feasts. The first and most valuable was the loving care with which all edibles were prepared. With true Gallic thrift the Sister Housekeeper marched off to market each day and shrewdly stretched her shopping allowance to its most profitable limits. Trundling back her well-stocked baskets, she devised ways of turning an inexpensive turnip or onion into a titbit of note. Nor did she lack originality in dressing up left-overs, for her battle against waste bordered on parsimony. Beyond doubt, the convent cook was a high priestess of her art.

Secondly, the device by which ordinary repasts were rendered extraordinary had to do with the manner of serving. Each dish was made a separate course, to be eaten by itself. This bit of sorcery glorified each morsel and assured it the maximum of attention. It also dramatized our homely mass-feeding into five- or seven-course collations, and planted in us a permanent revulsion against that gastronomic horror, the loaded plate. We learned to judge a broth or fricassee on its own merits without overtaxing the palate by the addition of extraneous flavours. Thus we discovered that by monastic standards a perfect bouillabaisse, chicken gumbo, mushroom patty, blancmange, compote, or gruel might be no less deserving of recognition than a properly rendered Gregorian chant, a sample of fine embroidery, or a Sapphic ode.

The reason for this was not sybaritic self-indulgence, but rather the most keenly developed evaluation and respect for the fruits of God's earth. It has been argued that the Roman clergy's rare discernment in culinary matters derives from the substitution of permissible *sensuous* for forbidden *sensual* delights, or the satisfaction of the lesser senses of taste and smell in compensation for the sex taboo. Certainly the nuns took pleasure in their victuals, for we heard them chortling merrily in the shuttered privacy of their own dining-room. But this was hardly proof of gastronomic intemperance, as most of them were spare, almost haggard, of frame.

There was no overweight among students either, possibly

because one convent regulation served as a distinct deterrent to hearty appetites: the meal-time readings. Enthroned on a narrow platform in the centre of the refectory sat our study-period supervisor, Madre Solórzano, armed with the *Tales of the Christian Martyrs.* As mentioned before, we were regaled from soup to soufflé with heroic, though bloodcurdling accounts, of the atrocities suffered by the faithful for their faith. There was Jeanne d'Arc, burned quite thoroughly at her stake. There were Saints Lucas, Toribio, Engracia, and Timoteo, tossed to the lions in some ancient circus arena. There was the Holy Child of Tibet, a little lad so imbued with the missionary spirit that he braved capture by the heathen and never stopped preaching even while they gouged out his eyes and broke the joints of both his arms and legs. Stylistically these accounts left nothing to the imagination. In vivid prose the fullest measure of lurid detail was marshalled for an assault upon the listener's ear. As horror piled upon horror one might easily have suspected sadism rather than piety lending inspiration to the writer's pen. Actually the author of these chronicles was generally anonymous or else a purported translator into whose hands some "ancient manuscript" had fallen. At the same time there was an artful mixture of violence and theology as, in the midst of almost voluptuous tortures, an airy moral was driven home to the effect that faith alone enabled the good martyrs to rise above their pain.

It was hard on our stomachs no less than on our reason. While some of the listeners gulped and laid down their spoons, others sensed an element of casuistry and contradiction. If the holy victims suffered no torment when they rose hale and hearty from a bed of sizzling coals, was it not absurd to wince in contemplation of their woes? On the other hand, since martyrdom was usually a requirement of sainthood, could anyone who had undergone no torment be accurately classed as a martyr? Or a saint? The older girls bedevilled Madre Solórzano with questions:

"How could that little boy in Tibet keep on talking and converting people while he had a hot poker in his eyes?"

Madre Solórzano pointed out the miracle of believing. "He remained unhurt. No matter what the heathen did, they could not blind him."

"Then he didn't *really* get hurt?"

A look of bewilderment appeared on the nun's face. She had not intended to convey the idea that the saints had had an easy time of it. There must be a way out of the dilemma.

"You have misunderstood," she said, with gravity, "because

your spiritual grasp is not yet developed. The martyrs all suffered intense pain and mortification, but their saintliness was such that they rejoiced and asked only to endure still more for the glory of God!"

Having repaired the damage, Madre Solórzano turned over a new page.

In time episodes like the above no longer dimmed meal-time cheeriness. By the law of diminishing returns the youthful listeners became immune (like the martyrs?) to the impact of continued horror. With each instalment in the interminable annals of Early Christian misery the ear grew better conditioned. Most of the students took calamity in their stride and coolly reached for another helping of prune fritters with cream sauce.

It was not so with newcomers. During my first fortnight at the convent I had difficulty in assimilating the trials of the Apostle Peter with my Vichyssoise. The Elder Apostle, it will be recalled, had been persecuted by the Romans after Christ's death and, in memory of the Master, crucified. But with a difference. In atonement for that shameful hour when the cock crowed, Peter was said to have chosen the added ordeal of perishing head down on an inverted cross. This ghastly deed had not only been perpetrated by pitiless infidels—Peter had asked for it!

An easy victim of nausea, I suffered agonies through this recital. I dared not close my eyes for fear of seeing the dining-hall turn topsy-turvy, with tables and benches swinging from the rafters. Nor was it any good arguing with myself that the antidote of faith nullified suffering. Even if in his ecstasy Peter had felt no pain, I was feeling it for him!

My only refuge lay in deliberately shutting my ears to outside sound. I could not press both hands against my head, as this would have drawn attention upon me, but by intense concentration on some object within my range of vision I achieved a kind of deafness.

What was there to look at? The cutlery, for one thing. Each set of engraved spoons, knives, and forks came from a different home and bore its own separate design. There were simple shell patterns, heavy gadroons, and endless variants on the theme of Louis Quinze. I studied them exhaustively before sizing up the drinking-cup situation. Here my eyes were rewarded with an array of mugs, tumblers, and goblets of gleaming silver. Many had obviously been baptismal gifts, as dents and scratches betokened hard use through their owners' nursery and early childhood days. My own baby cup had proved inadequate for school needs, being too small; it was also badly battered after I had stood on it one day. In consequence, I now owned a handsome new mug of satin finish, with gold wash inside and a gracefully convoluted handle. Over my name and number a rambling floral design was etched into the metal.

I loved my cup, though not for æsthetic reasons alone. Its contemplation provided a respite from chapter after chapter on the vicissitudes of early Christendom. The finer points of flagellation, burning, quartering, impalement, and lapidation have long since escaped me, but like some fervent Knight of the Grail I can describe that drinking-mug down to its most precious detail.

Owing to a time-saving if none too hygienic practice, our silverware never left the refectory. At the end of each meal a number of small steaming cauldrons were brought in and set at opposite ends of each table. Without needing to be told, we licked our forks and spoons quite clean before swishing them briskly about in the scalding water. A towel was passed from hand to hand for polishing, after which we wrapped the cutlery in our serviette, with corners folded over to keep out dust, securing the whole thing with a napkin ring. The latter operation called for some proficiency, as rings sometimes refused to clear the bulge at one end of the roll or else slipped off at the other. By watching the older girls, however, I soon learned to lay my pieces counterwise, distributing thickness at both ends and forming a concave middle. By the perfection of her "silver roll" one could tell how long a girl had been at the convent.

There were other signs that would mark the Sacré-Cœur alumna. We were not allowed to sit astride benches or chairs, or to cross our legs (except at the ankles). When it was learned that I rode horseback boy-fashion rather than side-saddle, eyebrows arched with disapproval.

Ladylike behaviour was prescribed for even such casual tasks as the carrying of a chair across the room. No reason why this operation should lack grace. A nun illustrated: walk up from behind and seize the chair by the 'shoulders,' as one might a person, propelling it neatly before you. It was ladylike all right, but difficult when dealing with a heavy piece. Years later, in another city and another country, I saw an earnest young woman apply this technique to an overstuffed armchair that would not budge.

"Sacré-Cœur?" I asked superfluously.

"Yes," she nodded. "Detroit." Whereupon we burst out laughing and gave the chair an unorthodox shove. It seemed to me at that moment that Marion Dupont and I had known each other for a lifetime.

The most conclusive badge of identification was, of course, our penmanship, taught in the majority of Sacré-Cœur convents according to an angular Gothic pattern. For some reason curves were frowned upon as plebeian. The way Mère de Campou put it well-bred people employed a writing style that was "sharp, pointed, *chic*. . . ."

It took daily drill in calligraphy to acquire this kind of *chic*. We filled copybook after copybook with angular scrawls that looked like picket-fences. Mother Piccard, the art teacher, had charge of these exercises. She paced up and down the classroom, beating time while our pens scratched jerkily along. After finishing a page we were admonished to write diagonally across it, and again at right angles, so as to utilize every inch of paper. The resulting criss-cross maze resembled nothing so much as the stencil from which Mama's dressmaker traced a never-ending variety of patterns. Like an experienced seamstress, too, Mother Piccard checked our work. With practised eye she caught each faulty line, every break in rhythm.

"Drill, drill, drill," she hammered at us, "until perfection is automatic!"

Automatic it became, though not permanent. At least, not for me. Schools everywhere look for an overwhelming percentage of pupils to retain throughout later years the script once taught in the classroom. But there are always those who depart from the norm and evolve a hand unmistakably their own. Graphologists may sometimes detect vestiges of early discipline in even a highly individualistic scrawl, but usually the last semblance is gone. To teachers of penmanship this must be discouraging indeed. Mother Piccard would have found it calamitous.

On the other hand, it is for me a disconcerting experience to receive, more than a quarter of a century later, letters written with the same naïve precision which I remember employing when I was mentally and physically aged ten. Wonder, and perhaps a kind of envy, overtake me. How, I am forced to ask, can Time have failed to mark and modify that hand? How, even if only in one's writing, can one remain so happily a child?

37

THE MOTHER SUPERIOR

I HAD been at the convent more than a week before meeting the Mother Superior, Louise de Charon. In fact, up to the moment of seeing her, I had had no idea that there *was* a Mother Superior. Isabelle de Campou's masterful personality had so insinuated itself into my consciousness that I could allow none above her. Yet suddenly the cold fact was before me: a higher power occupied the throne.

The Mother Superior was blue-eyed, rosy-cheeked, and round as a butter-ball. She concealed her hair-line, but it was easy to guess that she must have been a flaxen blonde of the Flemish type immortalized by Rembrandt, Rubens, and Franz Hals.

We addressed her as Révérende Mère, never using her personal name. Though of a sunny, smiling temperament, she remained aloof from daily school affairs. On the rare occasions when we caught sight of her, usually in chapel on ecclesiastic holidays, a hush made known her presence. Mère de Campou as well as the lesser nuns and lay sisters curtsied as though to approaching royalty. For her part the Reverend Mother accepted this tribute with the majestic composure of one to the purple born. On silent slippers she padded through the nave and ascended the steps to her special prie-dieu, where her ample form reposed in stately piety. Here was the true queen-bee.

I puzzled a great deal about the Mother Superior. What, for example, did she do? Where did she sleep and eat and take her exercise? On second thought, her physical dimensions precluded mobility on any but the most limited scale; the climb to the prie-dieu was in itself a strain. There remained nevertheless the merry twinkling eyes, the lips parted for ready laughter. Could it be that the chortles we often heard issuing from the nuns' refectory were the Reverend Mother's own? Did she, like some fabled prioress straight from the pages of Balzac or Rabelais, preside at table and regale her flock with salty persiflage? Assuredly the meek sisterhood would never have indulged in such animation unless encouraged from above.

If the activities of the Mother Superior remained veiled, no mystery clothed Isabelle de Campou. The Mother-General seemed at all times to be everywhere. She ran the convent both in front of and behind the scenes. With her small clapper she marshalled faculty, lay sisters, and students to their respective chores, clamouring always for greater speed.

"*Vite, vite, vite, vite, vite!*" was her favourite outcry, brought forth in rapid pizzicato.

We hopped at her slightest command, scrambling to breakfast, chapel, classroom recess, or the nightly litany, as though Beelzebub himself were at our heels. Everybody in the place scurried up and down stairs or in concentric circles all day long. Despite her electrifying energy, Mère de Campou was senior in age to all nuns, yet on her shoulders rested full responsibility for the convent's spiritual and economic subsistence.

She kept a tiny office, no bigger than a cubby-hole, at the foot of the main staircase, where the stream of student life flowed constantly past her door. But this was not enough. To keep further abreast of all that went on she had had the plyboard ceiling lifted from the flimsy structure, thus gaining a view of the world overhead. By the same token it was possible for anyone with even a passing interest in Mère de Campou's sanctum to take stock of its layout and of the business transacted there. Yet, though the Mother-General always looked out, we seldom looked in. There was that about peering into a roofless chamber that brought a flush to the cheek, quite as though one had stooped to eavesdropping. Moreover, even the most discreet ogle from some vantage-point on the stairs was certain to collide with Mère de Campou's own Argus-eyed stare. I do not recall anyone to whom this happened twice.

Outside the door of Mère de Campou's nook was a letter-box into which confidential messages were dropped. Through this means every student with a complaint to lodge could request a private conference with the Mother-General, the exact hour for the interview being conveyed to the applicant in a formal written reply. As there were few grievances, Mère de Campou often grew bored with herself. Seeing the letter-box empty, she reversed the proceedings and showered the student body with invitations of her own. Since an 'invitation' was in reality a summons, the good nun assured herself thus of a steady stream of callers.

It so happened that a conference with Mère de Campou was by no means dull. To begin with there was her fabulous accent. Merely to sit quietly by while she murdered the noble tongue of El Cid was an egregious treat. We memorized her linguistic howlers and regaled each other with them gleefully, never realizing that our own mistakes in French might conceivably be even more bizarre.

Another reason for the popularity of these private interviews was the fact that classes could be cut to attend one of them, for the Mother-General was never so unsporting as to claim our recess period for herself. It was fun to escape algebra and relax instead in her cosy roost, with its books, pictures, and heart-warming French *bibelots* that tantalized the eye. In one corner of the so-called office stood a little desk (everything was perforce of almost dolls'-house dimension) where convent accounts and bills were scrupulously filed, but it was clear that the Mother-General's off-keel nose did not always keep to the grindstone. She managed many an hour of leisure and contemplation in the snug graciousness of her den.

We were allowed to browse and poke an exploring finger among the trinkets on her shelves.

"But yes," cried Mère de Campou expansively, "*amusez-vous*! It is all yours, and the convent's. A *religieuse*, she owns nothing. . . ."

This made me think. From earliest childhood I had been acquisitive, yearning to possess and clutch to my greedy heart anything that was unguarded, portable, and not nailed down. My lawless instincts had reaped frustration and shame, yet they had not been conquered. It was the nun's words that now wrought a small miracle.

"Enjoy everything! It is yours. . . ."

Suddenly a new knowledge took hold. Enjoyment, not possession, was the essence of happiness. A jewel, a place, a person, need not be owned to be held everlastingly dear. On the contrary, property rights forge the heaviest of chains and warp the heart's enthusiasm into a grudging passion. We rejoiced in Mère de Campou's treasures, which were not hers nor ours, yet everybody's, like the sun and stars. For once I did not yearn to stuff my pockets and cart off what smote my giddy fancy. I had found a secret. The lovely things in life remained desirable only if one did not destroy their desirability by seizure.

The most important function of Mère de Campou's office was, however, its status as a court of justice and appeal. Two girls in the upper grades made use of it on one occasion which struck a faint echo in my memory. They were foreign children, an English girl named Sibyl Towers, and an American, Georgianna Watkins. They were fine students, who, as far as the rest of us were concerned, spoke the same language. Yet differences arose between them, which called eventually for settlement by an unbiased mediator.

To begin with, Georgianna did not—by Sibyl's standards—speak English. She pronounced the last letter of the alphabet "zee" when it was "zed," and she did not know the difference between the verbs "to bath" and "to bathe," the former (as every Britisher agreed) being a tubbing, whereas the latter could mean only a dip in the ocean. They also came a cropper over the word "schedule," which was "shedule" to one, and "skedule" to the other. Here the American child indulged in a bit of devilment, asking whether in England *shool*teachers taught in *sh*ools?

This touched off a patriotic spark. After all, Sibyl decided, Americans didn't know any better. How could they? Great Britain was on top of the world.

Georgianna could not let that stand. The United States had made big strides since breaking away from England in the Revolution——

"You mean the Rebellion?" asked Sibyl icily.

At this point Mère de Campou entered the debate and re-established international accord.

For me the incident recalled other verbal duels. Had not my own Solymár kin exulted long ago in the unique glory of the Magyars and their boast of a thousand-year-old realm? What about the Berlin nursery, where my brothers and I had entered a brawl with race-proud Prussians who scoffed at Attila's spawn? Mynheer Thoma no doubt believed in a resurgence of the once-mighty Netherlands, while Spain still dreamed that she was mistress of one half of the globe. But how could every one be right? If each nation insisted on placing itself at the head of the line, what was to happen to the world?

38

MIRROR OF CONSCIENCE

TWO PRIESTS officiated at the convent.

One was elderly, tired, uninspiring. He mumbled his Latin liturgy in a listless monotone and performed the rites of his office with weary mien. In retrospect I recall that he had a bilious, parchment look, due doubtless to a sluggish liver. I have forgotten his name.

The other was Padre Salvador. Darkly handsome, with clean-cut features and a Byronic air, this young cleric took our hearts by storm. Much of his charm derived, of course, from that superior Jesuit training which matched the poise of diplomats with the authority of churchmen. But some credit must also go to the slim fit of his cassock. Beside the arthritic and corpulent older priest Padre Salvador was a frocked Apollo. Unfortunately we saw him only on alternate Sundays, when he heard confessions and officiated at the ceremony of the Eucharist.

As the Sister Sacristan had to set out sacramental wafers in advance, the exact number of communicants was listed the night before. For this purpose special name-cards were dropped into Mère de Campou's letter-box; from here the convent kitchens received notification regarding late breakfasts, as all communicants were excused from early study periods so as to end their fast with delicious cocoa and hot pastries. The regular menu, for less pious folk, consisted of milk, bread, and apple-butter.

Confession too was by appointment. Once a week Mère de Campou went through her box for the names of all penitents who wished to be cleansed of their sins. With an eye to the moral welfare of her charges the Mother-General kept a book in which all scores were neatly entered. She could on a moment's notice poke her finger at anyone guilty of spiritual backsliding.

Needless to say, when Padre Salvador was due to arrive, a wave of repentance overtook young and old. The Mother-General's letter-box bulged with name-cards, of pupils and faculty members alike, all headed for the confessional. Predominantly this betokened recognition of the young priest's intellectual and pragmatic merits, no doubt. But for my part, I wanted to go to Father Salvador because of his marvellous profile.

Unfortunately I did not know the first thing about confession, besides which I had not yet been issued with a name-card. But, in my eagerness to share in the excitement, I gathered up courage and knocked on Mère de Campou's door.

"*Entrez!*" she answered from within. Then, on recognition, there followed the usual detonations: "*Eh bien, ma petite, là-là-là-là-là-là!!*"

I crossed the threshold, kissed her hand, and smelled the cough-drop. "Please," I said, picking my way in unfamiliar French, "I want to go to confession."

She treated my request with flattering courtesy. "But certainly!" She consulted her chart. "Let me see—there is time to-morrow at seven-twenty."

I basked in the adult importance her attitude shed upon me. For a moment I even put on a pensive expression, as though considering whether the available hour suited my own plans. But in the end it became necessary to inform Mère de Campou that I had never been to confession and hadn't the faintest idea on how to go about it.

It was Mère de Campou's turn to wear a pensive air. One by one she was adding up loose facts concerning my background until a comprehensive picture must have emerged. What she had pieced together proved fairly accurate; mine was a worldly family, nonconformist, free-thinking.

"Pauvre enfant!" sighed the Mother-General, raising her eyes heavenward.

At that instant I felt very poor indeed, for it dawned upon me that I had not lived in wickedness entirely alone. Those nearest and dearest to me shared my dreadful plight. Certainly, in the years I remembered spending with them, Papa, Mama, and my brothers had not been seen entering a confessional.

"Sit down," said Mère de Campou, taking me firmly in hand. For the balance of that afternoon I learned the ritual: cover the head (black veil), enter chapel fifteen minutes early so as to read special prayers and induce proper degree of contrition, remain in line with other penitents, and step up to the confessional promptly in turn. From here on the technique grew more involved, as there was dialogue to memorize. You knelt before a small grilled window of the box-like confessional and waited for the priest to say, "In nomine Patris et Filii et Spiritus Sancti!" To which the answer was, "Amen . . . Father, I have sinned."

Next came the "Vitam impendere vero" or pledge of truthfulness, which was followed by a painstaking recital of one's iniquities.

This was the outer form. But Mère de Campou wisely pointed out spiritual pitfalls for the unwary. Let no one take the Sacrament of Confession lightly! A single sin deliberately withheld would nullify absolution granted for all admitted wrongs, besides constituting in itself an added burden of guilt. Likewise, confession without honest remorse became automatically invalid. Intent to repeat an offence even while seeking pardon for its previous commission, ditto. In short, by extending forgiveness the Church did not issue a passport to wrongdoers with delusions of advance immunity. No priest could intercede for him who feigned repentance while nurturing evil in his heart.

Of greatest importance was the distinction between venial and mortal sin. The former, or run-of-the-mill brand, did not constitute a complete fall from grace. That is, in case of sudden death (without opportunity for extreme unction) the venial sinner faced Purgatory, but not eternal damnation. As for the second category, it drew inexorable punishment in the cauldrons of Hell.

It was shockingly easy, I discovered, to commit a mortal sin. Anyone deliberately failing to attend Mass on Sundays must count himself among the damned. To partake of Holy Communion while in this state of gracelessness doubled the hazard. Furthermore, any of the previously listed deceptions practised in the confessional belonged in the same fatal bracket. Thus, whoever took the above chances with his soul's salvation had better be in good health and mindful of accidents, as unforeseen demise augured the worst. Only a reckless gambler counted on last rites to accord him blanket absolution. In this uncompromising threat lay the great power of the confessional.

"One must live as though one were to die to-morrow," said Mère de Campou cheerfully.

Her words threw me into sudden panic. I certainly could not afford to die to-morrow. My religious life up to now had been confined to simple night-time prayers. I had never even been to Mass, yet ten years of existence lay behind me. I felt myself practically buried under an accumulation of mortal sins. Worse than that, my parents and brothers at home staggered under the same burden, if not, being older than myself, an infinitely heavier one! Now, it was bad enough for me to contemplate permanent residence in Satan's fiery domain, of which I had a graphic picture, based on an illustrated copy of Dante's *Inferno* in the convent library. But the thought that my dearest of kin might suffer a like fate caused me the most cruel torment. I particularly could not bear to imagine Papa in pain. Kind, generous, wonderful Papa!

The least I could do was to cast off the weight of my own misdemeanours, and that quickly. Eagerly I pounced on the hour set by Mère de Campou. To-morrow, at twenty past seven. This would leave me ample time for preparation.

I felt that I needed "ample time," considering the period I had to cover. Yet on careful self-examination it developed that my list of sins looked rather sketchy after all. I had perpetrated nothing spectacular. Apart from riding horseback on Sundays instead of attending church, and being addicted to thievery in extreme youth, there was little to show for my years of godlessness. True, disobedience, sulky behaviour, and impudence towards elders (parents, teachers, servants, etc.) were infractions against the Fourth Commandment, since "Honour thy father and thy mother" was interpreted to mean all authority. I could also put hair-pulling incidents between my brothers and myself under this heading, thereby bringing up my average. But the total still struck me as a meagre showing, hardly worth Father Salvador's time.

It was now that the "Mirror of Conscience" came to my aid, as Mère de Campou had intended when she pointed to a section so named in my prayer-book. The "Mirror of Conscience" was a tabulation, in fine print, of every conceivable form of wrongdoing. In short, a catalogue of sin.

Until confronted by it now, sin in its canonical definition had been unknown to me. At home I had been taught right and wrong from the standpoint of cause and effect, good breeding, and good sense. Lies were reprehensible because they stamped one as untrustworthy and without honour. Disobedience revealed lack of respect for law. Cruelty aroused hate and brought only punishment in kind. Thus, human behaviour controlled individual destiny to a large extent, by inviting happiness or catastrophe according to man's use or abuse of reason. This, of course, left out the Devil altogether.

I was now to learn about him, and about the presence in the world of evil for the sake of evil.

To the convent His Satanic Majesty was very real. Through every hour of day and night one needed to be on the watch, as the Tempter waited only for a chance to corrupt our bodies and souls.

He lurked behind even our smallest misdeeds, such as a rude snigger when Mother Piccard fell over her drawing-board. But there was a sphere of wickedness upon which Lucifer concentrated with special fervour—namely, sex. The "Mirror of Conscience" treated this subject at fascinating length under the Sixth Commandment, where the reader was asked point-blank:

> Have you done anything indecorous? Have you indulged in impure thoughts, visions, wishes, or desires, deliberately and with pleasure? Did you listen to unclean words or employ language of salacious double meaning, laughing and taking delight in it? Have you sinned by unchaste glances or by reading lascivious books, such as novels and the like? Were you immodest in dress and carefree with persons of the opposite sex? Have you touched your own body or that of another in lewd fashion, or permitted such lustful action? How often? Note: be particularly specific in this last matter and withhold nothing. If in doubt, ask your Father Confessor. . . .

I was pop-eyed. To begin with, here were strange new words that far exceeded the limits of my vocabulary. I had never heard anything described as salacious, lustful, or lewd. Oddly, the very terms employed in railing against sex seemed to grow tainted by association. It was impossible to read about prurient thoughts, lascivious glances, or carnal contacts without feeling an impact from the words themselves. Such was the power of Lucifer that he could twist even the alphabet to his purpose, causing a given combination of vowels and consonants to evoke a voluptuous tremor. At least, this was the case with me as, for the first time in my life, I came head-on upon the problems of the flesh. Before scanning the revelations printed in the "Mirror of Conscience" I had vaguely deplored the dull character of my confessable material. But the unmistakably lecherous delight with which my startled eyes now devoured disclosures the existence of which I had never suspected tore asunder the veil of childhood innocence. Though I had not the remotest grasp of libido, there was libidinous pleasure in dalliance over the more perturbing passages in the text. It is shocking to admit, but I had a marvellous and thoroughly wicked time absorbing this new knowledge.

Something told me that this febrile excitement in itself constituted sin. Without any action whatever on my part, my inventory of guilt had expanded, for I would certainly have to tell Father Salvador how much I had enjoyed the "Mirror of Conscience." What puzzled me to the point of irreverence (and this, too, probably called for confession) was speculation regarding the nuns versus the Sixth Commandment. Did these saintly souls examine their own hearts as I had done, and stray equally far afield while luxuriating in the contemplation of evil? In determining the exact nature of what they must *not* do, were they in danger of focusing too lovingly upon it?

Then there was the matter of chastity, a major preoccupation at the convent. In company with my fellow-classmates I had only a confused idea regarding the meaning of this word. We believed it described the human body fully clothed, as opposed to its 'unchaste,' or disrobed, state. The reason for this grotesque notion was not hard to find: immediately upon enrolment at the Sacré-Cœur each child was issued a 'bath shirt,' to be donned before stepping into the nightly tub. Younger girls were bathed by prim attendants, thus giving no rise to blushes. The older ones, in turn, were spared the perils of seeing their own epidermis.

To me this concept was not only new but wholly incomprehensible. Until only a few years ago I had shared the nursery at home with my brothers, both of whom were given to prancing about indiscriminately with or without their breeches. As for the shock of discovering our nakedness, impatient servant-girls had shortened many a bath-hour by plunging all three of us into the same hot tub. When informed of this Mama had emphatically questioned our cleanliness rather than our morals.

The convent 'bath shirt' intrigued me. It was a huge garment of grey linen, cut along Mother Hubbard lines, with voluminous folds, and sleeves that reached to the wrist. On first contact with warm water the skirt was apt to balloon out, wrapping itself about the wearer's neck. If this did not lead to slow strangulation it played right into the devil's hand by exposing the more critical areas of human anatomy to full view.

The actual scrubbing process *avec chemise de bain* was necessarily complicated. In my own case, Sister Elena had charge of the dousing. Wielding a great sponge, her experienced hand dived in and out of my tent-like toga, working up through the sleeves, down my back, and under the choking rim of the collar band. Yet in spite of all this activity there was something unreal about the whole process. It was like a bath in a dream, a bed-wetting, or an accidental fall—fully dressed—into a nice warm lake. There were times when I stole a quick glance at my feet, as the sensation came over me that they might still be encased in shoes.

One thing was certain, this new outlook on nakedness greatly amplified my glossary of sin. I worried no longer over paucity of material. Memory brought back to me past scenes of uninhibited childhood when prudery had been unknown. Visions returned, which formerly had aroused no more than healthy curiosity, yet now took on a darker meaning: servant-girls careless of a bursting button over their round bosoms, or Petronilo pinching the Chamaca as she climbed a ladder. There was also the time when I had inadvertently crashed into the sewing-room, where our governess was being fitted with a stylish corset; embarrassed shrieks and whoops put me to rout, but not before I had marvelled at the mighty circumference of Fräulein's buttocks. In reviewing the matter it now became my earnest conviction that Father Salvador would have to hear about this.

Altogether, these meditations endowed me with a sense of importance. No minor petitioner was I, approaching the confessional with a petty load. Perusal of the almanac of evil had swelled my store of sins and lent an edge to that which lay ahead. My past life had been placid and on the dullish side. Now it was fraught with a mixed tingle of fear and excitement.

I had not met the devil before.

39

CONFESSION

In anticipation of my imminent regeneration I dropped into bed that night to sleep the sleep of the righteous. My mind was at ease. To-morrow I would make my peace with God, and, after receiving a clean bill, I was not going to sin again.

The big event, nevertheless, did not go off without a hitch. On the morrow I entered the convent chapel promptly and knelt down in prayer, observing at the same time the technique employed by my predecessors in line. As they stepped one by one to the confessional box the girls drew their veils well forward and held the ends over the grilled aperture. This kept their faces hidden from view and, more important, foiled accidental eavesdropping on the part of the next in turn. Locked in the gloom of his curtained chair, the priest, of course, could see us sharply silhouetted against the sunlit chapel windows.

My prayers were interrupted now and then by speculation regarding the girls around me. Were they as heavily burdened as myself, or was I an exceptionally black sheep? It occurred to me that I should have consulted some of them and compared notes. But then again, perhaps they all came from pious families; they might have minor mischief to confess, but never the grave sin of missing Sunday Mass. On second thought I could not bear to expose Papa and Mama to their censure.

It was my turn to walk up the aisle. The confessional, shaped like a telephone-booth, loomed now before me, and I knelt at the base of the nearest aperture. As I did so a blurred whisper reached me from the opposite side, indicating that a confession was still in progress. I should scarcely have been human if I had not strained to listen, but the low buzz remained indistinguishable. The upholstered confessional, which might well have doubled for an old sedan-chair without shafts, reduced sound to a mere purr.

After a minute or so there were creaking vibrations to indicate that the priest had turned in my direction. He intoned in crisp Latin: "In nomine Patris——"

I caught the rhythm of his breathing as he leaned well forward. He must have seen plainly that I was a small girl.

The full realization of his presence came over me now. This was Father Salvador, whose mere advent threw the convent into a delicious flutter. I choked over my well-rehearsed responses. My mind was suddenly a total blank.

"In nomine Patris——" repeated Father Salvador. Then, obviously master of any situation, his voice changed to easy conversational Spanish. "Well, my child? What did you come to me about?"

I was struck dumb. With each second my embarrassment increased as I ransacked my vacant brain.

"This is your first confession?" he prompted. It was the key that unlocked my prison.

"Y-yes." I had found speech.

"Well, then, you've probably done some things that you shouldn't have?"

The sluices had opened. "Oh," I blurted out, anxious to prevent his judging me too lightly, "I've done *everything*!"

Father Salvador cleared his throat. "My, my—suppose you tell me all about it."

It was now that I made a clean breast of my 'lifelong' failure to observe the Sabbath, my early embezzlings, and those carefree but immoral years without a bath-shirt. Just how shocked Father Salvador was at my depredations I cannot say. He listened with evident patience, breaking in occasionally to ask a question. Regarding the Lord's Day, he wanted to know whether I disobeyed my parents by not attending Mass. My reply to this was silence at first, then a small "No." It made me unhappy that Papa and Mama got into my confession. I realized that, without my saying so, Father Salvador knew now about my parents' not attending.

Nevertheless the ordeal wound up satisfactorily. On exhausting my repertoire of guilt I listened to the priest's instructions and his words of absolution. I was to offer up a Paternoster, an Ave Maria, and the Salve thrice repeated, in atonement for past wrongs and as a pledge towards betterment in future. Then Father Salvador made the sign of the Cross and spoke the Latin blessing. As I rose he added in Spanish: "Go forth and sin no more. . . ."

It was with airy step and a light heart that I went through the rest of that bright day. My state of felicity was indescribable. I felt uplifted, reborn.

This new-found blessedness carried over into Monday's school routine. I attended classes in a glow of virtue and eager application; my spiritual rebirth, not to say odour of sanctity, registered alike with teachers and fellow-students. During sewing class, the last period of the day, my study-hall neighbour, Margarita Canseco, nudged me and asked, "What's the matter with you?"

Though never shy about whispering in class, I now lowered my eyes and continued silently to sew a fine seam. It was the kind of needlework for which convents the world over were noted—painstaking, delicate, infinitesimal stitches, which brought admiring praise and shortsightedness as a reward. In Latin countries the hallmark of well-bred young ladies was a Sacré-Cœur handwriting and myopia. The former looked well on deckle-edged notepaper, while the latter launched the fashion of disguising prescribed lenses in casual sun-glass frames.

Margarita gave me a quizzical sidelong glance, as though she could not quite fathom my passion for rolling a proper hem. And it was now that the devil, assuredly lying in wait, employed the unsuspecting girl in order to lay his snare.

"Guess what?" said Margarita under her breath. Her question was put in the one way that was sure to catch a listener off-guard.

"What?" I came back before I could stop myself.

"Mother Piccard has a *furunculo* [boil]!"

Never having had a boil, I looked blank. But Margarita explained its nature and, in this case, its unfortunate location.

"Bah, I don't believe you! Did you see it?"

She was offended. "I suppose you don't know that my father is the convent doctor? He can make the Reverend Mother herself take castor oil or swallow a stomach pump."

I was nonplussed. Somehow the thought had taken root in me that nuns (or monks, for that matter) were not people in the ordinary sense. For instance, perhaps before she took the veil Mère de Campou might once have been a child like ourselves, though I harboured doubts about this. In any case, by donning the habit she must have undergone some sort of transmutation for which I knew no name. Without being able to explain myself, I saw nuns as a species apart, disembodied and ethereal, composed of feet, hands, faces, and a preponderance of billowing black cloth. Under that cloth I visualized (if I thought about it at all) a neutral zone of nothingness, incorporeal, and certainly without gender. The floating, monastic walk, which was more of a glide, only intensified this astral quality. Castor oil and stomach pumps certainly had no place in this picture. I flatly rejected the implication of any physical need for them.

"Did your father *tell* you," I challenged Margarita, "about Mother Piccard's—er—*furunculo*?"

She giggled. "No, but I went home yesterday and I heard him tell Mama." She explained further that Dr Canseco had trouble treating the ailment as the patient's modesty forbade inspection of the affected part.

"Not even a peep," said Margarita.

We both giggled.

At this point the awful realization smote me that I had taken a tumble from my new-found state of grace. For the ribald mirth with which my companion and I greeted Mother Piccard's unhappy plight was rank irreverence and an abomination in the sight of the Lord.

Too late now to lower my eyes and hush our impudent tongues. I might ply my needle and finish the most meticulous of seams. I might stay after class and help Sister Marina pick up scraps from the sewing-room floor or put away the work-baskets. But I well knew that no outward show of virtue would cancel the shameful lapse.

My thoughts went back to Father Salvador, who only yesterday had cleansed my soul of sin. He had scarcely left the convent, yet already I had need of him again.

40

RETREAT

THE CONVENT's single and uncompromising function was to save souls. If in addition to the gift of eternal life it also furnished its charges with an education this was but a gratuitous plum. God's work came first. Worldly interests remained at all times secondary. "It is the Hereafter that one must be prepared for," said Mère de Campou firmly.

I did not take easily to this idea, rooted as I had always been in the immediate present. Vaguely I accepted the prospect of Jehovah waiting for me in a commodious Heaven, but I was in no unseemly hurry to join Him there. From my parents I had imbibed a great zest for life here and now, with little thought of hypothetical to-morrows.

This point of view was to undergo modification as Mère de Campou enrolled me among those who before the end of the school year were to receive their First Communion. Fourteen other children were to become communicants with me. In addition, I was the only one who would also be confirmed, the rest having been administered this sacrament at the baptismal font when they were infants in arms, as is usual in Spanish countries.

"What is Confirmation?" I asked in catechism class, for I was anxious to know what made me different from my companions.

The teacher, Madre Estrada, flicked open her textbook at just the right spot. "'Through the Sacrament of Confirmation,'" she read aloud, "'the true believer reiterates for himself those principles of faith pledged for him at Baptism by his sponsors (godfather and godmother).'"

In other words, baptismal vows entered into by proxy and in babyhood were not permanently binding until the Age of Reason (an elastic term) was attained. Theoretically the individual must have a chance to speak for himself and, if so inclined, to change creeds. After being confirmed, however, he was no longer free to leave his Church without becoming an apostate and a perjurer in the sight of God.

"Is that perfectly clear?" inquired Madre Estrada. Her tone implied that nothing could be clearer.

Unfortunately I seemed to be in a fog. Confirmation, as defined, presupposed mature judgment and a voluntary decision scarcely to be expected of a pre-adolescent like myself. How then could my classmates have been "confirmed" while they were yet in napkins?

Madre Estrada showed great patience. "Their parents had them baptized in the True Faith, which no one would think of repudiating in favour of some misguided heresy. Then why delay confirmation?"

I could not take this mental hurdle. What about well-meaning parents who baptized children in the *wrong faith* and, believing themselves right, made the damage irreparable by confirming it? Would it not be better to save even Baptism itself until people grew up and knew, or at least thought they knew, what they were doing?

"Impossible!" cried Madre Estrada. "There is the danger of dying unbaptized and being damned through all eternity!"

"Even babies?"

"Certainly—they are born in Original Sin, and no time must be lost in cleansing them."

I floundered hopelessly. Here was that strange, cruel God again, whom I had met in Hungary—Grossmama's and Aunt Cornelia's God, who not only burned sinners in hell but sent infants to a sad place called Limbo. I did not know what to think of so ungodly a deity.

Needless to say, Madre Estrada's further elucidations were of little help. By baptism, it developed, we were to understand specific admission into Roman Catholicism. Protestants, Budhists, Mohammedans, and other hapless infidels were simply out of luck.

Far from lifting my spirits, this information plunged me into despair. I could not properly rejoice in the safe embrace of my own Catholicism for worrying about all the miserable non-Catholics scattered throughout the world. Was it fair to hold anyone responsible for whatever label (religious, political, or racial) he fell victim to at birth?

"What about Chinese babies," I asked desolately, "or Eskimo children?"

The nun answered, with a deploring gesture, "Lost, all lost, unless our missionaries convert them in time."

Having as yet no sound grasp of history, I failed to realize that the Church of Rome and Christianity itself were finite rather than infinite institutions, since mankind had lived for countless centuries without either. Had I known this, my confusion would have doubled and I should have given Madre Estrada no peace until she explained how God dealt with those prehistoric millions for whose salvation He had made no possible provision. Were they all damned *a priori* because they had not been baptized in a faith which to their knowledge, and to that of some primitive peoples to-day, did not even exist? In short, was the Creator's wrath (which struck at infants in their cradle) also retroactive? If so, I could take little cheer from the fortuitous circumstance to which my own 'redemption' was due. There was something spine-chilling about the realization that, but for my accidental Papist ancestry, I too might be heading straight for Limbo. It was spine-chilling, yes, and more than a shade unsporting. Beset by this mental conflict, I entered Retreat.

"Anda con Dios!" said Madre Estrada, glad to have me out of her catechism class. "Go with God!"

The fortnight that followed was like a dream spent in a realm of fantasy. A potent mysticism cloaked the period known as Retreat, during which we were schooled and prepared for the holiest grace of the Church. To begin with, my fourteen companions and I were separated from our remaining schoolmates and housed in a special dormitory, where in turn we were segregated from one another by means of our well-screened cubicles. From the start of our retirement we had been bound by a vow of silence.

It is impossible to convey the tremendous excitement that this vow of silence engendered in our childish breasts. Lively magpies that we were, the self-imposed ban on speech filled us with an unaccountable sense of importance, quite as though an earth-shaking secret rested in our keep. We particularly loved to be seen by fellow-students, who spied on us during their 'breaks' as we perched on an upper convent gallery and gazed back at them in mute smugness.

"Like a tree full of owls," said the older girls, smiling at our solemnity. But the younger children stared in unabashed admiration. We had been glorified in their eyes. An aura amounting almost to transfiguration had attached itself to our small persons.

This was intensified, of course, by our apparel. Like miniature nuns we wore black veils and carried a prayer-book and rosary through every hour of the day, though normally these appurtenances were used only during religious services. For me this bit of panoply lent a picturesque touch. I felt myself part of an absorbing drama, or rather, since we were speechless, a solemn pantomime.

We received a gratifying amount of attention, not only from the school faculty, but from the Reverend Mother herself, as well as the two convent priests. Following exact rote, each of these mentors conducted daily lecture periods, during which theological tenets, the etiquette of Communion (correct swallowing of the Host), and other ceremonial matters were expounded in minutest detail. Beautiful rhetoric floated about us, and we were encouraged to keep a notebook of pious quotations, including such personal effusions as might burst spontaneously from our own inflamed fancy. Once a day Mère de Campou gathered up these notebooks and read aloud from their somewhat florid contents. An indescribable thrill swept over each young author (anonymous, of course) whose literary efforts were thus made public. Nor did genius remain long unidentified. By none-too-subtle squirming, sheepish grins, or coy batting of eyelids, the perpetrator of some particular fustian was able to dispel all doubt. "Hear that?" each of us learned to convey with expert mimicry. "C'est moi!"

The reward in mutual admiration was blissful. We furnished our most appreciative audience. But this was not all. Each time Mère de Campou singled out a passage worthy of attention she succumbed to a quaint monastic urge. In medieval times, when handprinting was almost exclusively a monkish art, highly decorated initials on so-called illuminated manuscripts were the fashion. The practice had survived into modern times, one of its most eager exponents being Isabelle de Campou. Whenever the Mother-General encountered some especially unctuous euphemism among our scribblings she reached for her stippling-brush and her box of water-colours. A happy sigh went through the class as we speculated enviously on the lucky one to be 'illuminated.' For with swift, deft strokes Mère de Campou applied herself to the formation of lacy frets and garlands, etched in black ink and filled out with enchanting gilt, silver, or mixed rainbow hues. On occasion the good lady outdid herself. Reaching into her own psalter (always at hand), she brought forth a miniature *santito*, or holy picture, of which she had a seemingly endless supply. With a dab of paste the image was anchored opposite some remarkable bit of verbiage, framed, of course, in a flourish of traceries and fleurons all its own. Thus it happened that my own notebook, though by no means outstanding among the rest, boasted a series of elegantly prinked initials plus an exquisite engraving of St Anne and a tiny portrait of the Sacré-Cœur founder, St Madeleine Sophie Barat, clasping a crucifix to her breast.

But maxims and meditations did not take up all our time. There were questions of dogma to be explored and understood. There was the ritual of the Mass to be memorized, from the first *Introibo ad altare Dei* ("I shall approach the altar of God") to the closing *Ite missa est* ("Go, it is the dismissal!"). For this we enjoyed the tutelage of Father Salvador, whose charm continued to be such that we would have picked up Sanskrit or Swahili with equal abandon. Merely to hear his flawless intonation of the *Sanctus*, the *Mea culpa*, or the likewise thrice-repeated *Agnus Dei, qui tollis peccata mundi*, made eager Latin scholars of us all. That, and his unpardonable good looks.

41

THEATRICAL INTERLUDE

"We have wonderful news!" announced Mère de Campou one morning midway through our fortnight of Retreat. "The Archbishop of León will officiate at your First Communion!"

Gasps of excitement greeted this disclosure, though we had the presence of mind not to break our silence. A flock of questions stormed through my head. Would there be a fiesta? I had heard from older students that high dignitaries visiting the convent were always fêted in style. The nuns bestirred themselves, organizing pageants, a bazaar, and theatrical performances in which the most talented children took part. This time Mother Piccard's art class would rehearse a suitable French comedy, while the Hijas de María (Daughters of Mary) held a procession.

The Daughters of Mary was a senior student society whose influence extended far beyond school years. Its members wore a special medal on a chain. During their convent days they set an example in virtue and scholarship, while later years saw them—whether married or not—promoting good works and charities. It was axiomatic that any pageant calling for an impersonation of the Virgin or other holy characters fell into the domain of the Hijas. A flowing madonna costume was part of the society's permanent equipment; it was kept in the small meeting-room, boxed in tissue-paper and mothballs. Periodically, just before an important holiday, the folds were shaken and aired.

As for the theatrical performance, Mother Piccard had already assembled her cast. From the balustrade of our top-floor cloisters we could see rehearsals progressing in the patio below. Bolts of cloth in snowy white, emerald green, Magdalen red, and Virgin Mary blue were unfurled near by for the cutting of biblical garments to be used in the pageant, while carpenters could be heard hammering at the stage props. From now on Mother Piccard shuttled back and forth between her classroom and the Sister Seamstress's quarters, trying to settle upon a proper outfit for the male characters in her comedy, which was to be a modern piece.

She had a problem, Mother Piccard. It would have suited monastic requirements far better if the playlet of her choice had stipulated an all-feminine cast. But, alas, French comedies did not come that way. There seemed to be always a *papa*, a *curé*, a notary public or counsellor-at-law, an unhappy suitor, and a prefect of police. The *curé* constituted no dilemma, to be sure. Any reasonably slender girl—or even a corpulent one—could be sheathed in a black cassock, with her hair pinned up under a clerical biretta. With measured step and solemn speech she could interpret anything from exalted prelate to lowly beadle. But secular characters of masculine gender were another matter. Trousers were not only forbidden in the convent—they were ignored. Bifurcation itself was so offensive to the chaste nuns that, though our weekly laundry fluttered openly in the breeze, all panties—even those of kindergarten size—were hung in a special shed, well out of sight. Only the school laundress took cognizance that such garments existed. The rest of the convent seemed tacitly to agree that women and girls were built like mermaids, with hands and feet operating like fins. This was never more evident than when we assumed our 'ladylike' posture on a chair.

It was in this connexion that Mother Piccard's theatrical plans ran into trouble. The ban on trousers left only wigs, moustaches, neckties, starched collars, and walking sticks to convey the general idea that the prefect of police, the unhappy suitor, the counsellor-at-law, or the heroine's *papa* had just walked on stage. From the waist down the performers were in skirts.

Oddly enough, so great was the love of histrionics, both among participants and members of the audience, that dramatic action did not suffer. From the Archbishop down to the youngest novice in the convent scullery, not to mention the student body, every one was sure to relish and applaud the *comédie* presented by Mother Piccard and her French stars.

My own regret at not taking part in the present proceedings would be palliated later in the year, when I was sought out to play not just a father but a grandfather of *quatre-vingt-dix ans*. In my portrayal of this ninety-year-old gaffer I wore a straw hat, beard, smoking-jacket, and wool muffler above my knee-length uniform skirt and patent-leather pumps. The smoking-jacket was the prize piece among Mother Piccard's scant costume supplies, having been donated years ago by a helpful and sympathetic parent. It did double and sometimes quadruple duty, being passed between scenes from one character to the next, according to shifts in the plot. Thus, during my own third-act climax, Grandfather noticeably lost ground and a mere stripling named Maurice hogged the limelight. The evidence was unequivocal—Maurice wore the smoking-jacket, while I had only my beard and muffler.

What with the air of suppressed excitement that hovered over the convent, heightened by the preparations downstairs, we had a difficult time getting through our second week of Retreat. At dusk, while we knelt for the long litanies, a crescendo of voices reached us from the lighted patio, where rehearsals were increasingly accompanied by squeals and giggles. There were moments when we groaned with envy and despair. To think of what we were missing!

As the tension mounted the curve of our behaviour took a downward turn. We had been docile, dutiful, and pious in our spiritual preparation for the mystery of the Eucharist. Without protest, since we were bound by our vow of silence, we had soaked up the prescribed quota of canonical teachings. Thus it came as a distinct shock when, at the start of our second week of Retreat, a wave of mischief overtook us. We seemed to fall prey to restlessness and an attack of fidgets.

It began with inattention during lecture periods and our bedevilling the nuns in charge with needless signals to be excused. We also nudged one another and developed a telegraphic code that did duty for conversation. But our worst malefactions occurred at night after lights had been doused and we were supposed to slumber sweetly in our cubicles. It was then that a thousand demons possessed us, as we romped about and cooked up every manner of prank.

Our iniquities were as silly in character as they were juvenile. We held pillow fights in the dark corridor outside our dormitory and in general raised a considerable rumpus. As a result we were all subjected to a new regimen of extreme austerity, designed to fix our flighty minds on the purpose ahead. This included the setting of a date for our "Day of Personal Atonement."

The "Day of Personal Atonement" marked the end of Retreat in one last soul-searching exercise that included a confrontation with our respective families. The object of this confrontation was to obtain a blanket pardon for all wrongs ever committed against our kin. Before receiving the Holy Sacrament we must be cleansed not only through the confessional but by direct self-abasement before those most likely to have been affected by our lifelong depredations. This meant parents, brothers, sisters, uncles, cousins, aunts. . . .

Mère de Campou coached us in the procedure to be followed. On the appointed day, towards evening, we should be ushered into the reception parlour where our relatives waited in separate groups. Relieved of the ban on speech, we were to address each of our kin individually and as follows:

"Dear Papa [Mama, Brother, or Sister, etc.], I beg humble forgiveness for every wrong I have ever done you, so that with your blessing I may enjoy a perfect Communion!"

We rehearsed this speech in silence and recited it with mere lip movement until each word was letter perfect. The half-hour in the reception parlour, when a special dispensation allowed us to talk, left little time to spare. This was particularly true for those who had large families. We could see that the "Day of Personal Atonement" would be no picnic.

In retrospect it appeared that Mère de Campou, despite her tireless zeal, overlooked an important angle. Our families too should have been prepared for the "Day of Personal Atonement." As it was they completely misunderstood the purpose of the 'get-together.' To most of them the occasion promised a preview of our white dresses, veils, and other finery, combined with a social call. Thus the bleak parlour filled in no time with ebullient visitors; there was much banter and chit-chat among the various clans, all of whom had a bowing acquaintance with one another.

Baffled looks greeted my companions and me as we filed in, wearing our black-and-white schoolday uniforms. Fond mothers exchanged informative glances; evidently this was to be no dress-rehearsal after all. An instant later the joy of reunion blotted out this minor disappointment. Greetings were loud and stormy as we flung ourselves into outstretched arms and exchanged shy kisses. Soon a maddening chatter filled the room, with our childish voices topping the rest. Two weeks of silence set our tongues wagging now at record speed.

It was wonderful to see my family again. They had become strangely dim, these loved faces, receding into a world of distant shadows. Now they emerged suddenly, warm, cheerful, gay, with voices and gestures that were poignantly familiar. It was good just to look into Papa's eyes and to hear Mama's laugh. Just to listen and take a quick journey in time, until you were home again in surroundings that had once seemed so safe, so timeless, so immutable. . . . The convent had taught me my first lesson in separation. . . .

A dozen precious minutes must have slipped by, when Mère de Campou and the Mother Superior put in a sudden appearance.

Every one rose while they graciously made the rounds, greeting each individual family group. On the surface this gesture brimmed with solicitude and bonhomie, but my companions and I caught the hidden purpose behind it. In the happy turmoil of visiting, we had forgotten the underlying reason for this meeting. Our time was running out, and none of us had yet made the slightest move towards seeking that pardon for derelictions against kith and kin. The appearance of the nuns was a reminder.

Actually we had not forgotten at all. It was simply that not one of us could bring herself to make that stilted speech, memorized so many days in advance. Immature as we were, we still knew that sort of rhetoric could not be employed in the family circle.

"My brother Jorge would die laughing!" whispered María Rivero, as she nudged me confidentially.

I gave her an agonized look. "What about *me*? I've got *two* brothers, and an uncle who jokes all the time!"

We looked about the room and saw the same dilemma everywhere. Each girl was stumped by the problem before her.

Five more minutes passed, and the Mother Superior neared the end of her round. She had discoursed affably with all the parents while Mère de Campou, only a few paces behind her, tapped each child's shoulder as a signal that the vital moment was at hand.

"Le pardon!" she urged sharply. "Alors, demandez le pardon!"

We could see that the Mother Superior had run out of conversation and was headed for the door. But Mère de Campou lingered, grimly determined to await the results of her prodding. Only on being summoned from the door by the Reverend Mother did she rejoin the latter in the antechamber. We were left to our own devices, face to face with an impossible task.

To our credit it must be said that we made a desperate effort and acquitted ourselves with some histrionic distinction. Covering our embarrassment, we sized up the battery of relatives and arrived at a unanimous conclusion: the pardon speech was out. But we kept conversational balls rolling, in all directions as a matter of fact, to disguise the failure of the occasion. Our lively —nay, scintillating—efforts would have done honour to Mother Piccard, had this performance been under the auspices of her drama department.

But with twenty futile minutes ticked off on her pocket watch, Mère de Campou could contain herself no longer. She shot through the door of the antechamber and, a desperate smile distorting her lean face, stepped once more on to the scene. She was frantic. Flitting across the crowded parlour, she bobbed up here and there, glowering, gesticulating, and emitting meaningful coughs.

Now it was twenty-seven minutes by my mother's dainty gold timepiece, which she wore suspended from a *fleur de lis* brooch. Three more minutes to go.

Mère de Campou was, as she herself might have put it, *au bout de son latin* (at her wit's end). Dropping all further pretence, she came out into the open and shook an angry finger at each of us in turn. Her eyes glared threats of unspeakable punishment in Hades if we allowed the deadline to pass unused.

Two more minutes. Then one.

A bell rang and everybody rose to say good-bye. To right and left of me Lala Pinero, Amparo Garza, and the Madero girls plucked each other's sleeves, then nudged me in turn.

"What are you going to do? Are you going to say it?"

We were hysterical by now, giggling, snorting, and snuffling. Our embarrassment knew no bounds. We were at the same time panic-stricken and on the verge of tears.

My own family thought us all a little crazy or possibly overwrought by the rigours of Retreat. They were certain of it a moment later when I hugged each of my brothers and, blushing to the roots of my hair, gulped a high-toned phrase which they had never before heard me use:

"Please forgive me for my sins——"

It sounded awkward, maudlin, and absurd. My brothers grinned foolishly, as did Jorge Rivero, whose sister had obviously startled him with a bit of the same.

Having taken the plunge, I now dropped into my parents' arms and forced myself to repeat the difficult phrase. However, I whispered it half under my breath, with face averted as I pressed close to them. Perhaps, I thought hopefully, they would not hear me. But now I saw them exchange blank looks.

"Forgive you?" asked Papa, with a puzzled shake of head.

Mama added, "In Heaven's name, what for?"

"There, there," said Papa, patting my head. Mama and Uncle Bichteler joined in magnanimously, "Just forget all about it!" With this they walked serenely from the room.

I breathed a sigh of relief. I had my pardon. It may not have been exactly what Mère de Campou had in mind. But—and of this I was dead certain—the condensed version I had substituted for the planned "Day of Personal Atonement" speech was absolutely all my particular family would stand for.

42

FIRST COMMUNION

Our first Communion fell on June the 3rd, which was my father's birthday. For me this fact of course lent an added significance to the occasion. But there was another circumstance not to be overlooked; I would have the rare distinction of being confirmed, alone amid the group, by an archbishop. The other girls had missed this privilege because they had undergone Baptism and Confirmation in one operation, with no Prince of the Church conveniently at hand.

The day dawned radiantly in a burst of tropical sunshine. We were up with the birds, primping and preening in feverish excitement. As a special concession, our hair was to be worn loose, and brushed to a high sheen, rather than tightly braided and skinned back from our brows. The long white dresses, slippers, gloves, and veils had a bridal air about them. This was further enhanced by the white-ribboned candle and ivory or mother-of-pearl prayer-book each of us carried, together with an exquisitely filigreed rosary.

Our only piece of jewellery was a gold chain with a religious medallion, chosen and presented to us by our respective *madrinas*, or godmothers (not to be confused with baptismal godmothers). My *madrina* was Doña Guadalupe Martínez, daughter of a Monterrey surgeon, and herself a graduate of the convent. She was an Hija de María, with a pronounced monastic vocation; soon after these events she took the veil and, years later, became the school's youngest Mother Superior. Since the Order of the Sacred Heart, unlike other convents, permitted its members to retain their names, my godmother was to be known as Madre Guadalupe.

Her present to me was a gold pendant representing Our Lady of the Immaculate Conception, wrought after the Murillo painting. I wore also a second medal, given to me by my parents. This was an enamelled image, on gold, of the Indian Madonna of Guadalupe, exactly as she could be seen above the altar of her votive shrine of Tepeyac Hill, outside Mexico City. The choice of this madonna was a courtesy towards my *madrina*, who would naturally have preferred to give me her own namesake and patroness for a talisman, but felt constrained by modesty and good breeding from doing so.

My ivory prayer-book with hinged clasp of gold and mother-of-pearl arrived at the eleventh hour from Europe, after I had almost despaired of ever receiving it. Purchased in Vienna, this was a present from my baptismal godmother, Baroness Marosffy-Fehéregyházy.

Since early morning Sister Elena had been on hand to supervise our coiffures and hook up our frocks and sashes. But it was Mère de Campou herself who pinned on the billowing veils and placed the coronet of white rose-blossoms on our heads.

She was walking on clouds, our good Mère de Campou. All the chagrin attendant upon our bungled "Day of Personal Atonement" had given way to a glow of warmth, now that the sacred hour was at hand. Her eyes crinkled with happiness as she lined us up in the sacristy, just off the convent chapel, for a final inspection.

"Fifteen little brides!" she exulted, giving our crisp tarlatan coronets a last tap.

Inside the church a chorale resounded and the doors were thrown open. The high altar shone in a flood of lights, with tapers flickering from sconces and candelabra as far as the eye could see. We were unaccustomed to such splendour, for the convent practised strict economy; on ordinary Sundays six large candlesticks were in use, reduced during week-day services to a single pair. We always counted candles and judged the importance of a religious function by the amount of illumination it called for from the Sister Sacristan.

At ten o'clock the procession started, and we filed one by one up the flower-decked aisle. A white-draped prie-dieu awaited each communicant in a semicircle near the altar rail. Behind us, veiled in the incense-laden air of the long nave, loomed the expectant faces of the congregation.

In passing the pews we searched with overt glances for our respective families, who nodded and smiled at us in return. It was now that I felt myself beset by one of those torments peculiar to childhood, for I suddenly noticed that my mother looked different from anybody else in the church. Alone among those present she wore a hat, while all Mexican ladies had put on their lace mantillas. What was worse, my mother's head-covering represented the last word in Paris fashions, being a copy of a prize *chapeau* straight out of her favourite magazine, *Femina*. It was a magnificent cartwheel of Milan straw, trimmed with a garland of bright blooms. The shawls of the pious Monterrey señoras were black, as were their sober dresses.

I suffered acutely through the long ritual of the Mass, forgetting even the pangs of hunger that gnawed at my inside (our fast had not been broken since the night before). I felt exposed and pilloried before my fellow schoolmates.

Actually, Mama had not put on her prettiest hat for the purpose of defying local custom. It was simply that, being no regular churchgoer (in fact, no churchgoer at all), she was unaware that Monterrey ladies, unlike Mexico City sophisticates, clung to their provincial shawl when attending religious services. To my parents a Spanish mantilla was as much a part of fancy-dress costume as the kerchief tied under the chin of a *csárdás* dancer in Hungary. Garbed with a mantilla, Mama would have believed herself en route to a masquerade rather than the Archbishop's Mass.

Plagued by my vexing thoughts, I missed most of Father Salvador's eloquent sermon as well as the Archbishop's special address. During the *Sanctus* I recovered somewhat from my distraction, aware that I had forgotten to strike my breast, much earlier, half-way through the *Confiteor*. I made up for it hurriedly: "Mea culpa, mea culpa, mea maxima culpa——"

And now the supreme moment was at hand. Solemnly we stood up and approached the Communion rail. At an almost inaudible click of Mère de Campou's clapper, we knelt on the strip of velvet cushion and placed our hands under the houselling-cloth. The Archbishop of León stepped forward with the gold ciborium in his hands. He made the sign of the Cross.

"Corpus Domini nostri Jesu Christi custodiat animam tuam in vitam æternam. Amen."

To these words each of us in turn received the Host. For an instant I felt myself tremble, lest this morsel of the Saviour's body touch my teeth. But fervid practice had borne fruit as I swallowed without committing sacrilege. So great was my relief at this that I neglected sinking into a suitably meditative trance. Instead, I looked eagerly at my fellow-communicants to see how they were getting on. It was thus that I noticed Teresa Magaña on my left, blocking the proceedings.

Teresa was an affected young creature who pursed her lips so people would say she had a small mouth.

"Hasn't Manuela a *tiny* mouth!" she would remark about some other child, the while she pinched her own lips into a dainty rosebud calculated to draw loud protests.

"Not so teeny-weeny as *yours*, Teresa," she hoped we might exclaim, though we never obliged.

At the Communion rail the long-nurtured affectation proved Teresa's undoing. She failed to open her mouth wide enough for the Archbishop's broad fingers to manœuvre the Host on to her tongue. As a result the sacred bread broke and fell on the silver tray held under each communicant's chin by the assisting acolyte.

The interruption set up faint whisperings, while Teresa felt herself the target of untold mocking eyes. But now the Archbishop reached for another wafer. He held it aloft, as if to urge the silly girl to gauge its circumference. This time Teresa relinquished all thought of pulchritude. Opening her mouth as far as it would go (which, to my surprise, was quite far indeed), she received the proffered Host.

It was only now that I observed a slight difference in the ritual as applied towards the other children and myself. Not only did I have a special sponsor, but while the Archbishop stood in front of me he had lightly struck my cheek with two fingers of his right hand, anointing me with the chrism oil and murmuring a phrase I did not comprehend. By this brief act I had undergone Confirmation.

At last the ceremony ended and the recessional began. In order of rank the clergy and nuns paced slowly down the aisle, followed by the white-robed communicants, their relatives, and students and lay sisters.

A luscious *déjeuner* awaited us in the refectory. The food differed considerably from our daily fare, and the most loving touches had gone into its preparation. Our cocoa had been beaten with a whisk into a mellow froth, while each bread crescent and *brioche* fairly popped with crispness. A platter of assorted jams, a basket of fruits, and a tray of Swedish titbits, including every variety of smoked fish, completed the repast. Coffee was brewing in an urn on the console for those who did not drink chocolate.

Having kept our fast for eighteen hours, we displayed voracious appetites. Also, since the ban on speech had been definitely lifted, our tongues wagged at double speed. To-day no Madre Solórzano sat on the reader's platform, rendering a selection from the *Tales of the Christian Martyrs*. Throughout the convent a spirit of joy and care-free gaiety held sway.

The festive note reached a climax at two o'clock, when the

afternoon theatricals began. Late the night before, a stage had been set up under the main cloister off the patio, with chairs and benches extending for some twelve yards. Here the audience arranged itself according to a singular pattern: at the far end, commanding a full view of the stage approach, sat the Archbishop beside the Reverend Mother, the visitors, and the assembled convent staff. Upholstered sofas and great roomy armchairs were assigned to the more portly spectators, particularly the Archbishop, whose rotundity exceeded even that of our Mother Superior.

In front of this august gathering and reaching all the way to the footlights lay a completely empty space, to the right and left of which the student benches had been set up. These benches did not face the stage, but were placed sideways, or at right angles to it, so that we might give no offence by turning our backs on the visiting prelate. While such an arrangement demonstrated our excellent manners, it wrecked any chance of enjoying the show. As we sat facing one another across the gulf that furnished the archiepiscopal party with an unobstructed view, we had only a distorted idea of what went on to our left or right. That is, we heard the actors on stage, as well as the applause issuing from the preferential seats. But we saw precious little of the performance.

My unhappy reaction to this unreasonable set-up was one of rebellion. Not docile by nature, I found it difficult to yield under discipline. Besides, like every one else in the convent, I was wild about theatricals. I couldn't bear to miss a tittle of Mother Piccard's wonderful show. So great was my disappointment at the position of the benches that I forgot the holiness of the day and my own state of spiritual regeneration. In a fit of temper I muttered something about preferring the French comedy to a view of our fat Mother Superior, whom we could see every day.

It was an ugly remark and a very sinful one, for I had used the word *gordiflona*, which meant bloated and belonged in the servants' vocabulary at home. What was worse, Teresa, the girl who pursed her mouth into a rosebud, heard me. She told Madre Solórzano, who at that moment was ushering us to our places.

A crisis was precipitated. Not hearing clearly through the thick folds of her coif, Madre Solórzano thought at first that my blasphemous language had been directed against the Archbishop. The good nun paled.

"His Grace will have you expelled," she whispered, "for such an insult to his person!" She seemed unable to decide whether to

file past, flaunting their badge of excellence. Resplendent in my white regalia, I had become a full member of the Church, with my first sacramental privileges that set me free from adult authority.

It was a strange sensation, this knowledge that I had entered a sphere beyond the reach of even parental control. The nuns made it quite clear that in religious matters each new communicant was henceforth on her own. Nothing could come between me and God.

Though I had seldom chafed under excessive family control, my new estate was accompanied by a peculiar elation. I was inflamed with the flattery of my spiritual independence. It seemed almost as gratifying as the new name I had acquired through the addition of yet another godmother. I was now Bertita Carla Micaela María de los Santos Guadalupe. . . .

43

THE MISSIONARY ZEAL

MAMA WAS not happy.

"I don't like the change in Minka," she said on her way home from the convent. "That child is a born extremist. If we don't put a stop to it she will become a religious fanatic."

This was true enough. From my earliest years I had displayed an alarming lack of emotional balance. I was given to extravagant reactions in the face of outside stimuli, and showed a shocking readiness to follow every impulse, permissible or otherwise. This trait culminated in an urge to lose myself and become identified with whatever force swept across my path. Thus, while listening to music, I could react only in the most personal terms, with a vision of myself on the concert stage taking bows amid salvoes of deafening applause. I would be another Clara Schumann, Teresa Carreño, Yolanda Merö! Similarly, a casual photograph of Anna Pavlova sent me off on a different tangent, so that I practised standing on my toes and dreamed of joining the Imperial Russian Ballet.

My parents had always been disturbed by these disquieting tendencies. What would happen one day when I discovered love? Would I be satisfied with my individual share or must I embrace the world? An expansive nature such as mine might well clamour for the passions of the universe. . . .

"She'll be a nun or a street-walker," sighed Mama, "and I don't know in which capacity she'll make more trouble!"

Whatever the basis for her suspicions, Mama was right. On my eleventh birthday I declared that I would take the veil.

It had been Mère de Campou who first brought my 'vocation' to light. During one of those private conferences in her office the Mother-General pried gently into the unclouded recesses of my mind, for she wisely believed in watching early which way the twig would bend. Her questions were tactful but to the point. What, she wanted to know, did I plan to be when I grew up?

The afternoon sun shone brightly through the cloisters, while jasmine blossoms wafted their perfume over the convent garden. In Mère de Campou's cosy study the knick-knacks glistened on their shelves, diffusing an air of indescribable contentment. The Aztec nightingale called *zenzontle* sang in its swinging cage above the desk, and over it all the benison of God lay like a protecting hand. The world was far away. I felt neither need nor curiosity for it. And so, in the language that was second nature to me now, I answered, "Je voudrais être religieuse. . . ."

At no time, the world over, is there a plethora of candidates for the conventual life. Hence the pardonable gleam in Mère de Campou's eye as she spotted in me a new recruit. With considerable emotion she kissed my brow and blessed me by making three signs of the Cross (a gesture we knew in Spanish as *persignar*).

Almost simultaneously with this event my parents decided to remove me from the Sacré-Cœur. Their resolve was not easily arrived at, for they had previously reviewed the city's educational possibilities and fixed on the convent as the most acceptable choice. Nor did they feel that my time under the care of the nuns had been wasted; I had learned many things. Almost too many, Mama thought. But I was now fetched home.

Not until I returned to the house on Matamoros Street did I discover for myself how great a change had been wrought within me. The old surroundings, once familiar and so dear, appeared quite strange. I looked up at the walls and saw that nowhere in our home was there a picture of a saint, or even a votive candle before some hallowed statuette. At once my missionary instinct was aroused; I must remedy the oversight. Among my convent possessions, carefully stowed away in a suitcase, were the cherished trinkets out of my desk. With these I now set up an oratory in my room, before which I knelt and offered up prayers for the salvation of my godless kin. I had embarked upon a crusade to snatch my dear ones from the thrall of Satanás.

Soon I became convinced that such private devotions were ineffective. On Sunday mornings before the household stirred I roused Petronilo and ordered him to take me to church. I had heard of a six o'clock service known as the Servants' Mass in the shabby neighbourhood of San Luisito. An anæmic-looking priest in tattered vestments read the liturgy to a congregation reeking with what Mama called *arme-Leute-Geruch*, or the odour-of-the-poor. Puzzled eyes stared at me—an incongruous apparition in that dusky gathering. Shy Indian children ducked as Petronilo made room for my passing. With his red bandanna kerchief the manservant wiped a place for me in one of the less dilapidated pews, then stationed himself respectfully a few paces away.

Although my parents had taken note of the pietistic trappings in my room, they were unaware of these Sunday expeditions. Invariably I managed to return before the family gathered for breakfast. It was not until some weeks had gone by that my activities were discovered. A tropical storm had broken at dawn, just as Petronilo and I marched off to church. We wore raincoats and carried an umbrella, but our path was obstructed by swift torrents gushing through the streets.

"Shall we turn back, *niña*?" asked Petronilo.

I was uneasy and almost willing to give in. But the lesson driven home during catechism classes, and later in the confessional, weighed heavily upon me. To miss Mass on the Sabbath was a mortal sin, punished by eternal damnation. Was it not sufficient tragedy that my whole family faced this lamentable fate? On no account must I flinch. It was up to me to appease the angry heavens.

The lightning crackled and the thunder roared until I shuddered with fright. But my fear of the elements was no match for the terror of Jehovah, whose wrath had been painted for me in lurid flame. I ordered Petronilo to take off his sandals and carry me across the stream.

We reached the little church square, only to find it completely flooded. Above the swirling waters the house of God rose like a forlorn island. On the church steps stood the priest, ankle-deep in mud, wielding an ineffectual broom. In the low campanile the bell hung silent, for it was obvious that no one would come to Mass to-day.

The storm grew more violent every minute as the clouds poured down a veritable cataract. Drenched passers-by retreated from flooded pavements into houses where the water was already lapping across stone floors. A woman screeched, "The river is rising!"

This was the ever-recurring nightmare that threatened Monterrey—the sudden floods of the Santa Catarina. For years the freak stream lay dry as a desert, yet suddenly its sluices opened in the hidden Sierra gorge and loosed a major catastrophe upon the helpless city.

Petronilo paled under his brown skin. "The *jacalito* of my mother is near by, *niña*. If you wish, we can take shelter under her roof——"

I had always wanted to visit a *jacalito*, or native compound, with its thatched hut, adobe oven, and surrounding fence of prickly organ cactus. To think that I should at last get my chance, even if at the risk of possible disaster!

"God couldn't really expect us in church, could He, Petro?" I strove to ease my conscience of its burden of responsibility.

The manservant shook his head firmly. "Petronilo cannot swim," he declared, pointing to the swirling maelstrom. "The good Lord knows that."

This reassured me. Confidently I put my hand in the Indian's and asked to be led to his mother's house.

We made our way across cobblestones and rolling boulders, up an incline that lay safe and dry above the flooded square. At the top of a green hillock rose the spiked cactus columns that surrounded the compound.

There was no gate, but simply a gap in the fence permitting entry and egress. Beyond this lay an earthen courtyard, soaked now by rain, which formed a meeting-place for beasts, birds, and humans from the surrounding huts. A flock of children splashed about in a puddle and shouted greetings as we passed.

With dignity Petronilo showed me to his mother's door. We knocked and entered a small room, dark and windowless, with only a primitive hearth glowing in a corner. Out of the murk rose the frail figure of a wizened crone.

"This is the señorita," said Petronilo, in explanation of my presence.

The old woman's dry fingers closed over mine. "You bring honour to our house," she greeted me. I stood awestruck, marvelling that this damp hole should be referred to as a house.

Petronilo meanwhile poked about in the darkness until the place came suddenly to life. As my eyes grew accustomed to the shadows I realized that there were other occupants stretched out above and beneath a square table, which evidently did service as a community bed. Never had I seen human beings crammed into such restricted quarters.

"These are my brothers, Honorio and Gavilán, with their families," introduced the servant. His gesture encompassed several in-laws, as well as small nephews and nieces, who stirred and stepped over one another in heavy-lidded stupor.

"Good day," they chorused, bewildered at this early intrusion. But now there was a bustle of activity as the women stirred up the fire and brought forth a jug of goat's milk. Would the employer's child partake of their humble breakfast? Madre Santísima, this was going to be the talk of the neighbourhood!

I felt touched by their goodness and sincerity. As the cooking went on, my stomach turned at the assortment of odours that assailed my nostrils, but I did not know how to extricate myself from a situation for which no one but myself was to blame. By now the place teemed with life, for the animals too had awakened. From the low rafters came the cackle of chickens, while dogs, cats, and a brace of piglets pushed their way through the door and out into the open. I remained speechless as the whole crawling scene etched itself upon my mind.

Fortunately the elements came to my rescue. As suddenly as it had arrived, the rain subsided, and a smiling Mexican sun swept across the heavens. Two rainbows appeared, one inside the other, above the rim of Saddle Mountain.

"*Arco iris! Arco iris!*" cried the children, pointing to the wondrous sight.

I thought abruptly of my brothers asleep in their snug beds while I was gazing at a double rainbow above the town's most miserable slum. What extraordinary discoveries I had to report! Sylvester and Arnim would be fascinated to hear that Petronilo's relatives wore no night clothes, but slept in the same rags that served them day after day. My brothers were at an age when such an arrangement held a positive allure. They would also appreciate the indiscriminate association of man and beast within the *jacalito* confines. Though we had no piglets at home, every other household pet was smuggled into our beds at night and smothered with affection.

"Let's go home," I said to Petronilo.

We found the family distraught with worry. Breakfast stood untouched on the table, while Mama grilled the servants and Papa telephoned the neighbours regarding my disappearance. It happened that the cook, the Chamaca, and the maid Virginia knew about my Sunday expeditions; they were in full sympathy with my soul-saving efforts, hence they staunchly guarded my secret. With exasperating monotony they replied to every query: "*Quién sabe?*" ("Who knows?")

My reappearance, bedraggled though unharmed, relieved the worst fears. But the inquiry that followed quite upset my parents' peace of mind. They were profoundly shocked to learn how great a spiritual gulf had opened up between them and their daughter.

"The school problem must be tackled once and for all,"

declared Papa at the end of that morning's conference. "If there is no other way to a secular education we shall move back to Europe."

Mama agreed. She felt no inclination to conform to a small girl's fierce bigotry. My heretic family refused to be converted, and my career as an evangelist had ended.

44

CITY UNDER SIEGE

Two events of historic importance, though in vastly different degree, barred our projected return to Europe. One of these was the assassin's shot fired at Sarajevo, which precipitated the First World War. The other had no such far-reaching reverberations, yet it affected us in a more direct manner, since it concerned Mexico alone. This was the climactic turning-point in the Villa Revolution.

Much had happened while I was behind convent walls, concerning which I had no information. The course of Mexico's civil war had been punctuated by successive crises—the shooting of Francisco I. Madero, the usurpation of the presidency by the Federalist General Victoriano Huerta, an interchange of acrid notes with Mr Woodrow Wilson regarding border incidents in Villa territory, and the rising threat of intervention by the United States. The tide of revolt did not follow an evenly laid out plan. It surged and declined sporadically, taken up here and there by minor guerrilla leaders who joined in the fighting without any clear idea of its fundamental aims. Among these lesser figures there arose two brothers, Emiliano and Venustiano Carranza, who gained a large following which enabled them to consolidate into a party known as El Partido Constitucionalista. Ostensibly their aim was the drafting of a new and liberal constitution. In essence the Carrancista slogan was the same as that of the Villistas: "Down with peonage! Bread and land for the Indian!"

So long as the incumbent President, Victoriano Huerta, held Mexico in an iron grip, Villa welcomed help from any quarter. He would put no obstacle in the Carranza path. Later, when the Federals were beaten, there would be time to make clear who was master.

It was during this period of uncertainty that our father was summoned by his Canadian firm to a meeting of the board of directors at Toronto. At the same time my brother Sylvester was to enter Upper Canada College, a preparatory school in that city.

They left reluctantly, disturbed by rumours that a force under the leadership of Venustiano Carranza was converging upon the Government-held city of Monterrey. Only the assurance that Uncle Bichteler would look after us dispelled Papa's alarm somewhat and allowed him and Sylvester to board the train for Laredo. Shortly after their departure the political skies darkened and the storm broke loose. We awoke one morning to find the city under siege.

At first we misunderstood the signs. The sound of booming cannon, coming from far away, resembled thunder. Then it drew nearer and became more insistent, until we grasped the truth. But who was doing the shooting? And, for that matter, why?

The morning paper brought out an extra which informed puzzled readers that an army of Carrancistas had broken through the Mamulique Gorge to the north and could be seen approaching the suburb of Topo Chico. However, so stated an editorial, the Federals had the situation well in hand.

The magic that attaches itself to printer's ink caused people to be reassured. A thing must be so, if it was there before you on paper. Only a sceptic like Uncle Bichteler or Papa would have doubts. "Das Papier ist geduldig," Papa often said. "Paper is long-suffering; it will stand for anything." Monterrey, at all events, went calmly about its business, only vaguely annoyed by the sounds of battle beyond its gates.

Uncle Bichteler was not particularly well at this time. His lungs had always been weak, and of late he had developed a persistent cough. On the first day of the siege Dr Martínez came to call and ordered Uncle Bichteler to bed.

The second day of fighting found Monterrey citizens less placid, though by no means panicky. According to the morning journal, we—that is, the Federals—were admirably holding our own. The fact that shells seemed to be exploding now at closer range did not temper editorial optimism. The rebels hadn't a chance! White-collar Mexicans and foreigners alike had been conditioned to a classic line of thought—by definition all revolutionaries were tattered malcontents who defied law and order, but lacked the intelligence to see what was good for them. It was the job of established authority to deal with this ragamuffin element by swift and ruthless means. In earlier days Porfirio Díaz had leaned on his trained military police, the Rurales. Bring out the Cossacks! Victoriano Huerta looked on his Federals as his Iron Guard.

"The bandits are running out of food and ammunition," cheered the confident Press. "Our heroic forces are covering themselves with glory!" Gullible readers failed to perceive the contradiction in these claims. If the enemy was made up of obtuse incompetents, who lacked weapons and fodder, it was hardly a feat of heroism or grandeur to carry the day.

Another twenty-four hours passed, and the public began to revise its early views. On the edge of the town great columns of smoke were rising against the sky. The glow of spreading fires lighted up the night.

"Topo Chico is burning!" reported one paper, while another printed the shocking news that the Cuauthémoc brewery on the edge of the town was in the hands of the enemy. Another extra followed within the hour, describing the railway station as littered with dead. A Federal bulletin read: "The marauders have decapitated a whole platoon of our men and impaled their heads on fence-posts!"

It may have been the constant din which caused Uncle Bichteler to take a turn for the worse. His fever rose alarmingly, and the doctor diagnosed double pneumonia. "I don't know how long I'll be able to continue my rounds," the harried physician said. "There's going to be street-fighting soon."

By evening Uncle Bichteler's condition had become critical. "He must be sent to hospital," telephoned Dr Martínez, declaring at the same time that he could make no more calls to private homes, as his horse and carriage had been commandeered by the defenders. This last disclosure came as no surprise, since every motor-car in our street had been commandeered only an hour before.

Because no ambulances were available for civilian use, Petronilo scoured the neighbourhood and returned at last with a creaking surrey. In this hack the sick man was propped among blankets and pillows. Under cover of darkness he was transported to the only accessible institution, the Hospital Gonzales, where normally only charity cases gained admittance. The private Canseco Clinic, within the zone of battle, was reported in flames.

The Hospital Gonzales consisted of big crowded wards with two dozen beds in each. After considerable debate, coupled with monetary persuasion, a single room was made available. This turned out to be a guard's quarters in the wing for the insane, a fact that remained undisclosed until a female patient came running down the corridor, ripping her nightgown to shreds. Alas, Uncle Bichteler was much too ill to take umbrage or to care.

For the rest of that night our mother and Petronilo kept a vigil at his bed. Throughout the small hours the air was rent not only by artillery fire, but by the wails and screeching of the sleepless mad. Uncle Bichteler heard none of this, for he was a dying man. Losing consciousness, he remained also impervious to the frantic efforts at conversion engaged in by the hospital nuns, who had learned that their patient was a Lutheran. That anyone should depart this miserable life did not appal the good sisters, whose main concern was the saving of souls. Had they succeeded in winning Uncle Bichteler over to Catholicism his death would in their eyes have been an occasion for rejoicing, since he was certain of entering heaven without another chance at sin. As it was, the delirious man died unregenerate. The nuns held a gloomy view of his prospects in the hereafter.

The funeral took place at once. Without ceremony or flowers, Uncle Bichteler's body was carried in a hospital coffin to the Panteón for hasty burial before the besieging armies cut off the way to the outlying acres of the dead.

A lone grave-digger shovelled the earth. His assistants had been called to man the guns on Obispado Mountain. "Soon I won't be needing this," he said, indicating his spade. "We'll just piles up corpses, pour on the oil, and set them afire."

The callous words were uttered with matter-of-fact candour. The gravedigger's face was lined with age. A veteran of Juárez's campaign against Maximilian, he knew the way of revolutions.

We returned home and felt a great emptiness. The passing of Uncle Bichteler was, for my brother Arnim and me, our first knowledge of personal loss. Our father's and Sylvester's absence at this critical time contributed to the impact of danger and death. Seeing now three empty places at table filled us with ominous foreboding and a sense of abandonment.

In the days that followed a phrase beat more and more often upon our ears. "When the street fighting begins——" Better than any official bulletin it revealed the course of battle. The Federals (our side!) were not holding up as had been originally boasted. The enemy had now reached the broad Calzada Unión, later to be renamed Madero Avenue like Mexico City's fashionable shopping street. From here it was only a stone's throw to the military barracks which formed Monterrey's main line of defence.

Long ago the shops in town had closed down. Now even the market of El Parián boarded up its stalls. Except for the ceaseless rumble of cannon the city lay still and lifeless, as no one ventured forth from the safety of his home.

It was at this moment of crisis that Papa arrived suddenly out of the blue. Our mother could not believe her eyes, for it was well known that all train service to the border had long been interrupted.

"I didn't come by train," said Papa. "I pumped my way down with three other men on a hand-car."

He had cut short his journey to Canada at Buffalo, near the border, where newspaper headlines had informed him of the Monterrey siege. Arranging for Sylvester to be met by some one from the Toronto school, Papa had turned back and reached the Mexico border, only to learn that there was no more travel across the Rio Grande. What followed now was a tale out of Harun al Rashid. With the aid of a fisherman's smack he had crossed the shallow river at Nuevo Laredo, where, it appeared, numerous other travellers were stranded at the overcrowded Hotel de la Frontera. One of the men had found a small hand-car used by railway workers for inspection trips along the lines. There was no motor, but the hand-pump seemed in good order, though it called for considerable muscle.

The distance from Nuevo Laredo to Monterrey was just over 160 miles, given a flawless, unbroken road. With dynamited lines, blown-up bridges, and rocky ravines to negotiate, the mileage became something else again. The gentlemen at the Hotel de la Frontera showed little enthusiasm for such an undertaking. Instead, the little band of involuntary exiles gathered nightly in the bar to ponder the problem over a swig of *tequila*.

It was no surprise to me that Papa's arrival among them put an end to vacillation. A short debate ended with all the travellers wanting to get on the hand-car. But there was room for only four —the self-styled "owner," Papa, and two others.

They set out with two loaves of bread, a sack of oranges, and a jug of *tequila*. The latter is vile stuff, but it sustains you under stress. Mexicans tell the story of a frightened mouse that dipped its nose in a spilled drop of this liquor, cocked its sombrero, and shouted, "Throw me that cat!"

The foursome setting out for Monterrey found the journey beset with hardships. Despite some stretches of usable line, there were long gaps where the rails had been ripped apart. This necessitated pushing the hand-car over wild desert country. Luckily the rainy season had barely started, so that the ground was still hard and resistant; otherwise the steel wheels would have cut deep into the mire, forcing the expedition to bog down.

Even with the advantage of firm terrain the four men had

hardly enough strength to manœuvre their vehicle across deep gullies littered with boulders and the debris of shattered bridges. More than once they considered abandoning the hand-car and continuing their journey on foot. But the hope of recovering speed over the next interval of undamaged rails caused them to grit their teeth and hold on. Actually, whenever the going was good, two men alternated at the pump while their companions took quick naps. On a hike no such impromptu dozing would have been possible without bringing the travellers down to a halt. Thus, under a blazing sun by day and a chilling wind by night, the men pushed on. They lugged their heavy hand-car over intervening obstacles while, like a Fata Morgana, visions of smooth bands of steel and endless lines of sleepers flashed tantalizingly before them.

They reached the little village of San Nicolás de las Garzas after four days, having survived mostly on oranges, skin and all. At San Nicolás, however, they meant to gorge themselves on the gustatory speciality of the place: big, juicy *enchiladas* topped with onions and crumbled white cheese.

Alas, their hopes were dashed before reaching the main plaza, for the village lay deserted and only a few hungry dogs could be seen wandering about. Don Filiberto's tavern, formerly replete with luscious odours of pepper sauce and toasted *gordas* (a very fat *tortilla*), now stood empty and forlorn.

It was in Don Filiberto's back yard that the famished travellers spotted a narrow patch of Indian corn bearing half a dozen ripe ears. They fell upon these and roasted them in a near-by barbecue pit, then went back for some unripe figs and devoured these as well. There was no piped water, but the trickle of a fresh spring at the far end of the garden satisfied their thirst and served also for some perfunctory ablutions.

At San Nicolás the hand-car was finally abandoned, since there appeared to be no chance of getting through the battle lines. The rumble of artillery could be heard plainly in the village, and there was evidence that no tracks led past the zone of firing. They had better dodge the northern approach altogether and make for the west, where there seemed to be no shooting.

This proved a correct analysis. Although no one in Monterrey as yet suspected it, the Federals no longer felt heroic and covered with glory. They were losing heart. The Obispado garrison had bolted during the night and was well on its way to Saltillo, while the enemy, busy on the opposite side of town, had not yet occupied the vacated heights. It was owing to this that the four wanderers, footsore and exhausted, managed to reach the San Gerónimo highway and to enter the town at dusk of the fifth day. At the gates of the amusement park of Quinta Calderón they parted, each heading for his own home.

Thirty-six hours had passed since Uncle Bichteler's funeral when Papa stood suddenly before us. He carried no luggage, and his clothes were tattered, with lapels torn and pockets bulging out of shape. His skin was burned a deep mahogany.

It did not take long to tell him that death had touched our house. As he listened Papa put the back of his hand against the raw burn on his forehead. We knew that he had loved Uncle Bichteler.

A moment later he turned to Arnim and me, while his fingers explored the pockets of his coat. "I didn't get to Toronto," he explained, "but I saw one of the world's great wonders, Niagara Falls!"

With this he spilled an assortment of trinkets on the dining-room table. There were quartz curios for Arnim, a photographic cyclorama of the falls and a souvenir teaspoon for Mama (she collected these atrocities), and an exquisite necklace of clouded crystal beads for me.

Papa took particular pride in this last-named bauble. "It's very remarkable," he said. "Each bead comes from the salt deposits on the wall of the great cataract."

Just then a violent tremor shook the house as a shell exploded in our immediate neighbourhood. Above the roof-tops rose huge billows of smoke.

45

TURN OF BATTLE

DURING THE night of Papa's arrival the street-fighting started. We were awakened before dawn by sharp, short blasts that seemed to ricochet from our own walls. A whistling sound cut through the air as bullets flashed overhead. Intermittently there came the *rat-tat-tat* of machine-guns.

"That's a *mitrailleuse*," exclaimed Mama, employing the French term used by the Austro-Hungarian army. Papa said *Maschinengewehr*, while Petronilo called it by its Spanish name, *ametralladora*, which best conveyed its nerve-racking clatter.

Noise is fatiguing. The distant booming of the past week had been bearable enough, but the detonations at close range, to which we were now subjected, began to tell on us. Conversation was almost impossible, except by shouting at one another. This in turn caused tension and needless alarm. Mama finally went about suggesting that we all took naps. But nobody could sleep, either by night or day. At best we merely dozed, jumping up in panic when some near-by target exploded with a bang.

I was terrified. My stomach seemed to have turned over, and my throat grew constricted. I could swallow no food.

"Are we going to die?" I asked Papa in bleak certainty that, regardless of his answer, these were our last hours.

He took me on his knee, as though I were still a small child. "Nonsense," he shouted above the din. "Why, you and Arnim are lucky to be going through such an experience as this. Just think—a city under siege! That's something most people only read about, but you'll be able to *tell* it!"

This was bleak comfort. "To whom?" I asked half-heartedly.

Papa hadn't really thought the matter out. "Oh, Grossmama, and your friends in Solymár."

Our food-supply was meanwhile running out. Apart from the closing of butcher's-shops, bakeries, and the market itself, there was no delivery of milk. Our cook, Luciana, wept into her apron as the pantry shelves grew bare.

"What shall we do, señora?" she wailed. "There is not even corn to make *tortillas*!"

Mama's knowledge of country life in Hungary now stood her in good stead. "We have salt, water, and a good supply of flour," she said. "That will make a kind of bread."

It did, though we had never tasted anything like it before. The texture was strange; without leaven the loaves did not rise. In fact, they weren't loaves at all, but just flat, elongated pancakes baked to cardboard stiffness.

On the sixth day of the siege the newspaper presses stopped operating. One final bulletin, made up of a single sheet, warned the public to shutter all windows and under no circumstances to walk out on to balconies or roofs. The enemy had stormed the battlements, and there would be fighting from house to house as the last remnant of Federals was smoked out.

We obeyed promptly. After all blinds were drawn Petronilo fetched step-ladder and blankets so as to drape transoms and skylights. The house had a deserted appearance.

"Whatever will that nosy Widow Pancracia do?" wondered Mama. "She can't bear to keep indoors!"

The Widow Pancracia, living across the street, was known throughout the neighbourhood as an incorrigible gossip. Her favourite post was a parlour window from which she could keep an eye on everybody who passed by. Besides this, Doña Pancracia liked to stroll up and down outside her door at dusk. The present injunction to keep under cover must drive the old busybody to distraction.

It was the Chamaca who brought us the news.

"I saw it myself!" she screamed, with a flush of excitement. "I peeped through the garage door, and there was the head of the Widow Pancracia craning out from her curtains. Poof! They popped her one."

We couldn't believe it, and Mama forbade us to go and look. But Petronilo and Arnim sneaked out to the patio and climbed to the top of the pomegranate-tree. From here they could barely glimpse the street. The Chamaca had told the truth. For there, decked in a beribboned boudoir-cap, hung the lifeless head of the Widow Pancracia, like a lampshade knocked askew. It continued to hang there for days, until the occupying forces ransacked the little house and carted off the decomposing body. By that time there were other stiffened shapes dangling from lampposts and telephone-poles as the siege ended in a burst of ferocity.

At the eleventh hour a remnant of Federals who had been cut

off from their fleeing comrades put up a brave last-ditch fight. This ended in bitter hand-to-hand clashes, with each man taking personal issue against his adversary. Up to now the artillery match had been a mechanical performance which evoked from us the same awe we felt before a tornado or an earthquake. But men engaged in individual slaughter somehow lost this objectivity. Their deeds, though reduced in scope, seemed to grow large in repugnance and horror.

I felt nauseated. I wanted to vomit, not from the fear that had for days convulsed my stomach, but in order to rid my whole being of the ugliness that bore down upon me. Horses and mules lay dead outside our windows, their bellies hugely bloated in the sun. These sights could not be kept from our prying young eyes, so the next best thing was to give a straightforward explanation: the process of decay formed gases. At night, under the hot glare of burning buildings, the stench of rotting flesh was almost unbearable.

Inside our own house sanitation had gone by the board, as Papa hoped to save his saddle horses by stabling them in one of the bedrooms. Floors were made sound-proof with blankets and straw, but there was no way to keep the nervous beasts from neighing and making their presence known. This became particularly important during the final hours of battle, when the last fleeing Federals requisitioned all transportation facilities that lay in their path. Clearly we could hear the rolling southward of caissons, wagons, and motor-trucks, plus such cars and carriages as the departing stragglers could snatch in their flight. There was no longer any doubt. The defenders had called it a day.

At the height of the evacuation there was a loud knock at the door to our mews. Luciana, the cook, answered, and took on the intruders. She showed them the empty stalls, then taunted: "So! You have come to look for animals? Well, you are late, *amigos*. It is only half an hour since your *comandante* passed through here and took his choice!"

A suspicious trooper pushed his way into the stable. "There's a carriage," he grunted to his glowering partner. "Maybe we ought to search the house and find something to hitch it to."

Luciana paled but recovered quickly. "Oh, that old crate!" she snorted. "The rear axle is broken. Why do you suppose your *comandante* left it?"

The foot-sore troopers spat across the courtyard and scratched their heads before turning to go. Luciana's able tongue had won the day. But how much longer could we hold out?

The family no longer slept at all. Overwrought and tense, we could not relax sufficiently to lie down. We dreaded being separated from one another, and no one left the dining-room, where Papa performed card tricks for Arnim and tried to teach us all the Austrian game of Tarock. This was played with a special deck of handsome cards that were the same in width but twice as long as the ordinary sort.

Just before the end of the siege all public utilities gave out, as the power- and gas-plants were shelled, and the water reservoir was breached. The city now lay high and dry. It was at this point that the Carrancista forces swept in, led by their chieftain, the grey-bearded and bespectacled Don Venustiano. And now a surprise awaited us. With the Carranza horde rode a pale, well-built officer, wearing the cap and uniform of the beaten Federals, in contrast to the cowboy hats and *ranchero* clothes that characterized the 'rebels.' One sleeve hung empty at the officer's side.

"Alvaro Obregón!" gasped startled onlookers, rubbing their eyes. The tidings spread. "Obregón has left the Federals—he's on the Carrancista side!"

This was significant. Obregón, the erstwhile supporter of Huerta, had broken with his party, though he had once sacrificed an arm in its defence. Had there been a clash of personalities? President Huerta was a tyrant of the old school, harsh and unyielding, whereas the younger man showed liberal proclivities and a distrust of the iron fist. A legend accompanied Obregón wherever he went, and he made no effort to dispel it. Fair-skinned and without trace of Indian blood, he was said to be of Irish origin and really named O'Brien. In any case, his presence in the Carranza vanguard brought reassurance to Monterrey citizens, who had feared looting and violence after the city's fall. Obregón was a military man who knew how to keep even an untrained revolutionary band under control. Apart from a few isolated cases of pillage, the Carrancista occupation took place in orderly fashion.

After the noise of battle a strange silence settled over the smoking, rubble-strewn town. Slowly, timidly, people opened their shutters and peered out, recoiling quickly at the first onslaught of the effluvia of war. The odour of blood and putrefaction was everywhere. Before digging itself out the city would first have to learn to live with it. For destruction was always rapid, but recovery took its own good time.

46

WAITING FOR VILLA

WE GOT used to the new régime.

It was frightening at first to walk among men fresh from battle. They stood in every square, on every street corner, wearing a peculiar flushed look (even the thin and old ones among them) such as one associated with drunkards. The fever of the firing-line, the smell of gunpowder, the fumes of death so long in their nostrils, had puffed and distorted these tired faces. These were the victors. Yet they did not look particularly happy.

"It takes time," Papa said, "to get over killing." Triumph was not necessarily beautiful.

Even less beautiful was the condition of our city. But the invading army set promptly to work, repairing water-mains and clearing the debris. Streets and public squares were made passable, while human casualties were piled in mounds and, as the gravedigger at Uncle Bichteler's funeral had said, drenched with petrol before being set on fire. Dead animals were given the same treatment, then buried in quicklime. All in all, the victors seemed eager to prove the worthiness and efficacy of the constitutionalist cause. It must not be forgotten that Venustiano Carranza carried in his pocket a draft of Mexico's new Magna Carta.

Monterrey co-operated. Licking her wounds, the city rose on tottering feet and resumed 'normal' activity. Such business houses as had remained undamaged opened their doors, while in the market-place a few hucksters offered their skimpy supplies. Newspapers reappeared, though only in broadside format, with tentative headlines announcing the dawn of a new era. No use to look backward, proclaimed the editorial column, or to cry over spilled milk. (The Federals, no longer "heroic and covered with glory," presumably were the spilled milk.) What Mexico needed, and would now receive, was a blueprint for prosperity.

Alas, before any sort of blueprint could be approximated, there came the rumblings of a fresh storm gathering on the horizon.

From the north-west, muffled at first, then growing gradually more discernible, rose the familiar boom of cannon.

Could the Federals be coming back? People shook their heads incredulously. Had Huerta sent reinforcements by a surprise route, unaware that they were much too late and the city had fallen?

The behaviour of the Carrancista garrison soon cleared up the mystery. "Pancho Villa!" The name travelled from tongue to tongue as a wave of excitement seemed to spread through the occupation forces. Simultaneously a rumour made the rounds that Don Venustiano, who had Presidential ambitions of his own, was making a hasty departure for San Luís Potosí and thence to Mexico City.

People did not know what to make of it. Had it not been expounded through every propaganda channel that the cause of liberalism was upheld by a single united force? Did not the Revolution, regardless of its component leaders, pursue one purpose only—namely, the extermination of the Díaz heritage as embodied by Victoriano Huerta? The various *caudillos* who organized uprisings in their respective provinces were presumed to be in complete fraternal accord. Then why the present angry voice of cannon? Why the fearful whisperings of Pancho Villa's approach? Could it be that all was not well among the *caudillo*? The noble dream of liberation seemed to have crystallized into a general scramble for the Presidential chair.

There was no time to ponder these things. Monterrey had become once more an endangered city girding its loins for battle. Only this time military defence was even more questionable, food stocks were almost non-existent, and public morale had dropped to its lowest ebb. No one understood the new issues at stake, nor were we certain of our present defenders, if indeed the unsettled Carrancista garrison qualified as such. There was something about the very name of Villa that planted terror in men's hearts. For years the exploits of the chieftain from Chihuahua had inflamed popular imagination until it was no longer possible to separate fiction from fact. The bandit of the north-lands was both an ogre and a Robin Hood, whose mercy was as hard to win as his fury was easy to arouse. What had peace-loving, industrious Monterrey to expect of him? The approaching cannonade augured the worst.

Without awaiting official orders the townspeople once more closed their shutters, boarded up balconies, and barricaded front doors. Pails, jugs, bath- and wash-tubs were filled with water, while matches and candles (wax tapers for the rich, tallow among the poor) were laid out within easy reach. As to further preparations, there was neither time nor opportunity. Such foodstuffs as had remained on grocery shelves after the Federal evacuation had long been commandeered by hungry Carrancistas, whose campaign rations were notoriously skimpy.

Our own pantry now contained a sack of flour, half a ham, the rind of a once-luxurious side of bacon, and fourteen cans of English plum-pudding which Papa had been able to locate in an otherwise bare food-store. In addition there were the stable bins, about two-thirds filled with corn, barley, and oats.

We also had a cow. That is, on the second day of the Villista attack, Petronilo arrived with a half-starved beast from his *jacalito*. "This is Clarinda, my mother's cow," he explained. "We raised her from a heifer. But our neighbours are hungry, and they want to butcher Clarinda for meat."

I was puzzled. "But, Petronilo, that day when I visited your *jacalito* you had only a goat!"

He thought back, then brightened. "Clarinda was at the house of my *compadre* Julio, who is the father of my godchild Juan. Julio's wife just gave birth to her fifteenth baby, and we let them borrow Clarinda because ever since the last three Julio's wife has had no milk. She is not the right kind of woman, Julio's wife. No milk."

Petronilo hoped he might be allowed to stable Clarinda with our horses and assure her of a share in their fodder.

"Only a small amount, like this," he pleaded, cupping his hands to show the modesty of Clarinda's appetite.

Mama was touched. "She shall have as much as she needs, while our supply holds out. But what about your family? How will they get along?"

The servant shrugged his shoulders in a helpless gesture.

"Bring them here," said Papa, "and let them spread out their bedding in the garage. We'll manage, if the siege doesn't last too long."

It was thus that not only Petronilo's parents but his brothers, their wives and offspring, all came to dwell under our roof. They camped in the rear patio, making no sound or bother. Also, they brought with them a flock of scrawny chickens and a stray pig which they rounded up in some abandoned *jacalito* along the way. This raised them to the status of paying-guests.

We led a strange communal life during the days that followed. Like a tribal matriarch, Mama doled out each meal in carefully computed portions. A bite of tinned plum-pudding for adults and Clarinda's milk for the children at breakfast. Lunch was a cup of thin bouillon made from an inch of bacon rind and a few grains of barley. For the evening meal we fell back on the ham, which was extended by the Hungarian trick of baking a crust of unleavened bread around it. Night after night another slice was carved off this *pièce de résistance* and distributed in tiny fractions, to be reverently chewed with more plum-pudding. As for the last-named item, it earned alternate praise and condemnation. Without sauce or trimmings the famed British Christmas dish tasted a trifle dry, but its concentrated food value was so great that a single mouthful could safely tide us over from one meal to the next. Meanwhile, every one waited eagerly for the stolen chickens to make up their minds whether they would lay eggs or end up in a stew, while the starved piglet was allowed to batten on rations of corn and oats prior to its execution.

By far the best-fed creature on our premises was Petronilo's cow. For Clarinda's sake the needs of both man and beast were trimmed to the absolute minimum. To us this meant no squandering of corn for bread or muffins. Clarinda did not like corn, but made up into a mash it was pushed down her gullet.

"Clarinda gives something in return," Papa explained the cow's preferred treatment.

This was true. There seemed to be no end to the benefits derived from one lone farm animal. First there was the milk, which, left standing in low pans, formed a layer of cream. This cream was spooned off carefully and whipped into sweet butter. The watery whey left during the process made a wholesome drink. In addition, any milk that soured over-night (we had no ice) could be eaten like Bulgarian yogurt, or else gathered in a clean cloth and hung up to transform itself miraculously into cheese. Altogether, here was a marvellous cycle of productivity running its course before our eyes.

On a smaller scale this soon became true of the chickens. After two days of hysterical cackling they adjusted themselves to their new surroundings and gave promise of settling down. Their food consumption was almost nil, for they took a tip from the sparrows and chased the latter off the stable dung. On this ignominious diet they flourished and presently went about their daily manufacture of eggs. I could not get over it.

"Nature certainly is messy," I commented, on comprehending this phase in the chemistry of life.

"Yes," agreed Papa, "but there is no better teacher of economics."

For the rest, we quickly fell back into the pattern already adopted during the first siege. As the new "enemy" drew nearer and the din of artillery fire increased, there was the same strain on nerves, bringing on general sleeplessness. Again we gathered about the dining-room table and watched Papa's card tricks. We also listened to Mama's inexhaustible store of folk-tales, most of them set in Imperial Austria.

When Mama ran out of Habsburg stories she turned to music. Songs were revived that brought back happier days: Schubert's *Am Meer*, the *Batti, Batti,* of Zerlina in Mozart's *Don Giovanni*, or a medley of Magyar gipsy airs. Hers was an immense faith in the sustaining power of the arts. With destruction at our door it was irrational for Mama's mind to move in æsthetic channels, yet we did not perceive the paradox. In a way this was the strongest proof of her claim. We might not be alive to-morrow, but our souls were certainly being refreshed with melody and conversation.

It did not take Monterrey citizens long to realize that the coming of Pancho Villa would bring on far greater sufferings than anything the city had yet experienced. The bombardment itself was more violent in character, indicating that our new attackers were practised in the art of war. As the shelling gained in intensity the Carrancista garrison barricaded itself in the inner town. Street fighting began before the end of the second day.

Late that night Obregón left. His decision did not spring from craven impulse but merely the realization that the city could not be held. The Carrancistas, in gaining their objective at Monterrey, by defeating the Federals had spearheaded the way to Mexico City, where Victoriano Huerta must be entrapped. In the impending struggle for the Presidency Alvaro Obregón had as good a chance as Don Venustiano. It was this fact which drew the younger man southward, though not before he had hammered instructions into the battalions he left behind. There must be a stubborn delaying action for the benefit of the main army elsewhere. Monterrey must hold out as long as possible.

Astonishingly, the order was obeyed. Without leadership, the Carrancista garrison fought desperately for nine terrible days. During that time the terrors of the first siege faded into insignificance as we came face to face with another side of war. Famine stalked the city. From outlying villages and the river slums came bands of marauding refugees, maddened by hunger and thirst.

There was a rumour that the suburban mansions of the rich Sada, Botello, and Treviño families had been looted and the mob was pressing into the heart of the town.

We did not live in a mansion, but Papa looked worried. "The people down the street know we have a grain reserve for the horses. We must share it with them or they will turn against us."

He was right. To Mexico's working-classes corn was the staff of life; hence at a time like this we ought not to be using it as fodder for our animals. Clarinda and the three horses would have to manage on a residue of oats and whatever greenery they might find palatable in the garden.

"Who knows," said Mama hopefully, "they might eat geraniums!"

Meanwhile Petronilo went out into the street to tell the wandering beggars that they could have our maize. "Bring your bowls and baskets," he said. "It will be divided evenly until there is nothing left."

Our father learned too late that unthinking magnanimity could invite danger. In less than five minutes a howling, pushing mob besieged our door, hysterically demanding admittance. A heavy iron bar provided a strong bolt within, but even so the thick wooden panels seemed to bulge under the human impact.

"The windows!" cried Mama. "Hand out the food through the windows!"

Her suggestion proved a life-saver. All our windows were protected by metal grilles, through which we could scoop out the precious corn. Instantly the mob rolled away from the front door and milled against the balconies. Nimble urchins climbed over the heads of their elders and hung on the grilles like monkeys. A sea of arms reached upward, while hoarse throats joined in a single shout:

"Ayuda, ayuda!" ("Help, help!")

We hadn't nearly enough. After the last grain was gone the crowd looked as big as ever, and as empty-handed.

"That's all," Papa shouted. "We haven't any more!" But no one believed him. Instead, the crowd grew bigger as stragglers from other neighbourhoods joined in the clamour. Faces grew hostile, jaws set. There were sneers and imprecations.

"There's corn stored in this house! Come on, you lazy rich, you robbers—let's have it!"

Curses were flung at us, and then some one picked up a stone.

"The shutters," Mama screamed; "quick, close the shutters!"

We all joined in a frantic rush to board up windows. Even as we did so the crash of splintering glass punctuated our steps. Not a single pane remained unbroken, but the iron grillework withstood the onslaught. We were safe within the walls of our small fortress.

Outside the frustrated mob turned finally on itself. Those lucky ones who had obtained a pittance of food tried to make their way through the throng and slip out of sight. But before they could head for safety the others had caught up with them.

"Friends of the plutocrats! Traitors to your own class!"

With fists and heels the wretches were belaboured until they gave up their small booty, which in turn was fought over by a fresh set of contestants.

The riot lasted several hours. When it ended there were cuts and bruises for every one, but the pinch of hunger was sharper than before. Our experiment in philanthropy had miscarried. Up and down the street, as far as the eye could see, the priceless maize had been ground into the dust.

47

SECOND SIEGE

We had been called lazy rich, and robbers. I was profoundly impressed.

"Papa," I demanded, "are you a millionaire?"

My question seemed to arouse amusement. "Far from it!" said Papa, with a smirk. "Whatever goes on in that head of yours?"

Memories of Solymár caused me to assume that ours was a high place in life. It was a shock to learn that Papa called himself a *Bürger*. "What the French mean by *citoyen*," he explained, "a middle-class citizen; it's the best thing to be."

I felt dispossessed. "But aren't we *rich*?" I persisted, unwilling to surrender that attractive fantasy. "Don't we have a cow and horses?"

Papa reminded me that the cow belonged to Petronilo. For the rest, economic values were comparative. Beside that hungry mob in the street, he conceded, we were indeed well off. But in the present crisis there was nothing to guarantee our preferred status. As if to underscore his words there was the sudden crackle of machine-gun fire overhead, indicating that our desperate defenders were now entrenched on the housetops, where they hoped to gain a vantage-point for sniping. This meant that the final stage of the siege was at hand.

We spent another night of terror, during which the tottering city was shaken to its foundations. A shell struck the Garrido home next door and breached the wall that separated our respective gardens. Scurrying through this opening, the family crept across the patio and joined our circle. Señor Garrido carried two bottles of beer. Some moments later another neighbour, an American named Himes, crawled over the wall with a box of poker-chips under his arm. Still shaky from the ordeal of dodging bullets, he proposed a game.

It was a corking idea. The Tarock cards were quickly brushed aside, and Mr Himes brought out his own deck. Since no one else knew the game, he took time to explain the rules, with the result that the children learned along with the adults. For the rest of that night our ears were deaf to the rataplan of shell-fire and hand-grenade. We were dazzled by the clatter of chips tossed into what Mr Himes called, in deference to the Garridos, *El* Pot.

The game had still another tonic effect. Stimulating enough to take our minds off the immediate danger, it paradoxically restored our capacity to sleep. For days we had sat, hollow-eyed and exhausted, yet afraid to leave one another's company. No one dared undress, for fear the house might be struck and we should be forced to flee. But a few rounds of poker released the tension. One by one we relaxed and fell asleep in our chairs. The card game went on without interruption as other players, refreshed by their naps, took up where some one else left off.

All this time Luciana, the cook, was praying in the kitchen. She had gathered our own and the Garrido servants together and, basing her calculations on the length of the first siege, started a novena. Surely nine solid days of bead-telling would benefit a household engaged in frivolous and night-long gambling. Not that Luciana disapproved. She welcomed the laughter and the occasional happy snore that emerged from the dining-room. Any pastime that had so beneficial an effect upon a distraught household was acceptable. But some one, reflected Luciana, ought to keep things squared with God.

She had trouble keeping Petronilo in line, for the manservant dodged the protracted orisons under the pretext of doing his chores. But this did not cause the novena to lag, for Luciana betook herself and her followers to the cowshed. Here, while Petronilo went on with the milking, an unbroken chain of Aves rose heavenward.

More than once I slipped away from the family circle and joined the servants at their prayers. But I discovered to my amazement that the religious fervour of my convent days had abated. The jolt received at Uncle Bichteler's death, when the hospital nuns assured us that his Protestant soul was damned, had torn my faith from its firm moorings. Never had there been a gentler and more selfless being than Uncle Bichteler. It was unthinkable that God should banish him to eternal hell-fire on a purely theological count.

Having lost the blind comfort of my convent faith, I now lacked the solace that Luciana and her servant-girls found in their beads. I had no balm against fear. God seemed far away, while the reality of artillery fire was nerve-racking and immediate. I despaired of living through it.

"We're going to get killed, we're going to get killed!" I screamed, running back to Papa's side.

He looked at me, then said quietly, "Bring out your school books. Sit down here and read."

I recognized by his tone that this was no time for dawdling. Obediently I fetched my school-bag and emptied its contents on the floor. An empty copybook fell on top of the heap, its blank pages gleaming invitingly. Suddenly the thought took hold. Instead of reading, why couldn't I write a story for myself? The story of my life! Not my real life, of course, since that struck me as hopelessly dull, but an account of the sort of fantasia one would have wished to live. Since my immature mind was mired in the notion that only the far-fetched and the extravagant deserved attention, I was going to allow myself ample leeway. My pages would be crammed with high-flown adventure. In fact, one copybook would hardly be enough. I ought to keep another on hand as a sequel to Volume One.

Now for the opening paragraph. Since reality did not measure up to my literary requirements, I speculated on the advantages of changing my background. Perhaps I did not belong to Papa and Mama at all? I might very well have been kidnapped long ago by those very gipsies who camped near our grandfather's house in Solymár. Having only dark-haired sons, my parents could have bought me from the Romanies because I was fair in colouring, and a girl. Here was a perfect opening sentence. "I do not know," wrote my deceitful pen, "where I was born."

Even while putting down these words I paused. The convent had given me a conscience which stirred at inopportune moments. It now caused me to wait for a bolt of lightning straight from the chiding skies. But nothing happened. God was busy elsewhere. This gave me courage. I continued my prevarications with impunity, plunging headlong into a florid account of my anonymous ancestors and their presumably exotic origin.

It was Mama who put an end to this excursion into autobiography. Glancing over my shoulder, she read a paragraph or two and snatched up the copybook. "What is this supposed to mean?" she asked, passing my writings round the table. "Why, it's out-and-out fabrication!"

Papa tried to soothe her. "The world's best authors have been known to stretch truth to make a better tale——"

Señor Garrido had likewise something to say in favour of fic tional embellishment. "Se non e vero," he quoted an Italian aphorism, "e bon trovato!" ("Though it be not true, it is well put!")

Such sophistries carried no weight with Mama. Years ago she had nipped my pilfering proclivities in the bud. She would deal as ruthlessly with falsehood, whether oral or on paper.

My career as a writer was closed.

48

AND VILLA CAME

IT WAS just as well that Mama ended my literary fling, for the events of the next twenty-four hours were to wreak havoc with our lives. In the midst of my autobiographical *débâcle* the city fell.

Again, before the entry of the victorious attackers, there was violence to be endured at the hands of a fleeing garrison. Before departing, the last remnant of Carrancistas perforce must supply themselves with food and equipment for the long trek south. They ransacked warehouses, homes, garages, schools. Whatever had been overlooked by the Federals was pounced upon now.

It was midnight when a scavenging party reached our door. "Open up!" came raucous shouts, as rifle-butts pounded against the panelling. "We know you have horses hidden in this house!" Resistance would have been useless. Besides, our fodder was running low, and shortly we should not know how to keep the animals alive. It was better to let them move southward with the routed armies, reflected Papa. He led the horses out himself.

"Where are the saddles?" demanded one of the raiders.

We had only English saddles, unpopular among rebel riders because of the short stirrups and lack of a pommel. But Papa ordered Petronilo to bring them.

The animals were made ready, one after the other. Our father's thoroughbred mare came last.

"Here you are, señores," he said, turning over the reins.

Two of the men leaped into the saddles, when the third paused nervously and eyed the mare with suspicion.

"She is a vicious animal, eh?" he inquired, indicating her snorting, dilated nostrils.

Father touched the mare's head. "No—just high-strung. She's a hunter."

Gingerly the trooper tried to hoist himself into the unfamiliar saddle. At last, with Petronilo's help, the feat was accomplished. But horse and rider parted company almost instantly. The mare had recognized the grip of a strange master, for she was not used to harsh bridling nor the sting of spurs in her flanks. She reared and bolted, tossing the man off her back.

He picked himself up from the dust, rubbing his neck and shoulder. His face grew purple with rage. As the mare halted her flight and ambled back he drew his revolver and pressed the muzzle into her ear.

"No! No!" shouted our father.

But it was too late. The trigger had been pulled, and the animal made one vast leap into the air, then fell heavily against the stone curb.

"Thank God," said Mama quietly. "This is better than turning her into an army nag."

Papa was instructing Petronilo regarding disposal of the dead beast, when a cavalcade of Carrancistas swept into our street. At sight of the fresh kill they reached for their lassos and soon improvised a litter; the fleeing troops were desperate for food.

By sundown the second siege had come to an end, and Villa's forces entered a plundered, prostrate town. For the second time the cessation of cannon and machine-gun fire was followed by a sudden uncanny hush that seemed more frightening than the preceding din. We had become so used to the ear-splitting noise of the past fortnight that silence was almost unbearable, ominous.

Behind half-opened shutters people peered into the streets to observe what manner of men our latest conquerors might be. The very word "Villista" struck terror in every heart, for the bandit leader from Chihuahua and his mountaineer horde had become legend. Their ferocity was celebrated in rhyme and song.

"They rape women and bayonet small children!" warned Luciana, as she summoned the maidservants to further prayer. Now, if ever, God had better listen to her pleas.

While frantic supplications echoed from pantry and kitchen my brother Arnim and I watched the Villista vanguard stumbling past our house. It was a raggle-taggle army, with nondescript clothing and torn shoes, though each man carried heavy cartridge-belts and a double holster with guns. On their heads these strangers wore the famous Pancho Villa sombrero, enormous, battered, and grotesquely curved, front and back, in the best tough-hombre fashion. Nowhere outside the super-sombrero town of Guanajuato had we seen hats of such circumference tilted at a more sinister angle. Yes, Luciana was right; these warriors looked savage indeed. They bore the same glassy look of battle which we had seen on Carrancista faces, the bloodshot eyes, the swollen lips, the indescribable lustfulness induced by carnage.

But there was something more that could not be defined. These men walked and rode with a stealthy, trance-like motion, as though hypnotized by some primitive force. That force was Pancho Villa.

And now we saw the terrible *caudillo* himself, riding at the head of his carabineers. He was a giant of a man, astride a giant charger, unmistakable in his garb and dominant manner.

"He looks like Petronilo!" I whispered to my brother. "That is, if Petronilo had tight trousers, a belt with pistols, and a hat as big as a windmill."

We stared at the notorious leader in awe and wonderment, for he was that rare phenomenon, a man outside the law, who lived by his own law. A killer whom no court dared bring to justice, he looked every inch the part assigned to him by legend. He sat far back in the saddle, leaning on his spine, with an indolent, leonine arrogance that was fraught with menace. The broad brim of his sombrero was tilted backward too, exposing heavy brows and eyes that gazed lazily ahead, while the thick lips hung half open in a self-confident smile. Here was a man who knew his strength and feared no one.

I noticed that Villa wore a sash. But this was not an ornament draped picturesquely over one hip. It had been slung *ranchero* fashion about the waist and twisted securely into place as a belt above his high leather chaps. Our Petronilo wore exactly the same kind of sash, whipped several times round his middle so as to form alternate layers of pockets for tobacco, cornhusk cigarette wrappers, and a few coppers in change.

"Es hombre del pueblo," said Villa followers, of their chieftain. "He is a man of the people." I could see exactly what they meant.

The city held its breath. Rapine, murder, destruction, all had been predicted by the departing Carranza forces, if Monterrey fell into Villa's hands. Yet, though we cowered in fear, none of these horrors occurred. The horde of battle-scarred warriors swarmed over the town, but there was no sign of brigandage or pillage.

In our kitchen prayers were interrupted as the Chamaca observed resignedly, "They're not coming for us after all." Whereat the cook cuffed her ears and bade every one get back on their knees. The devotions continued.

It was not long before we learned the secret of Villista discipline. Like wildfire the news suddenly spread through the town: "Felipe Angeles is bringing up the rear!" People opened their doors and rushed into the street. They hailed a slender, khaki-clad horseman, who smiled and waved back, campaign hat in hand. "There goes the saviour of our cities," men and women assured one another. "But for Felipe Angeles, Monterrey would be ashes."

We had heard for some time about this youthful intellectual who joined the Villa movement soon after Madero's death and lent prestige to the proletarian cause. At the cry, "Felipe Angeles is here!" we too rushed from the house to catch a glimpse of this quixotic figure, whose influence stayed the bloody hand of Villa and kept an army of desperadoes in check.

What was the secret of Felipe Angeles? It would be difficult to prove or disprove any legend woven on the loom of popular fancy. But this much was certain: whatever redeeming features won tolerance for the Villa movement at home or abroad must be ascribed to the efforts of this lone aristocrat. The original Chihuahua rebellion had started as a blood-bath; violence was all that Pancho Villa, the son of beaten slaves, could understand. In avenging the wrongs of Mexico's past this rebel chieftain squared accounts by a simple process of gory arithmetic. With bullet and *machete* he meant to annihilate the privileged classes that ruled only by whip and economic strangulation. Felipe Angeles, the idealist, was a child of privilege, but he shared the *caudillo*'s anger at social injustice. He differed with Villa only in the manner of seeking redress. Instead of violence, Angeles proposed peaceful reforms; following in the footsteps of Madero, he preached regeneration and humanitarianism.

Had one of his illiterate peasants voiced such altruistic views, Villa would have made short shrift of him. He had no use for chicken-hearted milksops. Yet on the advice of this Angeles he had once bowed to Madero, the son of wealth, who took up the cudgels on behalf of the downtrodden but frowned on carnage and the heavy hand of wrath. While Madero was in the field the banners of the Revolution floated on a clean and hopeful breeze. Only after the gentle dreamer's death had the Villa campaigns reeked once more of depredation and murder. The Revolution's hard-earned prestige collapsed, and with it the hopes of Mexico's inarticulate peon class, for the apostle of the poor had become again only Villa the bandit.

It was then that Felipe Angeles had once more asserted himself and saved the foundering cause, and for the second time the rebel chieftain showed a flash of wisdom: Villa, the bull, bowed again to a man of intellect.

He was not to regret it. With Angeles at his side, the *caudillo* recaptured popular trust and acclaim. Monterrey bore testimony to this. The city lay smouldering amid the ravages of the siege, but a curious populace wandered unafraid through avenues and squares. There was no instance of abuse on the part of the conquerors, no incendiarism or looting of homes. As for the violence anticipated by Luciana, the weary warriors appeared too exhausted for lechery, quite apart from the fact that the Villista army was accompanied by its own 'campaign women' or *soldaderas*, who kept a sharp eye on their men. Not only did these gun-toting squaws cook, scrub, and bear children beside the battle lines, but they banded together in a concerted front against outside competition. To cast inviting glances at a Villista trooper was to flirt with death at the hands of a female battalion in arms. Thus, without detracting from the efficacy of Luciana's novena, Monterrey womanhood owed something to the *soldaderas*. Chastity's best insurance is a homicidal rival.

As for Felipe Angeles, whom people credited with the virtues of a Knight Templar, there were sighs and fluttering heartbeats at his passing. Despite the grime and blood of battle there was about him a look of fastidious grooming, the hall-mark of a true *hidalgo*. As he rode up Bolívar Street between endless columns of spectators his hand was raised to his temple. Felipe Angeles saluted the conquered town.

"Viva! Viva!" cried the people, careful not to hail anyone in particular, lest jealousies be aroused among the invaders. Obregón's split with Victoriano Huerta was fresh in public memory, and it was no secret that the "Irishman" now vied with his new chief, Venustiano Carranza, for the Presidential chair. There might be similar rivalry between Angeles and Villa. One could never tell about political love-matches. Thus Monterrey burghers cheered because the sun shone and the siege had ended. They also raised a proper hubbub in the forlorn hope of wheedling foodstuffs from the conquerors.

In this they were due for a disappointment. Coming eastward by forced marches, the Villista horde had lived for weeks on roots and cactus pears, stripped from a landscape almost bare of sustenance. The territories over which they passed had long since surrendered livestock and grains to the Federals, and after them the Carrancistas, so that the pickings were laughable. Decidedly there was no prospect of replenishment for our larders. Even so, people went home that evening with light hearts and renewed confidence.

Because of this good beginning, what followed was an indescribable shock.

On the morning after the Villista occupation, Felipe Angeles left town, in hot pursuit of the Carranza armies. The *caudillo* himself remained behind and, with no high-minded counsellor by his side, went into action with some reforms of his own.

Having suffered privation all his life, Pancho Villa hated poverty; or rather, he hated those whom he believed to be the cause of it. Like Robin Hood, of whom the raw-boned Chihuahuan had never heard, Villa felt called upon to take action. He was no economist, and so only the most elementary remedy occurred to him. One must take from the rich and give to the poor. This happy theory called for definition, but Villa had no time to lose. Besides, by his standards the privileged classes included anyone with an extra pair of shoes. The *caudillo* himself was an enemy of the superfluous; ergo, he would persuade all who had more than they needed to share with their less fortunate fellows.

Persuasion, with Villa, was a simple process. He summoned people into his presence and, with each hand caressing the butt of a revolver, told them what to do. The alternative was stated with cool candour: the firing squad for Mexicans, and Article XXXIII (deportation) for foreigners.

We had heard of such scenes through fugitives from other provincial towns where all commercial enterprise had been dislocated by Villa's recipe for reform. But little credit was given to such reports. Besides, what had happened elsewhere did not necessarily threaten Monterrey. Confident that the worst lay behind them, people returned to their offices and shops. Amid the rubble of shelled and burned-out buildings they pluckily strove to set the wheels of industry once more in motion.

It was in the mist of these peaceable activities that the blow was struck. By special decree issued from Villa's headquarters in the Palacio Nacional all heads of business and industrial firms were ordered to appear at a general round-up. Anyone failing to obey this summons soon saw the error of his ways, as raiding-squads combed the city and ferreted out every merchant, banker, or professional man whose name was listed in the telephone directory. That list, of course, included Papa.

The meeting took place in a battered reception-hall of the palace. Here the bewildered townsmen waited in a silent group, their questioning eyes fixed upon one another. Some of the gentlemen, among them the financier Don Constatino de Tárnava, senior, had taken time to dash home and don morning-coat, striped trousers, and spats, though the majority assumed correctly that Pancho Villa was insensible to sartorial splendour.

The session that followed was an exact duplication of reported events in previously conquered areas. The *caudillo* needed money, a sizeable percentage from each firm, for the relief of destitution and the upkeep of his campaign. The amount asked for was not exorbitant. In all, less than a million pesos, which the town's wealthier men could easily have raised by concerted effort if given time. But no one had large cash reserves on hand in those revolutionary times when money had prudently been withdrawn from Monterrey. One of the spokesmen, a prominent lawyer named Berazaluce, explained all this to the *caudillo* and asked for the indispensable respite.

Instantly Pancho Villa's suspicion was aroused. Unversed in business procedure, the rebel chieftain brooked no delay. He set a deadline. "To-morrow noon, señores! Anyone stalling beyond that hour will find himself under arrest."

This automatically doomed the project to failure. Few of the men present were sole owners of the business enterprises bearing their names. The majority shared partnerships in corporations with main offices in Mexico City, Paris, London, or New York. Papa was the representative of a Canadian firm operated by absentee owners. They simply could not act without proper authorization, quite apart from the actual manipulation required for obtaining spot cash on such short notice.

By eleven o'clock the next morning only a negligible amount of coin had trickled into the Villista coffers. Most of the businessmen had spent the night at the telegraph offices, hoping to make contact with banking houses in near-by Saltillo. Some lost their heads and tried to cable Europe. But all communications with the interior were cut, and as for help from abroad, there was a world war blazing in Europe which reduced the plight of an obscure provincial town in northern Mexico to insignificance.

It so happened that, even before expiration of his deadline, the *caudillo* lost patience.

"I'll print my own money," he said. "I've done it before. My people in Chihuahua use nothing but *bilimbiques*." He referred to small bits of carton, similar to railway tickets, which —in Villa territory—had been declared legal tender. *Bilimbiques* were valueless, of course, but to refuse them was to risk one's life.

As for the hapless business leaders, they were rounded up for the second time and placed under arrest.

Papa was among them.

49

PRISON

WE COULD not believe it.

When first told that Papa had been fetched from his office and led on foot through the town streets, flanked by an armed escort, Mama shook her head in mock protest. This was no time for jokes. And, in any case, our father would be home for dinner.

But evening came and there was no word from Papa. Petronilo, who had spent the afternoon loitering about the police station, reported seeing a group of prisoners—some sixty of them—piled into trucks and driven off to the penitentiary, west of the city.

"Don Emilio walked right past me," the servant mumbled, flushing deeply. "He carried a bedding-roll on his back!" Petronilo's chagrin at this indignity was plainly greater than his worry about Papa's arrest.

We rushed to the prison that night, but were turned away at the gate with the statement that the men were being held *incommunicado*.

"For how long?" Mama wanted to know.

"That is up to the *caudillo*," replied a non-committal guard.

Mama worried about meals. "There's so little food in town. May I bring my husband a basket of fruit from our garden?"

The guard's face remained stony. "The prisoners will eat," he said, brushing her off.

We went home, and I sobbed myself to sleep. Terrible dreams tormented me through the night and I awoke long before dawn to the full impact of what had happened. This was no detective thriller or paper-backed adventure tale. In the grey light of day the fact rose before me that Papa was at that very moment locked in a prison cell, without comfort or news from us. What was it like, this cell? I recalled one of Sylvester's books, in which a man named Jean Valjean had languished for years in a damp, rat-infested dungeon. I could not eat my breakfast.

We were back at the *comandancia* by eight o'clock, having walked down Rayones Street and across the wide stretch of the Alameda Park. But at the prison door the guards again barred our way.

"No visitors——"

Seventy-two hours passed, and we were still without communication. The suspense was too much for Mama. Making the rounds among the families of the remaining prisoners, she learned that they too were frantic for news. At this she took a desperate step. Once, not so many years ago, she had faced the Emperor of Austria at Castle Schönbrunn. It ought to be no more difficult to stand before Pancho Villa.

She entered the Palacio Nacional and calmly requested an audience. This was promptly denied, but before she could be ushered back to the street a door opened and the rebel chieftain emerged. With heavy strides he clanked across the corridor and, catching sight of the caller, paused in front of her. Mama had prepared an eloquent plea. But before she could open her mouth the *caudillo* recognized that he was dealing with a petitioner. He broke into a roaring laugh.

"Those moneybags had their chance," he said defiantly, then walked ponderously on. "Let them stew in their juices. I'm printing my own money now!"

He was indeed. Within a week not only the city but the whole state had been flooded with bits of red, blue, and green pasteboard, no bigger than theatre tickets, a new issue of 'bank-notes' with printing on one side only. These bills were of astronomical denominations to keep pace with runaway inflation. As prices shot upward to insane heights all economic standards collapsed. The cost of one egg would in normal times have purchased a pair of shoes, while the price-tag on footwear looked like the down payment on a limousine.

At Villa's headquarters nobody cared, least of all the *caudillo* himself. Things were getting out of hand? *No importa!* It didn't matter. More money would be printed at a fine clip and the spiral could race upward indefinitely.

The chaotic financial picture was reflected in the food situation. Market-gardeners from the outlying district of San Gerónimo were loath to bring their crops to town in exchange for worthless paper. Villista currency was not accepted farther south than the state of Coahuila, which precluded the shipment of produce from other provinces. At the same time Venustiano Carranza was now starting to circulate his own brand of monetary tickets which trickled northward into Villa territory, only to be rejected as counterfeit. With foreign imports at a standstill, the deadlock was complete.

People despaired. The question was on every one's lips: what had happened to silver, gold, and legitimate bank-notes guaranteed by the Federal Government? The answer was clear enough. The Federals were on the run, dragging their guarantees with them. As for solid values like gold and silver, they vanished in time of trouble. Holes were dug in the earth under the floorboards of homes as hiding-places for jewellery, coins, negotiable securities, and the family plate. Automatically men turned into misers, enduring the pinch of hunger rather than part with a silver peso. Gold watch-chains became prized instruments of exchange, to be snipped off link by link in payment for comestibles.

"That is a good thing to remember at all times," said Señor Garrido, who had lived through revolution in Spain. "Watch-chains—they are better than money. Buy them up in pawnshops and put them away. Even if a country goes off the gold standard the metal keeps its value anywhere."

For myself, I could not see what all the worry was about. In financial matters I saw eye to eye with Villa. For some years now, when I neglected to balance my weekly budget and failed to make ends meet, I had been irritated by the strange workings of man's economic system. Since money was so desirable, and there didn't seem to be enough to go round, why weren't the printing-presses busy night and day turning out more of the lovely stuff? Why didn't governments give it away so everybody could buy all that he must have of life's good things? In short, to a child's mind there was nothing wrong with Pancho Villa's thinking.

Yet Mexico's poor did not grow rich. But the rich, paradoxically, swelled the ranks of the poor.

We were learning this at home. Papa's imprisonment in company with the city's moguls of finance was, to begin with, an absurdity. Such funds as he administered in the discharge of his duties belonged to his employers. Our own circumstances were comfortable, but by no means glittering. Yet with the shutting down of Papa's offices and the paralysing of all banking operations, we found ourselves suddenly without funds. To obtain daily necessities Mama began bartering with articles of clothing, jewellery, rugs, and whatever else was unessential to survival.

On the fourth day of Papa's imprisonment we were allowed to see him. The news was brought by Petronilo, who had bivouacked outside the *comandancia* day and night until the guards relented. We were to appear in the visitors' room between seven and eight in the evening, when the prisoners would file past behind a wire screen.

At the appointed hour we stood, with beating hearts, waiting for the familiar footsteps. And now we beheld Papa's face, very white and strange behind the wicket-like grille. Nervously his eyes counted our heads several times over.

"Hello, Papa!"

I could not get beyond the greeting, for my throat ached and choked off the words. No one else seemed able to speak.

"Five minutes!" a guard warned impersonally, yet prompted perhaps by a kind impulse. If we continued standing there tongue-tied the precious interval would slip by unused.

It was Mama who collected her wits. Touching Father's hand through the grille, she asked, "Shall I look up Lawyer Berazaluce?"

At this a fleeting smile lighted up Papa's face. "He needs a lawyer himself. Berazaluce is in the cell next to mine."

It was his voice which brought me out of my benumbed state. I had been unable, up to this moment, to believe in the reality of the scene about me. It must be a dream, one of the appalling nightmares to which I often fell victim, especially after those evening sessions when Sylvester used to read aloud from *Les Misérables*. French story-tellers, it seemed to me, inclined towards sending their heroes to prison—preferably for theft of a crust of bread—and then lining up their woeful families outside the bars. But surely this had not happened to Papa, nor could we be that family. . . .

"Ten minutes," said the guard. "The interview is over."

A soldier placed his hand on Papa's shoulder and led him away. We stood in silence, watching the slender, erect figure, the familiar walk; this was our father being taken to his cell. It was a shattering moment. No single incident during the long ordeal of the siege, the burst of cannon-shells, the hangings in the streets, the famine, fire, and destruction, compared with this. In the midst of havoc the family had held together, its solidarity unchallenged, perhaps even strengthened. Whatever fright we experienced had been purely physical and therefore far from demoralizing. Fear of sudden death curdled one's marrow without blighting the spirit. But this was different. I, for one, could not adjust myself to the fact that our father was under restraint.

"What are the charges?" asked our mother in the *comandante's* office.

"No charges," was the answer.

No charges. Men could be swept from their moorings, without cause or personal guilt, by a fatal tide that found them in its path.

No refuge. No security.

I went home that night stunned not only by Papa's lot but by the changed outlook which must inevitably spring from my new knowledge. The whole wondrous framework of love, within which I had been so carefully nurtured, revealed itself now as the most fragile of disguises. It had built a roof over our heads and planted a blind trust in our hearts, so that our childhood years were made gay by the certainty that we could not be hurt. But our parents, who had spun this web of sweet delusion, had no protection themselves.

A new kind of pain revealed itself to me as I grieved for the world of grown-ups. It did not seem a world I wanted to enter.

50

NEW ROUTINES

BACK AT the house on Matamoros Street a family council was held, with Señor Garrido and Mr Himes in attendance. Mama mapped out a plan. Rail communications were being re-established as far south as San Luís Potosí. She would travel this distance at once and continue to Mexico City by pack-mule, ox-cart, or on foot. Once in the capital, she hoped to stir up whatever Government was in power at the moment and to return north with an order for Papa's release.

"Perhaps I can get action through diplomatic channels," she theorized.

Señor Garrido was doubtful. "Diplomats mean nothing to this Pancho Villa. He hasn't the faintest notion of their function. If anything, their pompous manner will only antagonize him further."

Mama granted this possibility. "But I must still take the risk," she said, determined to go.

Before starting southward she worked out a set of instructions for us to follow. Petronilo and Luciana were to look after the house, while Arnim and I remained under the supervision of our neighbours. Meanwhile, some method must be worked out to keep in contact with Papa, either by letter or personal intermediary, in order to make certain that he continued unharmed. This was all the more important since rumours floated about the town that men were being shot nightly without trial in the prison courtyard.

"We'll go to see Papa every day," declared Arnim defiantly. "We'll take ropes and climb the wall!"

But Mr Himes had a more workable idea. He went before the prison authorities and explained that our father was a victim of stomach-ulcers, which called for a special diet.

The *comandante's* eyebrows rose. "*Ulceras*," he repeated thoughtfully, "that is a serious disease?"

Having invented the ulcers in the first place, Mr Himes added a few frills. "Not only serious but, in this particular form, highly contagious," he said mournfully. "So contagious that dishes carry the germs, and anyone eating at the prison is in danger of catching it!"

"Ah," said the *comandante*, frowning.

Without further delay, he wrote out an order permitting our father to receive meals from home, served in containers that did not pass through the prison kitchens. "But," he added an oral footnote, "food may be brought only once a day, and by a person who is above suspicion."

It was this requisite which caused the choice to fall upon me. An immature child, the *comandante* felt, would be of little use in furthering an escape plot. He approved an arrangement whereby I could visit my father each noon and spend an hour in his cell.

The food question was handled expertly by Luciana. We had little enough ourselves, but she managed to stretch available supplies and to borrow substantially from friends and neighbours. For transporting the meals Petronilo suggested a device used by Mexican workmen. This consisted of several graniteware bowls about the size of cereal dishes, each fitted on top of the other, and jointly gripped by a metal rod that formed the handle. The top bowl, of course, had a lid; the bottom one, usually black, while the others were white or of a mottled blue, had perforations round the sides and served as a brazier for glowing coals. In this fashion each dish remained hot, either by direct contact with the brazier or through the steam from the one immediately beneath.

We had often seen Indian children hurrying through the streets with one of these fascinating contraptions. Since my brothers and I were inordinately fond of native food, we knew the escaping odours mingled with aromatic charcoal fumes to be all but irresistible. More than once I deplored the fact that Papa was not a labourer, so that I might scurry after him with his 'steamer' of food, the little basket of toothsome *tortillas*, and a jug of coffee. For it had not escaped me that the young purveyors of these goodies sat down with their elders and shared a generous portion of all that they had brought. No cold sandwiches or paper-wrapped foods for Mexico's toilers! The family table followed them to work, with all the crisp-toasted, last-minute perfection of a meal at home.

Though in a manner I could not have foreseen, my wish was being granted. Like the brown-skinned and barefooted objects of my envy, I would start out each day with a crackling brazier to serve Papa his noon repast. The task in itself held such allure that I temporarily overlooked the grim circumstances that brought it about. Prison or no prison, I could hardly wait to get going.

Papa, happily, could take pleasure in small, unexpected things. The 'steamer,' for example! Quite possibly at one time or another he too had longed for the kind of treat we now shared—the suspense of lifting the top lid and then going from dish to dish, all the way down to the hot ash in which the *tortillas* could be toasted. Actually, I had seen at home what went into each container. But on my way to the prison I forgot the order of their arrangement, since from the outside the receptacles all looked alike. Hence my excitement was almost as great as Papa's. Together we explored each level, greeting the sparse supplies with exclamations of delight.

As for the prison authorities, they eased my comings and goings as far as regulations allowed. On my arrival, and again before departing, a guard inspected the bundles I carried, as well as every pocket in my dress. Each packet of cigarettes I brought Papa was opened and thoroughly fingered, but the messages which Señor Garrido and Mr Himes rolled in rice-paper (with tobacco inserted at either end) were never found. Once the *comandante* asked jovially for a smoke, and my heart stood still. I held my breath while he toyed with the packet. Would he reach for the wrong one—the message—and set fire to it? No, he was no smoker; he had only been teasing.

"You may pass, *niña*. And a good day to your father!"

The walk through the prison courtyard and down the long cell-blocks oppressed me. Here was a world made entirely of stone, with only the ubiquitous web of iron grille-work to break the monotony of grey. Nowhere was there a spot of green, a blade of grass, a wild daisy such as grew on the poorest field. Stone underfoot, irregular, cobbled, ankle-breaking. Stone overhead, to right, to left, as far as the eye could see. And everywhere the creeping mould, brownish-black, oozing from the damp floors.

I learned about prison architecture. From the outside all one could see were the crenellated walls forming a gigantic square with observation turrets at the four corners. But within this quadrangle lay the vast unit of the prison proper, built about a central tower from which the cell-blocks radiated outward like long rigid tentacles. A single guard in this tower could spy upon the slightest activity. Pressing a series of signal buttons, he could spread a general alarm or, in case of a minor disturbance, confine disciplinary measures to a limited area.

Actually, these buttons were seldom used. Whether due to tropic languor, or the natural placidity of Indian temperaments, the run-of-the-mill captives in the Monterrey prison were docile to the point of inertia. It got so that the guards yawned with boredom and all but snored at their posts. They would have welcomed anything, including a rip-snorting riot, to break the monotony.

On the day of my first visit matters had apparently reached a limit of endurance. The guard on duty in the central tower had decided to take action. Setting up a chair, mirror, washstand, and towel-rack, he established a prison barber's-shop within the confines of his post. With other guards eager to lend a hand, prisoners were fetched from all the blocks, one by one, for a haircut and a shave.

It soon became a clubby affair, owing to a certain casualness about returning the customers, each of whom paid a small tip, to their cells. Freshly shampooed, tonsured, and barbered, they cluttered up the cramped tower and hampered the gaolers at their amateur task (needless to say, there was not a professional barber in the place).

By a stroke of luck I found Papa in the midst of this animated gathering. He was sitting in the makeshift barber's chair, with head thrown back so that the small tuft of his imperial, now grown a trifle straggly, pointed straight into the air. A perspiring guard with a gleaming razor in one hand was pinching Papa's nose, while round about stood a number of gentlemen with whose faces I was familiar. Don Constantino de Tárnava, the banker, looked somewhat dishevelled and the worse for wear. Beside him hovered the lawyer, Berazaluce; the Zambrano brothers and their cousins, the Sadas, formed a coterie of their own. Altogether I recognized a dozen or more of Monterrey's top-drawer citizens. All circled about Papa's chair, holding forth on affairs in general while attentively supervising the trimming of his beard.

Between operations, as he paused to strop his blade, the 'barber' voiced some profound opinion of his own. This was either acclaimed or refuted, according to its merits, by the assembled listeners, thus opening new fields of discussion and inevitably slowing up the shave. There was time out for laughter, too, as humour leavened many a remark. Mexicans are extremely witty, and their mirth, even in adversity, is uproarious. The 'barber' himself, rocking with guffaws, was twice forced to pocket the perilous blade and bend over to slap his thighs until the paroxysm passed.

Coming upon this scene, with food-basket in hand, I froze in my tracks on the top step of the tower approach. A great halloo of welcome greeted me as Papa's friends rushed forward with outstretched hands. I almost toppled backward down the stairs.

"Don Emilio, look!" they exclaimed, turning to my father and lifting him bodily out of the chair. "You have a visitor!"

For the next minute all was confusion. Not only Papa, but each of his prison cronies, hirsute or shaven, pumped my arm and gave me a bear-hug. For no particular reason the others also threw their arms about Papa and slapped his back fraternally, receiving in turn a smudge of lather from his jaw.

Patiently, and with a sigh of complete understanding, the 'barber' wiped his razor. He could wait, for time was not of the essence of the contract.

His customers were not going anywhere.

51

MEETING MY FATHER

IT WAS in prison that I really came to know my father.

All through my childhood he had been a dominating presence, second only to the one whom in infancy my brothers and I needed most, our mother. This divided allegiance, dictated by Nature, prevails among normal families regardless of their degree of civilization. The young brood, helpless at first, is chained to the parent that gave it birth. Only with the first stirrings of independence is there an awareness of another authority and the recognition of the male as head of the house.

Through Mama's deference to him, we loved and respected Papa. This did not mean that our parents lived in passive and perpetual agreement. On the contrary, their differences of opinion were frequent and voluble. But even when Mama won, which was most of the time, she made the outcome look like a paternal victory. This gave us to understand that our father was important. We also thought him good, and enormously wise. But we did not know him very well.

Prison changed all that.

On that first visit, when my arrival temporarily disrupted the barber's-shop session, I discovered that Papa was no longer housed in the cell-block with the remaining prisoners. The *comandante*, haunted by fear of the allegedly contagious stomach-ulcers, had ordered our father to be removed to single quarters just off the women's wing. The cell assigned to him was actually no cell at all, but a guard-room that opened on to a tiny stone court. There was no window, and the furniture consisted of a bare *catre de lona* (canvas camp-bed), a table, and an upright chair. As to hygienic facilities, there was a water-closet at one end of the court, concealed by lattice-work and a sloping tin roof. No bathing equipment existed, but a pipe ran along one wall, with a spigot, and an old petrol can underneath to catch the water.

"It's not bad," said Papa. "If I wait for the afternoon sun the pipes get hot and I can draw myself a bath. That's more than those poor fellows in the cell-blocks can do."

He was right. The cubicle where he had first been held *incommunicado* measured scarcely four by six feet and was completely devoid of comforts. Dark and dismal, it had no ventilation except through a peep-hole in the door, which did not permit a head to be forced through. The men who had been arrested with him were still in those cramped cells, without light, air, or room to stretch out.

It was Papa's awareness of his good fortune which revealed to me a new facet in his personality. He was philosophical and capable of adjustment. The danger of his position had remained no secret to him. The record proved that Pancho Villa snuffed out lives like votive candles. In such circumstances a prisoner knew that each dawn might be his last. Yet Papa greeted me invariably with a flourish, as though we were playing a game.

"What are we feasting on to-day?" he would ask, surveying Luciana's meagre victuals and pretending that they were choice savouries. This baffled me the more since I had never known our father to make much of table pleasures. His appetite was small to the point of asceticism, and it could be choked off completely at the sight of an overloaded plate. He claimed to have dined once by merely looking at a mountain of spaghetti. How, then, account for his change of attitude? Was the approval he gave Luciana's humble pottage a show of gallantry for gallantry's sake?

We sat in the doorway, with Papa's table pushed out into the courtyard. The meal, in which he always insisted I should take part, was flavoured with conversation. That is, my father talked and I listened. It came to me now that his days must be long and desolate with emptiness, for he was allowed no books or magazines, no pencil or paper. Out of every twenty-four hours the noon interval seemed to loom for him like a spiritual oasis. During this break in the protracted silence his need for human communication was almost unbearable, so that words came in torrents. Never had I known Papa to be so loquacious.

He talked to me as to an adult, beginning with the food I set before him. His former gastronomic apathy changed to keen interest. He commented on the goodness of each dish and pointed out what made it so. "Simplification," he said. "Take this bit of cabbage; it's not chopped up and overcooked in some starchy white sauce. Luciana has no butter and flour to waste, so she just boils a few leaves with a bit of salt."

"She was unhappy," I interrupted, "because she had no meat to put in for a stew."

"But that's just it! This way the flavour is fresh as fruit. Dumping meat and cabbage into the same pot is what creates objectionable vapours and gives cabbage its bad name. All vegetables are better when not tampered with."

I listened appreciatively, for one of the horrors of my life was the eternal white-sauce with which European cooks blanketed their peas, carrots, kohlrabi, and green beans. The result, it seemed to me, was that one always tasted only the sauce. "Wall-paper paste," Papa called it. One virtue, at least, accrued from wars and revolutions: food shortages eliminated wasteful frills and put an end to much culinary malpractice. Simplicity was the secret of proper nutrition.

From food and philosophy Papa's thoughts turned to literature. With no distractions at hand, he fell back upon inner resources which braced and sustained him. Imprisonment was in a sense no different from conventual retreat or the anchorite's seclusion; it sharpened perception and forced the mind to feed upon itself. A cricket hopping on the table brought not annoyance but companionship. A stanza from Chamisso or Lamartine, grudgingly memorized in his school-days, now made my father's eyes glisten with pleasure at its new-found meaning.

He had much to say about language. "Words are among man's highest treasures. Without them nothing could be salvaged from the periodic violence of nature or humanity's wars." He pointed to the destruction of cities, of noble works of art, of human life itself. Yet from the ashes of dead civilizations there survived this dual heritage: music and literature. These could not be eradicated by earthquake or cannon. The solid mass of skyscrapers and cathedrals might blow away in a fine dust, but who could destroy a Shakespearian sonnet? Only annihilation of the earth itself would blot out the last symphony and the final measure of written speech.

I knew almost nothing of Shakespeare, and what I knew I had been taught in French. This alienated me from the original medium. That is, as Papa now recited passages to me in his carefully acquired (and still halting) English, the authentic Shakespearian text seemed to me archaic and remote. In translation, whether into Gallic, Spanish, or the powerful German version by Schliemann, the Bard's work gains immediacy because these languages forgo the obsolete flavour of Elizabethan speech. In modern idiom, as I knew them, Hamlet, Macbeth, Shylock, and

Iago evoked sympathy or horror with an urgency of to-day. The greatness and dramatic power were all there, as well as the heroic metre; what fell away was the mannered period touch. By the elimination of "forsooth," "what-ho," "methinks," and all the pristine terminology with which Shakespearian English is glutted, the ends of realism were well served.

By contrast, Papa pointed out, in Spain crude peasants quoted Cervantes or *El Cid* because there is no cleavage between the country's literature and its living tongue. In Britain the native idiom changed, causing Shakespeare's most throbbing lines to freeze into classics.

"The same thing happened to Homer," continued Papa, "only in more extreme degree. Modern Athenians read the *Iliad* and *Odyssey* in translation, since the original is—well—Greek to them."

The mention of Homer took our conversation into a related field, the Balkans. Here was territory with which Papa was familiar. In a flash of memory he recaptured forgotten scenes from his youth when, as a student, he had wandered through Siberia. Against the background of prison walls he now recounted the story of Alexander Obrenovich and Queen Draga, who were done to death in a night of horror at the royal palace in Belgrade. Slavic names and phrases returned, focusing his attention once more upon the fascinating subject of language.

"A nation's vocabulary is the measure of its culture," he repeated.

I was puzzled. My childhood, I clearly remembered, had been overshadowed by a permanent injunction against chattering too much. Yet now it appeared that there was a premium on words.

52

EMBRYO AUTHORSHIP

WALKING HOME from the prison that day, I was overcome for the second time in my life with a literary urge.

The question was not whether to write, but what? A poem, a song, a novel? Viewed through my limitations, there were distinct drawbacks to all of these. Poetic rhyme seemed too confining, while blank verse was simply prose cut like tape into regulated lengths. A song, on the other hand, called for harmonics (I should have to provide the tune as well), and here was my true Achilles heel. However strong might be the lure of music, I recalled that lessons in counterpoint had been sheer torture. It looked as if I should be a lifetime mastering the complexities of tonal script.

This left the novel. But here I struck another snag. From what I had gleaned up to now of grown-up conversation, particularly servant talk, novels hinged always upon an elusive pastime called *l'amour*. No matter what other ingredient went into the making of readable fiction—war, crime, adventure—the bone and marrow remained this thing I knew nothing about, the *grande passion*. Though countless books had already dealt with the matter through the ages, no one ever seemed to have enough of it. Yet, except for a few garbled and naïve notions on sex, I stood before a blank wall.

Our library at home held ample clues to the mystery. But there was a lock on the glass doors of the very cabinet that interested me most—the one through which adult visitors browsed with the greatest show of eagerness. Here, neatly grouped and shielded from dust (or from prying young hands?), were books with handsome bindings and exotic names: Tolstoy's *Kreutzer Sonata*, Flaubert's *Madame Bovary*, Artzibashev's *Sanine*. The last lay open on a table one day and I made a hurried inspection of its pages before being interrupted by sounds in the next room. During the scant interval at my disposal I absorbed two facts. First: in Russia both sexes insouciantly shed their clothes on beach or river-bank and swam together in the nude. Second: Sanine, a dashing rake in the Tsar's army, was embroiled in a violent love-affair with a blonde beauty named Lydia. Owing to events which I evidently missed, the young woman was pregnant, and responsibility seemed to fall on Sanine. At least, the paragraph I managed to scan indicated that Lydia's brother was going after "dashing rake" with a revolver.

For some years my imagination was inflamed by recollection of this passage. Unfortunately the book soon vanished through some forgetful borrower, and I was never again able to lay hands on an unabridged version. In those days of its first discovery, however, I often stared at the volume on its shelf and felt my fancy take wing across the world to a rustic setting outside St Petersburg (or was it Moscow?), where young officers and their lady friends disported themselves nonchalantly in a stream. Needless to say, all this brought about a conflict with the stern conscience I had contracted during convent days. The antics of those Russians caused me considerable embarrassment.

As for producing a novel, my encounter with Artzibashev defeated any such idea. No matter how lurid a situation I might conjure up, it was bound to pale beside the activities that presumably went on in *Sanine*. And here was the tantalizing question: Just what did go on?

Thwarted in any hope of further exploring Artzibashev, I could aspire to one other field of authorship. It was a form I had already tried, with signal lack of success: autobiography. Much had happened since the occasion of my first failure. I had seen Pancho Villa, and had trembled in a city under siege. I knew the inside of a prison. Perhaps of these things I could write.

One handicap stood in the way. My previous exaggerated outpourings had caused an uproar in the family. The riot act had been read to me, and I was made to promise never again to embroider reality for the sake of a good tale. "Stretching the truth," had been Papa's euphemism for my sin, but Mama called it out-and-out prevarication. In any event, a collective foot had been put down on further authorship.

In this predicament I presently discovered a way out. We had received news from Doña Pilar in Parras that our mother's trip to Mexico City was cut short at San Luís Potosí. Here Mama had turned back to the Madero estates in Coahuila, where a plan was being worked out to make contact with General Felipe Angeles. While these efforts were in progress a courier would carry letters back and forth. Mama asked all of us to write.

This was my chance. I would incorporate a new autobiography, unfortunately limited to contemporary events, in a series of fat reports to Mama. Whether she kept these or destroyed them did not concern me at the moment. The main thing was to get them off my chest.

The stratagem worked beautifully for a time, until the demon of exaggeration again led me astray. Life's daily occurrences, even at the prison, did not meet the requirements of my pen. With an *élan* for the macabre, I touched up my news. My melodramatic brush painted the State penitentiary at Monterrey as a house of pain, with torture chambers that echoed with wild cries in the dark of night. The minutiæ I thought up were worthy of Dostoievsky and caused Mama to fall ill with shock.

Actually, owing to the fundamental placidity of the Indian character, Mexican prisons were singularly free from brutal abuses. Guitars and gaiety were far more in evidence than irons or the knout. What screams I heard on my daily visits to Papa issued from the drunkards' pen, a large enclosure where vagrants slept off their hang-overs. Even here I saw no evidence of beatings or other mistreatment. On the contrary, the bibulous beggars were mostly in excellent spirits, often serenading one another with great zest, and beating time with their feet. Occasionally a fight started and spoons were twisted into makeshift weapons, but results would have been far more gory if the participants had been free.

Things were less peaceful in the women's prison, which I passed regularly on my way to Papa's cell. Here the town's lady crooks, shrews, and Magdalens dwelt in a permanent hullabaloo. There were hair-pulling scenes and fisticuff engagements originating not so much in the clash of tempers as from rivalry in love, for the women's wing lay within sight of the male exercise court and afforded ample play for coquetry. Fiery glances were exchanged, leading to inevitable conflict when too many eyes fixed on the same object. The men took such complications in their stride and, indeed, preened themselves on their popularity. But the women fought. With teeth, claws, hairpins, and long sewing-needles they fought until they drew blood.

These brawls were routine and called for routine measures. At the height of a fracas a team of guards came on the run, hauling the prison fire-hose. This they turned on the combatants, forcing them apart by sheer hydraulic power.

Punishment of this same sort was brought upon themselves by male inmates of truculent character. But quiet prisoners, like

Papa, suffered neither indignity nor injury. If anything, the monotony of confinement made an occasional skirmish in the women's wing loom in sight as a welcome diversion. At the first sound of pandemonium among the ladies Papa was at his bars, surveying the contest from a ringside seat.

"The curse of prison life is lack of exercise," he explained to me. "Those fighting tigresses at least make sure of their daily training."

All this was, of course, grist for my mill. I reported each tussle to Mama in vivid detail, without neglecting the heart interest. Judging from my letters, the prison throbbed with highly combustible intrigue.

I liked this business of writing. But an insidious effect was beginning to make itself felt; even to an embryo scribbler like myself everything turned into 'copy.' The most trivial happening, whether it touched others or myself, was filed away in the recesses of memory for possible future use. Even while listening to Papa I avidly sifted his conversation for gems with which to enrich my inadequate prose.

There were days when I found myself out of luck, for he grew moody with solitude and seemed too weary to talk. Once I came upon him drawing sketches on the walls of his cell: woodland scenes with trees and rolling meadows. His drawing materials were bits of charcoal saved from the brazier on which I warmed his daily food.

"Something to do," he said, without looking at me. "Something to do, or I'll lose my mind——"

It was Petronilo who thought of the chess-board. After five weeks of confinement, when Papa's resourcefulness seemed at an end, the servant pressed a package under my arm. It contained the familiar carved figures boxed with a folding board.

The idea was a godsend, though it likewise proved a strain. Papa rallied joyfully and forthwith instructed me in the execution of elementary gambits. But chess is no pastime for children. The daily matches in which we engaged, after finishing Luciana's bean porridge, were difficult for me and far from stimulating to my parent. Nevertheless, we staunchly went on with the game.

53

RELEASE

In the third month of our father's imprisonment a letter came from Mexico City, with special instructions for transmitting it safely into his hands. Evidently Mama had been able to get through to the capital and to deal with responsible authorities. "The enclosed note is too big to hide in the usual cigarette-packet," she wrote. "Instead, seal it in a glass tube and drop this into the neck of a beer-bottle. Recap bottle and keep shaking it so a thick foam will conceal the tube."

The directions were fine, but we had no beer. Neither did the Garridos next door. Luciana went to the Himes house, where pantry shelves were equally bare, but Señora Himes had a practical suggestion. Let Petronilo fill an empty bottle with soapy water, which would shake into a froth and could be coloured with a bit of brown dye from his shoe-polishing kit. In addition, because she regretted being of so little help, the good lady tucked a batch of old American magazines under Luciana's arm.

We welcomed the magazines, particularly those with pictures in them. But one, called *The Nation*, had no pictures and was pre-empted by Luciana for kitchen uses. Its pages made a good starter for her wood stove, and they also served as wrappers for Papa's daily *bolillo*, or roll of bread. As for the suggested beer substitute, it worked admirably. With infinite care a plausible decoy was produced, which I carried gingerly to the prison on the following day.

In my letter to Mama that same week I elaborated on the exploit. At the prison gate, so ran my trumped-up report, a brace of armed guards had detained and searched me. In the excitement the bottle had been knocked from my grasp and sent crashing to the stone floor. But with rare presence of mind I had snatched up the glass tube and held it concealed in my fist until I could safely place it in Papa's hands.

All this was, of course, preposterous. For eighty-six days I had wandered in and out of the prison, unmolested, and with no hint of melodrama. Beyond a cursory glance at passing visitors the guards appeared supremely indifferent. The only restriction they enforced with some rigour was the ban on newspapers and other printed matter, for the untried Villa régime must prevent collusion between prisoners and outside forces of revolt. This was the reason I could bring Papa no reading-matter. Nevertheless, a sheet from the advertising pages of *The Nation* now got past the prison inspector's eye. It was crumpled and food-stained, besides containing little in the way of intellectual stimulus. But Papa smoothed it out and saved it for thorough perusal, after he was done with the Mexico City note. A day or two later he asked me a startling question: "How would you like, some day, to go to boarding-school in the United States?"

Before I could answer he pointed to a small notice on the torn page from the magazine. The school was in Philadelphia, and its name was Drexel-Lankenau. I did not rally warmly to the thought, except to catch the polysyllabic beauty of the word "Philadelphia" and the even lovelier "Pennsylvania." No more was said about the matter. Yet this fleeting instant shaped the course of my entire future life. I did not know it, but before the year was out I should be entering the strangest of new worlds.

Before this, however, a momentous change had yet to be undergone in the *status quo* at Monterrey. It happened that the Villista régime was beginning to rock on its foundations. The apostle of the poor, Pancho Villa, had successfully conquered the northern states of Sonora, Chihuahua, Coahuila, Tamaulipas, and Nuevo León, but in the summing up his triumphs proved futile. The rival liberator, Venustiano Carranza, had managed to get himself inaugurated as President of Mexico in the gilt ceremonial hall of Castle Chapultepec. This was the news I had brought Papa in the little glass tube, together with the assurance that Monterrey was soon to be retaken by the new Government forces and all prisoners would be freed. Papa was to bide his time and not lose hope, said our mother's letter. At the end there was a postscript: "If you run short of entertainment, ask Minka to tell you the story of her life!" Obviously Mama had been warned from other quarters to take my correspondence with a pinch of salt. For the second time I had been found out.

The discovery nipped further creation in the bud. Life, I told myself at last, was not to be improved by letters. It must be lived on its own terms and without falsehood, even if it made dull reading. I resolved to be done for ever with autobiography.

My disillusion rankled for a while, then faded under the strain of following Papa's moves at chess. There was something else, too. For twelve weeks I had seen my father behind stone walls, imprisoned without charge or trial, for reasons still unexplained. Yet these days, weeks, and months counted among the most cheerful and stimulating I had spent in the company of any human being, for I had become initiated into the sorcery of the mind.

"There is no limit to the possibilities of the human intelligence," Papa had said on the day I first visited his cell. The words had been directed not so much at me as at himself, for he was rehearsing certain rules of conduct. Idleness, particularly when enforced, was but a step to illness. Inaction is the enemy of life, and even contentment becomes harmful if it engenders apathy, boredom, spiritual death. Philosophers spoke of "divine discontent" as the source of all creative effort, the mainspring of genius. Such thoughts had borne down upon my father, goading his brain to brace itself against the ordeal ahead: the dreadful test of living in emptiness.

Then, having recognized the challenge, he had met it with all the resourcefulness at his command. The first thing to be learned was the game of "what one can do without." This would be difficult for a mind conditioned to civilized living and to the tonic effect of work. Lacking books and writing tools, or even the means of performing manual labour, it became necessary to fall back entirely upon ideas. Only thus could the spirit, cut off from outside nourishment, gird itself against atrophy and madness. Here, then, lay the true value of a memory rich with accumulated knowledge; it furnished that "glorified attic of the imagination," the storehouse of the mind, wherein one might rummage at will in order to draw from it what countless treasures!

Together with my father I learned to dwell for a time almost entirely in that storehouse of the mind, and we had not nearly exhausted its manifold riches when the order for release arrived. In a mopping-up action the Carrancista forces, now officially recognized as the "Constitutionalists," moved northward from Mexico City and pacified the land. Villa acknowledged, not his own defeat, but his rival's superior timing. Both he and Don Venustiano had pursued identical aims—the abolishment of peonage and poverty. But in the uneven struggle the cards had been stacked by Fate against the Chihuahua mountaineer.

Again Monterrey citizens witnessed an evacuation, this time without panic or haste. Villa, the unbeaten chieftain, cleared the field and relinquished the citadel to an honoured adversary. As a last act before departing, he freed all political prisoners.

I walked home with my father in the sun.

His eyes squinted at the sudden brightness, and he stretched his arms as though to embrace the free air. I looked up at him.

"Don't you hate that Pancho Villa?" I asked, overcome by a resentment to which I had not hitherto dared give voice. Inside the prison walls even the stones had ears.

"Hate him? Of course not. By his own lights he is a patriot."

"But he locked you up——"

"Yes," agreed Papa, "because he saw that something was wrong with Mexico's social structure, and he felt that the class to which we belong is somehow at fault. He is right."

"But *you* didn't do anything!" I protested.

"That's just the trouble, and the trouble with our kind all over the world. We *are* our brothers' keepers, in exact ratio to the advantages that shaped our lot. If we refuse to recognize this it is brought home to us sooner or later by the catharsis of revolution—even world revolution. Pancho Villa is only one of many names for a national conscience outraged."

He held out his hand and pressed my fingers in a warm grip. It was almost noon. My brother Arnim had gone to meet Mama, due on the train from Mexico City. At home Petronilo, Luciana, the Chamaca, and the neighbours up and down our street had joined in preparations for the *fiesta de bienvenida*—the welcome.

My heart was light and my feet danced.

I walked home with my father in the sun.